OXFORD MODERN LANGUAGES
AND LITERATURE MONOGRAPHS

Editorial Committee

D. J. CONSTANTINE   T. F. EARLE

R. E. GOLDTHORPE   I. W. F. MACLEAN

G. C. STONE   R. W. TRUMAN

J. R. WOODHOUSE

Joseph Joubert: lithograph by Charles Vogt, based on a portrait attributed to Sophie Joubert

The Thought and Art of Joseph Joubert
(1754–1824)

DAVID P. KINLOCH

CLARENDON PRESS · OXFORD
1992

Oxford University Press, Walton Street, Oxford OX2 6DP
Oxford New York Toronto
Delhi Bombay Calcutta Madras Karachi
Petaling Jaya Singapore Hong Kong Tokyo
Nairobi Dar es Salaam Cape Town
Melbourne Auckland
and associated companies in
Berlin Ibadan

Oxford is a trade mark of Oxford University Press

Published in the United States
by Oxford University Press, New York

© David P. Kinloch 1992

All rights reserved. No part of this publication may be reproduced,
stored in a retrieval system, or transmitted, in any form or by any means,
electronic, mechanical, photocopying, recording, or otherwise, without
the prior permission of Oxford University Press.

British Library Cataloguing in Publication Data
Data available

Library of Congress Cataloging in Publication Data
Kinloch, David P.
The thought and art of Joseph Joubert, 1754–1824 / David P. Kinloch.
(Oxford modern languages and literature monographs)
Includes bibliographical references and index.
1. Joubert, Joseph, 1754–1824—Criticism and interpretation.
I. Title. II. Series.
PQ2311.J73Z77   1992
840.9—dc20   91-33685
ISBN 0-19-815183-7

Typeset by Latimer Trend & Co. Ltd., Plymouth
Printed and bound in Great Britain by Bookcraft Ltd,
Midsomer Norton, Bath

*For my
Mother and Grandmother*

Foreword

The enigma of Joseph Joubert was not made any the less impenetrable by the pretence that it did not exist. A secretive author, Joubert was addicted to the pleasures of reading and writing compulsively all his life, whatever his public activities happened to be at any given time. Initially a teacher, then secretary to Diderot, he became an administrator and Justice of the Peace during the difficult years of the Revolution, an inspector of the Université Impériale, and a welcome guest in the literary salons of the period. Pauline de Beaumont, Chateaubriand, Fontanes, Bonald, Chênedollé were among his friends. By the time of his death in 1824 his probing, speculative intelligence had accumulated a great wealth of ideas. Unable to choose among the infinity of doubts, solutions, and further problems it constantly discovered, his mind became hopelessly entangled in the web of analogies linking the arts, the sciences, and language to imagination and creativity. Except for letters, Joubert could never finish a text to his satisfaction. He became a prisoner of the written word.

In 1824, that was difficult to understand. The mass of jottings, notes, and manuscripts that Joubert had consigned to the now famous trunk concealed his true self, but rendered him vulnerable to interpretation. So when Chateaubriand and Duchesne perceived that certain fragments of his work fitted into a recognizable genre, or could be made to do so, Joubert was presented as an author of *Pensées*, as a moralist. The solution was retained, and more evidence to substantiate it was produced, four years later, in 1842, by Raynal in his collection of the *Pensées, essais et maximes*, which became the standard edition until 1938, when Beaunier published the major part of the *Carnets* in two substantial volumes.

After Chateaubriand, Raynal and Sainte-Beuve rediscovered, almost invented, Joubert, Matthew Arnold introduced him to the Anglo-

Saxon world of criticism, translations of selected 'thoughts' appeared, and his reputation grew on both sides of the Atlantic. At the same time his personality was transformed. It is true that, with the years, the urbane, sociable, professional, and family man was assailed by the weaknesses of age, but the critics imagined Joubert as an eccentric recluse, with peculiar notions about diet and sleeping attire and prone to destroy the books he in reality cherished. His name became associated with Platonism, Romanticism, Spirituality, and many other concepts. As David Kinloch points out, the 'recluse' has even been compared to Marcel Proust. Admittedly, the critical assessments of Joubert's aims and contribution to aesthetics were not always completely void, but they were of necessity founded on insufficient evidence, and often on hearsay.

As the *Carnets* published by Beaunier reveal, the working methods of Joubert were determined by his habit of writing down comments on the authors he was reading and dissecting their ideas. This discipline, and its results, constitute the starting-point chosen by David Kinloch. He has correlated the notes, usually made on slips of paper, with the marginalia Joubert penned in his books and with the draft texts that were either abandoned, or patiently reworked. This painstaking reconstruction of an accurate chronological framework has enabled David Kinloch to reveal the astonishing variety of Joubert's interests, his constant reappraisal of the philosophical and artistic principles debated in the polemics of the day, and his alert response to new ideas in the sciences and even in political theory. For the first time Joubert appears as an important witness to the changes that took place in the transition from Enlightenment to a spiritual revival in violent reaction to materialism.

Independent, individualistic, a convinced humanist, willing, even, to take his master Plato to task, Joubert rendered the interrogation of his century, of antiquity, of the forms of matter, of the cosmos, subservient to his obsession with the origins of art, of thought, of language. He was a poet whose intensely concentrated meditation upon the universal dynamics and resonances of his art reduced him to immobility, to silence, and to destruction. Yet, this slow negation generated its own poetry. The fascination of this paradox has been sympathetically and brilliantly conveyed by David Kinloch. His study lifts Joubert from the ranks of the more obscure writers and leads the reader to appreciate the unique vision of Beauty and Unity that inspired him to write:

> je joue de la lyre antique, de la lyre à trois ou à cinq cordes,
> de la lyre d'Orphée ...

London   Brian Juden

Preface

I am particularly grateful to M. and Mme Paul du Chayla and Mme la vicomtesse d'Arjuzon for allowing me access to their private archives in Paris, Villeneuve-sur-Yonne, and Bussy-le-Repos, for permission to quote from unpublished manuscripts of Joubert, and for the kind hospitality they showed me on all occasions.

The manuscripts of the *Carnets,* excluding *feuilles volantes,* some of which André Beaunier included in his edition of 1938, belong to M. Paul du Chayla and may be consulted at his home in Paris. The spines of the sixteen small leather volumes into which the manuscripts were bound during the nineteenth century bear the following dates:

i	2 oct. 1786–31 déc. 1795
ii	1 janv. 1796–21 juill. 1797
iii	22 juill. 1797–31 août 1799
iv	1 sept. 1799–23 oct. 1800
v	24 oct. 1800–18 mars 1802
vi	19 mars 1802–27 août 1803
vii	27 août 1803–4 juin 1804
viii	5 juin 1804–29 mars 1805
ix	29 mars 1805–23 avril 1806
x	24 avril 1806–16 fév. 1807
xi	17 fév. 1807–19 fév. 1808
xii	20 fév. 1808–18 fév. 1810
xiii	19 fév. 1810–31 déc. 1812
xiv	1 janv. 1813–31 oct. 1814
xv	1 nov. 1814–23 sept. 1816
xvi	24 sept. 1816–22 mars 1824

References to passages appearing in these volumes, but omitted by André Beaunier from his edition, take the form MSS *Carnets.* M. du

Chayla also owns the manuscript compiled by Joubert's nephew Duchesne for the use of Chateaubriand, entitled 'Pensees de M. Joubert. Manuscrit de M. Chateaubriand,' and the manuscript compiled by Paul de Raynal, in the process of producing his 1842 edition of the *Pensées*, entitled 'Pensées—Manuscrit'.

All other manuscripts referred to are the property of Mme d'Arjuzon and may be consulted at her home in Bussy-le-Repos, a small village on the outskirts of Villeneuve-sur-Yonne. I have chosen to refer to these in the form MSS Bussy.

These manuscripts include all the scattered materials published by Norbert Alcer in his thesis *Studien zu Joseph Joubert* and by Rémy Tessonneau in his collection of Joubert's *Essais*. They also include many *feuilles volantes* containing remarks, perhaps destined for the *Carnets*, lists of books read, and lists of quotations from books read. Most, but not all, of these manuscripts have been divided haphazardly into bundles, some of which are bound together with ribbon, others with bits of string, and several with frail elastic bands. They may be found in two large cardboard boxes. Most of these bundles have been numbered and a few of them given titles, such as 'Extraits des philosophes', for example. In his thesis, Dr Alcer used this as a basis for assigning these unpublished materials to *liasses*. Thus, *liasse* or bundle 11 contains the 'Éloge de Cook', etc. I have chosen to adopt the simpler method indicated above, first, because many of the sheets of quotations made by Joubert from his reading matter, as well as the *feuilles volantes*, do not belong to any particular *liasse*; secondly, because many of these *liasses* contain a great deal of extraneous material that has been included simply because no one could be bothered to invent a separate category to which they could be assigned; and, thirdly, because it is quite clear that many people who have handled these manuscripts over the past century have failed to return them to the appropriate *liasse*.

During his lifetime Joubert gathered together a substantial library of books on a variety of topics. Many of these books, some of which bear his own annotations, still exist and have been divided between M. du Chayla's family and that of Mme d'Arjuzon. The bulk of them may be consulted in Mme d'Arjuzon's house at Bussy and M. du Chayla's property in Villeneuve-sur-Yonne, where Joubert himself spent much of his time. A small number are kept by M. du Chayla at his home in Paris. When referring to books annotated by Joubert I have indicated their location in the notes.

Finally, I should like to record various debts of gratitude; first, to the late Professor Robert Shackleton, for the generosity and humanity with which, while in declining health, he supervised the thesis on which this study is based, and to Professor Brian Juden for all his unstinting help and advice in more recent years.

I am grateful for help afforded me by the following individuals, either in conversation or correspondence: Dr Norbert Alcer, Sir Isaiah Berlin, Dr Cyprian Blamires, Professor Yves Bonnefoy, Dr Richard Fargher, Professor Roger Fayolle, M. Hervé Goube, M. Roger Gouze, Mme Nuria-Illosa, Dr Neil Kenny, Dr David Klinck, M. Philippe Mangeot, Professor Alain Michel, Professor Valerie Minogue, M. Bruno Neveu, Dr Cynthia Stallman, Professor Alan Steele, Dr George Sutherland and Dr T. H. H. Vuong.

I should like to thank Mrs Valerie Jensen for the patience and interest she showed while typing this study and Mrs Hilary Walford for her help and advice in the preparation of the typescript.

Its writing was made possible by the generous award of a Major Scottish Studentship from the Scottish Education Department, and a Snell Exhibition given by the University of Glasgow and Balliol College, Oxford. Research in France was made possible by my appointment by the Universities of Oxford and Paris as 'Lecteur' at the École Normale Supérieur, Paris, and by the award of a Zaharoff Travel Grant. Work was completed during the first year of the Kathleen Bourne Junior Research Fellowship at St Anne's College in 1985 and revised for publication in subsequent years during a Research Fellowship granted me by the University of Wales and lectureships at the Universities of Salford and Strathclyde. I am very grateful for each of these grants and appointments.

I am also deeply indebted to my family and friends for their help and support, in particular to my mother, my late grandmother, my late father, Dr Robert Crawford, Dr Raymond McCluskey, Mr Nick Pacitti, and Mr Eric Samuel.

D.P.K.

University of Strathclyde
May 1991

Contents

	List of Illustrations	xvi
	Abbreviations	xvii
	Introduction	1
1.	The Early Years	23
2.	Politics and Aesthetics	56
3.	Platonism and Expressive Aesthetics	71
4.	The Status of Art in the *Carnets*	110
5.	Idea, Image, and Copy	144
6.	Imagination and the Form of the *Carnets*	164
	Final Profile	191
	Appendix: Joubert's Reading of Plato	200
	Select Bibliography	203
	Index	227

List of Illustrations

Joseph Joubert: lithograph by Charles Vogt, based on a portrait attributed to Sophie Joubert *frontispiece*

1. Experiments in magnification and refraction: an illustration from J. A. Nollet, *Leçons de physique expérimentale* (6 vols.; Paris, Guérin, 1764), *Trustees of the National Library of Scotland*. 114

2. An extract from the manuscripts of Joubert's *Carnets* (C i. 183–4), *M. Paul du Chayla*. 122

Abbreviations

BL	British Library
BN	Bibliothèque Nationale
C	*Les Carnets de Joseph Joubert: Textes recueillis sur les manuscrits autographes*, ed. A. Beaunier (2 vols.; Paris, Gallimard, 1938)
Correspondence, Raynal	*Correspondence de J. Joubert*, ed., with an introduction by, P. de Raynal (9th edn., Paris, Perrin, 1895)
Correspondence, Tessonneau	*Correspondence de Louis Fontanes et de Joseph Joubert*, ed. R. Tessonneau (Paris, Plon, 1943)
Critical Tradition	P. A. Ward, *Joseph Joubert and the Critical Tradition: Platonism and Romanticism* (Geneva, Droz, 1980)
E	*Essais, 1779–1821*, with previously unpublished material, ed., with an introduction by, R. Tessonneau (Paris, Nizet, 1983)
Studien	N. Alcer, *Studien zu Joseph Joubert (1754–1824), mit bisher unveroffentlichten Schriften* (Bonn, Free University, 1980)
Tessonneau, Éducateur	R. Tessonneau, *Joseph Joubert, Éducateur, d'après des documents inédits (1754–1824)* (Paris, Plon, 1944)

Note on the Text

André Beaunier's edition of the *Carnets* reproduces Joubert's own spellings, punctuation, and accentuation; when quoting from this edition, or from unpublished manuscripts, I have respected these idiosyncrasies. Joubert was in the habit of leaving sentences unfinished and I have indicated such occurrences with three dots. Editorial ellipses are enclosed within square brackets.

Introduction

> Joubert est le secret de quelques-uns. Ses lecteurs, rares, en sont venus à former une espèce de société secrète, à tel point qu'ils s'ignorent les uns les autres ... Il passe ... sorte de Monsieur Teste pour femmes et hommes du monde le meilleur, confident idéal.[1]

In these few words, Georges Perros has given an accurate summary of the commonplace judgements behind which critics of Joseph Joubert have sought refuge since the 1840s. The tradition of impressionistic evaluation is prolonged in his article, but its weaknesses are revealed with more wit than is often the case. An effete Proustian tourist in the hinterland of literature, Georges Perros evokes an

> Œuvre à elle-même posthume, qui respire légèrement dans une éternité du second rayon, un peu comme ces villages qui nécessitent un détour, que les routes nationales laissent toujours à quelques kilomètres de leur enfer motorisé, je pense à Vézelay, à Illiers ... D'où Joubert a la postérité qu'il mérite, qu'il se souhaitait. Peu connu, peu lu, mais passionnément, il passe en douceur les générations successives, montrant à peine ses papiers à la douane.[2]

This image of passport and customs reminds us of Joubert's real passport, displayed, along with the only known portrait of him, at the exhibition of 1954 in the Bibliothèque Nationale, commemorating the two-hundredth anniversary of his birth: 'Agé de 67 ans, taille d'un mètre quatre-vingts centimètres, cheveux (néant), front haut, sourcils châtains, yeux bruns, nez long, bouche moyenne, barbe châtaine, menton rond, visage ovale, teint ordinaire. Signes particuliers: portant perruque.'[3] The picture that emerges is as pale and skeletal as that which confronts most customs officials to this day; and the portrait of

---

[1] G. Perros, 'Joubert', *Les Cahiers du chemin*, 13 (15 Oct. 1971), 130–1.
[2] Ibid. 134.
[3] Bibliothèque Nationale, *Joseph Joubert, 1754–1824: Exposition organisée pour le 200ᵉ anniversaire de sa naissance* (Paris, 1954), 15.

Joubert by his niece Sophie, which attempts to flesh out these contours, is limited by being a simple profile of the writer's head. So Joubert remains for most a literary enigma, victim of a host of second-rate journalistic 'appreciations' which have saluted successive editions of his *pensées* and *maximes* since their first publication in 1838, some fourteen years after the author's death. In recent years a number of short studies by distinguished critics has done something to restore his reputation. Before referring to these, however, it is necessary to ask why it took over 120 years for anything approaching a proper understanding of the nature of Joubert's work to materialize.

The answer lies almost entirely in the nature of the manuscripts available to nineteenth- and twentieth-century editors of Joubert— when they took the trouble, that is, to consult them at all. What we now call the *Carnets* of Joseph Joubert, the term used by André Beaunier, editor of the most complete twentieth-century edition of Joubert's private journal, are in fact a collection of some two hundred small jotters and sixty bundles of *feuilles volantes* which the author used between 1774 and 1824 for the purpose of taking notes. At some unknown date during the late nineteenth century the jotters were stitched, sometimes carelessly, into sixteen small volumes bound in brown leather. To this day they belong to the direct descendants of Arnaud Joubert, a brother of Joseph, and they have been consulted in the research for this study.[4] The *feuilles volantes* mostly now belong to another branch of the family and may be examined at Bussy-le-Repos, near the Burgundian town of Villeneuve-sur-Yonne, where Joubert spent much of his adult life.

All these manuscripts were made available to Joubert's first editor, his nephew, Jean-Baptiste-Michel Duchesne. Until recently it had always been thought that Chateaubriand was solely responsible for the choice and publication of *pensées* from the original manuscripts, but, in 1976, Rémy Tessonneau published an interesting article proving that this was far from being the case.[5] There is no need to repeat every detail of Tessonneau's findings here, but it is necessary to dwell briefly on the history of the 1838 and 1842 editions, in order to show how Joubert's fate was sealed from the very first by the unscrupulous activities of his relatives.

[4] These manuscripts belong to M. Paul du Chayla and may be consulted in Paris. See Preface.
[5] R. Tessonneau, 'Chateaubriand, Éditeur de Fontanes et de Joubert', *Revue d'histoire littéraire de la France* (May/June 1976), 433–42.

When Joubert died in 1824, his widow opened the large trunk to which he habitually consigned his papers, and was the first to experience the kind of horror felt by future editors and critics of Joubert as they contemplated the apparent disorganization of a lifetime spent scribbling notes on the back of envelopes and sticking safety pins through fragments of scrap paper, somewhat in the manner of a dying Pascal. Mme Joubert gave the task of putting some kind of 'order' into her husband's work to Duchesne, who totally neglected the *feuilles volantes* and concerned himself solely with the selection of passages from the jotters. This selection was extremely inadequate, in so far as Duchesne included only those *pensées* he could understand and those which were written in a legible hand. His real and perhaps only merit is to have made careful notes of the dates Joubert had affixed to his various thoughts, thus providing a future editor with the possibility of producing a relatively chronological edition of Joubert's work.

This 443-page manuscript was handed over to Chateaubriand, who, far from checking Duchesne's material with the original manuscripts, proceeded to narrow down the selection even further by scoring out those *pensées* with which he personally disagreed or which he thought politically suspect.[6] Chateaubriand did not stop here either, for he was quite content to chop a *pensée* in half and replace the ending with another one. If a suitable example did not present itself, he did not scruple to finish it himself.

Today's editor turns away from this manuscript, with a mixture of interest and despair, to a large black folio volume of well over 620 pages that constitutes the manuscript compiled by Paul de Raynal, a nephew by marriage of Joubert, in the course of producing his 1842 edition.[7]

Raynal's manuscript is, in its own way, a thorough piece of work, listing in the wide margin of every page the date of each *pensée*, its number in the 1838 edition, and the new number ascribed to it in the forthcoming edition. The material *was* there for a bigger and better chronological Joubert. Certainly the 1842 edition does give us more: many of the letters he wrote to family and friends are included, but this version suffers from the same fault as the earlier one. For Raynal's manuscript contains just as many crossings out, rearrangements, and

---

[6] This manuscript is entitled: 'Pensées de M. Joubert. Manuscrit de M. de Chateaubriand'.

[7] This manuscript is entitled: 'Pensées—Manuscrit'. Details of successive editions of Joubert's *pensées* may be found in the bibliography.

personal additions as that used by Chateaubriand. The same process of editorial interference is visible if we look at Raynal's personal copy of the 1842 edition, which he annotated heavily in preparation for another edition of the *pensées*.

To a considerable degree, therefore, the figure presented to the critics of the nineteenth and twentieth centuries, until 1938, was an invention of Duchesne, Chateaubriand, and Paul de Raynal. Since most later editors continued, blithely, to reproduce Raynal's edition—'la vulgate du texte', as Claude Pichois puts it[8]—without recourse to the original manuscripts, there was little chance of anyone being able to penetrate the myth Joubert's family wove piously around him. As Patricia Ward points out in the introduction to her book on Joubert's 'Platonism', the use of the word *pensées* in the title of the first editions, 'with its apparent meaning of *maxims*, immediately placed Joubert within the great tradition of French *moralistes* such as Montaigne, La Rochefoucauld and La Bruyère'.[9] Raynal then capitalized on this initial identification by arranging his selection from the manuscripts into thematic chapters which were primarily moral, religious, and philosophical in emphasis, aesthetic and critical concerns receiving scant attention.

From the very beginning, therefore, Joubert's reputation was never allowed to be anything other than that of a fine purveyor of moralizing aphorisms. This suited the embalming tactics of a family who genuinely revered a much-loved relative. However, the remarkable series of financial calculations made by Paul de Raynal on the flyleaf of his 1842 edition bear amusing testimony to the way Joubert's loquacity had to be tailored to fit the pecuniary stringencies of a successful nineteenth-century publishing house.

A by-product of this myth was a less savoury tendency on the part of Raynal and subsequent editors to dwell on Joubert's delicate constitution, partly in an attempt to explain why he confined his energies to the small-scale art of the maxim. Mme de Chastenay's description of Joubert as an 'âme qui semblait n'avoir rencontré un corps que par hazard'[10] recurs with depressing frequency in much nineteenth-century criticism. Yet this is the most discreet formulation of a type of simpering intimacy that reaches sickening proportions in the preface by

---

[8] C. Pichois, 'Actualité de Joubert', *Revue des cercles d'études d'Angers*, 15–16 (Nov. 1954), 27.
[9] *Critical Tradition*, 22.
[10] *Mémoires de Mme de Chastenay, 1771–1815* (2 vols.; Paris, 1897), ii. 82–3. See also C ii. 716.

Matthew Arnold's niece, Mrs Humphry Ward, to her translation of selected *pensées* from the Raynal edition. In fact Mrs Ward does little more than paraphrase Raynal's own anecdotal emasculation of Joubert, but for some reason their evocation of a Joubert who spent 'whole days in bed, clad in the pink silk spencer that his friends remembered, couched there "like a horse in its stall, trying to feel nothing and think of nothing"' sounds more extraordinary in English than it does in French. Joubert's 'half-feminine interest in his own peculiarities' is dwelt on with a merciless relish that climaxes in a paroxysm of enthusiasm for a gentle androgyne who would 'retire to bed for days together, to avoid the excitement of friends and conversation. One day he will live on milk, another day on mincemeat,' she exclaims, and always, for her, Joubert is merely the 'friend, talker, thinker—the impulse and critic of other men's lives'.[11] Mrs Ward goes on to quote Chateaubriand's story, to be found in the *Mémoires d'outre-tombe*, according to which Joubert's library was full of books vandalized by their prudish and discerning owner, who would leave them, 'shivering in their half-empty covers'.[12] The story is apocryphal, but it is tempting to see in the persistence with which it has been repeated a proof of the laziness and prudence of critics and editors, loath to step out of line and only too willing to shelter behind the impeccable grandeur and 'integrity' of Chateaubriand.[13] Such an authority was not to be questioned, and so came into being the emasculated, official Joubert whose book was accepted by the nineteenth century as a 'livre de chevet par excellence'.[14] As Claude Pichois has written, 'toute bonne bibliothèque, à côté de son Montaigne, a contenu un Joubert. Emailler sa conversation de quelques maximes de Joubert' was proof of adherence to the culture of 'une société snob ... qui fleurissait et fleurit peut-être encore du côté de Passy et d'Auteuil'.[15]

Mrs Humphry Ward's preface, however, builds not only on Paul de Raynal's view of his relative but on the three most influential essays to appear on Joubert during the nineteenth century. The first two of these were by Sainte-Beuve, who played a considerable role in popularizing

---

[11] Katherine Lyttelton (ed.), *Joubert: A Selection from his Thoughts*, with a preface by Mrs Humphrey Ward (London, 1898), pp. xix, xx, xi.

[12] R. de Chateaubriand, *Mémoires d'outre-tombe*, ed. M. Levaillant and G. Moulinier (2 vols.; Paris, 1958), i. 450.

[13] See, for example, J. d'Ormesson's repetition of this cliché in his *Mon dernier rêve sera pour vous: Une biographie sentimentale de Chateaubriand* (Paris, 1982), 63.

[14] J.-P. Clarens, *Joubert* (Paris, 1893).

[15] Pichois, 27.

the early editions of the *pensées* and *maximes*. Much of his criticism was of the kind that gave added impetus to the type discussed above. Joubert belonged to 'cette classe d'honnêtes gens, comme l'ancienne société seule en produisait, spectateurs, écouteurs sans ambition, sans envie, curieux, vacants, attentifs, désinteressés et prenant intérêt à tout, le véritable amateur de belles choses', and Sainte-Beuve was the first to encourage even further selection from the choice of Joubert's thought already made: 'C'est de l'esprit distillé et fixé dans tout son suc: on n'en saurait prendre beaucoup à la fois,' he wrote. Therefore 'il sera convenable qu'un jour de tous ces chapitres métaphysiques, on n'en fasse qu'un seul, très-réduit, dans lequel on n'admettra que les pensées belles, simples, acceptables, rejetant toutes celles qui sont équivoques ou énigmatiques'.[16]

The importance and distinctive characteristics of Sainte-Beuve's essays on Joubert, however, are not fully apparent until they are compared with the article by Matthew Arnold which appeared in the *National Review* in January 1864, entitled *Joubert; or, a French Coleridge*. Arnold read *Chateaubriand et son groupe littéraire sous l'Empire* shortly after its publication in 1861 and his essay certainly bears the marks of Sainte-Beuve's influence.[17] There are significant differences, however, which need to be highlighted, since much, if not all, of the criticism that appeared after 1864 tended to polarize around the competing bias of these two critical stances.

As the quotation from his essay in *Causeries du lundi* indicates, Sainte-Beuve did not care much for Joubert's metaphysical speculations:

Les premiers chapitres du premier volume ne sont pas ceux qui me plaisent le plus; ils traitent de Dieu, de la création, de l'éternité, et de bien d'autres choses. A la difficulté particulière des sujets, s'ajoute celle qui naît de la subtilité de l'auteur. Ici ce n'est pas seulement du Platon, c'est du Saint-Augustin à haute dose et sans la liaison des idées.[18]

---

[16] C. A. Sainte-Beuve, *Les Grands Écrivains français*, ed. M. Allen (23 vols.; Paris 1930), xii, pt. i. *Philosophes et essayistes*, 190, 200. The two main articles are reproduced together in this volume, pp. 164–209; the first was originally published in *Critiques et portraits littéraires* (Paris, 1839), v. 396–427; the second in *Causeries du Lundi* (Paris, 1857), i. 159–78.

[17] The circumstances surrounding Arnold's reading of Sainte-Beuve are given in *The Complete Prose Works of Matthew Arnold*, ed. R. H. Super (11 vols.; Ann Arbor, Mich., 1960–77), iii. 451.

[18] Sainte-Beuve, *Philosophes*, 200.

Sainte-Beuve objected strongly to Raynal's attempt to present, from the outset, the portrait of an essentially religious thinker. Yet this was precisely what appealed most to Arnold. As Patricia Ward rightly notes, 'Unlike Sainte-Beuve ... Arnold delineates a portrait of a religious and moral critic. Although he notes Joubert's Platonism, he does not make a great deal of it.'[19] This divergence needs to be emphasized and gravitates around the important distinctions to be made between French and Anglo-Saxon understandings of the terms *moralist* and *rhetoric*.

Even when Arnold cites a number of Joubert's remarks on literature, it is in order to show 'the same sedulousness in him to preserve perfectly true the balance of his soul'. He compares him with Coleridge because he can find no one in France at all like him: 'Joubert had around him in France an atmosphere of literary, philosophical and religious opinion as alien to him as that in England was to Coleridge,' he writes. The comparison with Coleridge could have given Arnold the opportunity to describe their respective theories of the imagination, but what interests him is that 'they both had from nature an ardent impulse for seeking the genuine truth on all matters they thought about'. Finally, Arnold uses Joubert as a kind of morally self-righteous stick with which to beat the mischief out of Voltaire and the enervating passion from Rousseau. Joubert is the perfect *moralist* in the sense that he is 'disinterested', detached from his time, his value not to be found 'in what is exclusively intellectual' but 'in the union of *soul* with intellect', the 'most prepossessing and convincing of witnesses to the good of loving light'.[20]

The essential thrust of Sainte-Beuve's criticism, however, was rather different:

C'est quand il revient à parler des mœurs et des arts, de l'antiquité et du siècle, de la poésie et de la critique, du style et du goût, c'est sur tous ces sujets qu'il nous plaît et nous charme, qu'il nous paraît avoir ajouté une part notable et neuve au trésor de ses devanciers les plus excellents ... Malgré toutes ses religions de l'antique et ses regrets du passé, on distingue aussitôt en lui le cachet du temps où il vit.[21]

---

[19] *Critical Tradition*, 28.
[20] Arnold, ed. Super, iii. 201, 193, 189, 208.
[21] Sainte-Beuve, *Philosophes*, 201, 204.

These characteristics, identified by Sainte-Beuve, are of particular interest, because they correspond almost exactly to those of *le moraliste classique*, as defined and described by Louis van Delft.[22] Van Delft is careful to note Sainte-Beuve's own tendency to use *moraliste* and *philosophe* as interchangeable terms, in accordance with contemporary hesitation over the status of the former word.[23] In so far as Van Delft finds a common denominator, however, in the way in which *le moraliste* is expected to remain 'proche du vécu' in his speculations, then Sainte-Beuve's overt rejection of Joubert's metaphysical concerns and preference for his analysis of *mœurs* and *arts*, his expression of 'le cachet du temps où il vit', shows to what extent we are supposed to fit him into a distinct French tradition of *devanciers*.[24]

In particular, however, Sainte-Beuve's use of the word *mœurs*, as distinct from *la morale* or *le moral*, leads to the recognition of confusion or ambiguity present within the French understanding itself of the term *moraliste*. Van Delft points out that, if critics, past and present, have expected a *moraliste* to remain 'proche du vécu', they differ considerably in their appreciation of the point of view or state of mind from which these speculations may be directed:

Tout le long de son histoire le terme *moraliste* a subi l'attraction ou, plus exactement, ne s'est que difficilement dégagé de l'attraction exercée par le terme *morale*. Ce n'est que par intervalles—cas des Encyclopédistes ayant ... assimilé les idées de Montesquieu, cas de Sainte-Beuve—que l'on a considéré que le 'moraliste' pouvait se démarquer de la morale, observer les mœurs pour elles-mêmes. Cette ... sorte de subordination du terme *moraliste* à celui de *morale* explique que l'on ait si souvent attendu de ce type d'écrivain qu'il soit au service d'un impératif moral.

As Van Delft writes elsewhere: '*Morale* renvoie, non seulement en 1690, mais bien souvent au XVIIIe siècle encore, à ce qu'on appelle

[22] L. Van Delft, *Le Moraliste classique: Essai de définition et de typologie* (Geneva, 1982).
[23] Ibid. 32–3.
[24] Van Delft is of help when defining Sainte-Beuve's understanding of the term *moraliste*, yet this is particularly ironic when we consider that Van Delft blithely uses Joubert, *as categorized by Sainte-Beuve*, in his definition of this word. 'Le moraliste', Van Delft writes, 'revient toujours à la nature humaine ... Son ordre est celui de l'Homme; le mouvement, la pente de sa curiosité le ramènent toujours au vécu, '*le physique*' remplace '*la métaphysique*'. This is the 'lieu du moraliste' and Van Delft employs an antithesis Joubert himself uses to distinguish metaphysicians from the *moraliste* who operates 'non dans le ciel, mais dans la vie'. To quote Joubert in this way is to reject, as Sainte-Beuve did, the early chapters of Raynal's first edition of the *Pensées* and the 'intention aux choses du ciel', more comprehensively illustrated by the Beaunier edition of 1938. (Van Delft, 106, 31.)

alors très généralement "la morale chrétienne". *Mœurs* renvoie à une réalité pouvant être soumise à l'observation.'[25] It is noteworthy, in this context, that the *Dictionnaire de l'Académie* of 1762, perhaps stimulated by the example of the *Encyclopédie*, was the first to define *moraliste*: 'un écrivain qui traite des mœurs', in opposition to Furetière's 'auteur qui écrit, qui traite de la morale'.[26]

Sainte-Beuve, therefore, implicitly recognizes in Joubert an independent, perhaps even critical, attitude towards a subject-matter, much of which is rooted in 'le temps où il vit'.[27] *Mœurs*, indeed, can also be understood in the sense of the psychological characteristics of a given people or nation and it is clear how far such an interest is from the 'disinterested', timeless wisdom, the eternally valid message, which Arnold expects his isolated *moralist* to dispense.

Here it is worth drawing attention to similarities between Arnold's description of Joubert as *moralist* and the distinguishing characteristics of a group of men L. A. Selby-Bigge chose to call *British Moralists*. Writing in 1897, Selby-Bigge brought together selections from work which we now recognize as constituting British Moral Philosophy of the eighteenth century. Included in his selection are figures such as Shaftesbury, Hutcheson, Butler, Adam Smith, and Bentham among others, and, when D. D. Raphael produced a new edition of this work in 1969, he expanded it to take in Hobbes and Locke.[28] Significantly, Selby-Bigge starts his introduction by comparing the *moralist* to the *satirist*, but an attentive reader of Sainte-Beuve might be forgiven for wishing to substitute *moraliste* for the latter term:

The moralist and the satirist are not always suited to understand each other. The moralist seems to the satirist to discourse of a state of things which is not and never was, and to assume the prevalence of motives which never entirely determine and do not considerably influence the actions of ordinary men. When the moralist says that men ought to regulate their conduct on certain principles and ought to cultivate certain motives in preference to others, the satirist tests the possibility of these principles by asking whether in fact men do usually or ever act on them: he does not ask how far men recognize them as

---

[25] Van Delft, 35–6, 23.
[26] Ibid. 23, 17.
[27] Sainte-Beuve, *Philosophes*, 204.
[28] L. A. Selby-Bigge, *British Moralists: Being Selections from Writers Principally of the Eighteenth Century* (2 vols.; Oxford, 1897). D. D. Raphael, *British Moralists, 1650–1800* (2 vols.; Oxford, 1969).

ideals or standards of conduct ... Satire stops short of philosophy, even of sceptical philosophy.[29]

We can see here the same utopian disinterestedness present in Arnold's understanding of the word *moralist*, and there can be little doubt that Arnold would not have objected to conferring upon Joubert the dignity of the moral philosopher. It is to the point, also, that Selby-Bigge goes on to cite La Rochefoucauld, one of the stars in the French firmament of *moralistes*, as a *satirist*.

We can see, therefore, how partial are the descriptions of Joubert as *moraliste* and *moralist* by Sainte-Beuve and Arnold. On the one hand Sainte-Beuve neglects the genuinely metaphysical and spiritual dimension of Joubert's speculations in order to root him in a French tradition of social criticism, while pointing usefully to his merits as an aesthetician.[30] Matthew Arnold, on the other, neglects this last aspect and emphasizes his role as a religious philosopher, paying little attention to the question of tradition.

Sainte-Beuve's Joubert is, in fact, a less lonely figure than that of Matthew Arnold. However, one can hardly be blamed for wishing that Sainte-Beuve had been a little less emphatic in his assignment to Joubert of kindred spirits. At the conclusion of his 1849 article Sainte-Beuve relates how 'je me suis demandé quelquefois ce que pourrait être une rhétorique française ...'. This turns out to include Pascal, La Bruyère, Fénelon, and Vauvenargues: 'Puis, le cercle classique accompli, j'ai donné M. Joubert à mes jeunes gens pour dessert en quelque sorte, pour récréation, et pour petite débauche finale, une débauche digne de Pythagore! Et ma rhétorique française s'est trouvée finie.'[31]

In the light of evidence to be discussed later, Sainte-Beuve's reference to Pythagoras becomes slightly ironic, but for the moment all that is necessary is to underline the desire to provide some kind of historical context for Joubert's writing by the use of the word *rhétorique*.

Sainte-Beuve's *rhétorique* is that of the French scholastic tradition based on the examples of antiquity and taught since the Middle Ages as the staple unit of the school curriculum. Littré defines *rhétorique* as 'l'art de bien dire ou l'art de parler de manière à persuader; la dialectique

---

[29] Selby-Bigge, p. xi.
[30] As Patricia Ward points out, Sainte-Beuve also understood how 'thought and image were indissolubly linked in Joubert's mind: "sa méthode est de toujours rendre une pensée dans une image; la pensée et l'image pour lui ne font qu'un" ' (*Critical Tradition*, 25, quoting Sainte-Beuve, *Philosophes*, 199).
[31] Sainte-Beuve, *Philosophes*, 205–6.

des vraisemblances suivant la définition d'Aristote', following this immediately with a reference to its status as a 'terme de collège'. Van Delft notes the belief of the German philosopher Dilthey that the art of the moralist 's'apparente ... à l'art des sophistes et des rhéteurs de l'Antiquité: à la preuve méthodique se substitue l'art de persuader',[32] and this notion of *rhétorique* as dialectic, as debate, central to the French understanding of the term, inherited from Cicero, is far from the modern Anglo-Saxon conception of it which developed during the eighteenth century and which Arnold himself uses in his essay on Joubert. The *OED* defines *rhetoric* as 'a body of rules to be observed by a speaker or writer in order that he may express himself with eloquence', and here it is useful to consult W. S. Howells's work on eighteenth-century British logic and rhetoric, which demonstrates how the reforms of Ramus tended to limit rhetoric to questions of delivery and to the mere externals of style.[33] This led to the elocutionary movement of the eighteenth and nineteenth centuries, which was frequently identified with the whole of the art it should have served and completely neglected those other procedures such as *inventio* and *dispositio*, essential to the dignity of rhetoric as an art which aids Man to discover truth and improve his capacity to exchange ideas.

Howells reproduces a passage from an English translation of Fénelon's *Dialogues sur l'éloquence* which may be read as an accurate gloss on the differences existing between French and British understandings of the term *rhetoric*. Fénelon himself, of course, is distinguishing between two *ancient* rhetorics, but the description remains relevant to the point in question: 'Plato in his *Phaedrus* shews us, that the greatest Fault of Rhetoricians is their studying the Art of Persuasion, before they have learn't (from the Principles of true Philosophy), what those things are of which they ought to persuade Men.'[34] It is hardly surprising, then, to discover that rhetoric for Arnold is a pleasurable, essentially decorative form of discourse, liable to abuse and unfit for the teasing out of truth itself. In fact, he establishes a dichotomy between truth and rhetoric. Joubert could penetrate to the 'vraie vérité' of things, whereas someone like Lord Macaulay stopped short at rhetorical truth: 'Rhetoric so good as his excites and gives pleasure; but by pleasure alone

---

[32] Van Delft, 41.
[33] W. S. Howells, *Eighteenth-Century British Logic and Rhetoric* (Princeton, NJ, 1971), 78–9.
[34] Ibid. 506.

you cannot permanently bind men's spirits to you. Truth illuminates and gives joy.'[35]

If two distinct traditions of Joubertian criticism emerge from the divergent impetus of these different views, they do not organize themselves along exclusively national lines: the English and American successors of Matthew Arnold do not all follow obediently in his wake, just as the French do not blindly adhere to Sainte-Beuve. Partly, this is due to the complicating factors introduced by the publication in 1938 by André Beaunier of a 'complete' chronological edition of Joubert's journal. Suddenly Joubert was seen as a figure of far greater complexity than his description as a moralist by either Sainte-Beuve or Arnold allowed, however different their conceptions of this kind of writer may have been. Margaret Gilman, to take one example, was stimulated by this publication to examine Joubert's debt in aesthetic matters to Diderot, and thus provided a historical context for his theories, which was in accord with the thrust of Sainte-Beuve's criticism.[36] As Patricia Ward acknowledges, Sainte-Beuve himself hints at the influence of Diderot on Joubert's knowledge of art and literature.[37]

On the other hand, both André Monglond and Pierre Moreau, working before Beaunier published the results of his research, forced Joubert, despite discussion of his poetics, to adopt a more or less 'moral' attitude towards Rousseau, thus following the example set by Matthew Arnold.[38]

Of the two traditions, that coming from Sainte-Beuve *appears* to be the stronger, but—and it is from here that much of the confusion about the nature of the critical tradition surrounding Joubert stems—this is due to the unorthodox twist given by later critics to the comparison of Joubert with Coleridge in Matthew Arnold's essay. George Saintsbury's appreciation of Joubert's opinions about poetry could be seen as a tribute to the initial speculations of Sainte-Beuve; they are certainly related to Jules Lemaître's vision of Joubert as a precursor of the symbolists, in itself a development of Sainte-Beuve's concern with

---

[35] Arnold, ed. Super, 210.
[36] M. Gilman, 'Joubert on Imagination and Poetry', *Romanic Review*, 40 (1949), 250–60.
[37] *Critical Tradition*, 24.
[38] A. Monglond, *Histoire intérieure du préromantisme français de Prévost à Joubert* (2 vols.; Grenoble, 1929). P. Moreau, *Le Classicisme des romantiques* (Paris, 1932).

aesthetics.[39] The shadow of Matthew Arnold is there, however, in the insistence that 'In literature ... his time exerts remarkably little influence on Joubert',[40] and it was in thinking of Arnold's recourse to a comparison of Joubert with Coleridge and, perhaps, of the aesthetic parallels he did *not* draw, that Saintsbury went on to concentrate on just this aspect of his author's thought. Indeed, Saintsbury's criticism is of crucial importance for the future delineation of Joubert's position in the 'critical tradition'. We imagine him, weighing up the arguments of Sainte-Beuve and Arnold, noting the former's attention to Joubert's aesthetics, but missing the assignment of him to a distinct French rhetorical tradition, attracted by Arnold's suggestive comparison with Coleridge and ignoring his refusal to make aesthetic capital out of it. Saintsbury's combination of elements from both French and Anglo-Saxon attitudes to Joubert was to prove fatally influential over the course of the following century.

If this is an unnecessarily devious argument, then one should look at Saintsbury's successors, those of any distinction writing in America. Patricia Ward declares that 'In America, intermittent interest has been shown in Joubert, almost always as a critic or aesthetician,' and relates Irving Babbitt's praise of 'Joubert's gift of intuition' and interest in his 'intuition of the Many and intuition of the One' to this trend.[41] This should not obscure the fact, however, that these considerations serve a basically 'moral' purpose; Joubert's Platonic 'enthusiasm' is used to counter the 'Rousseauistic' enthusiasm of Mme de Staël, and Arnold's similar use of Joubert as an antidote or corrective to Rousseau is certainly not far from Babbitt's mind.[42]

Much later in the present century the influence of Arnold and Saintsbury is still apparent in the insistence of both René Wellek and Patricia Ward that Joubert stands apart from his contemporaries in his insights on the nature of poetry and in a comparison with Coleridge and a number of German romantics. By now the comparison with

---

[39] G. Saintsbury, *A History of Criticism and Literary Taste in Europe* (3 vols.; Edinburgh and London, 1900–4). J. Lemaître, *Les Contemporains*, 6th ser. (Paris, 1896), 302–7.

[40] Saintsbury, iii. 118. This statement could be seen, also, as a commonplace of spiritualist criticism seeking to rescue an author from the materialistic contamination of the eighteenth century.

[41] *Critical Tradition*, 31.

[42] I. Babbitt, *The Masters of Modern French Criticism* (London, and Boston and New York, 1913).

Coleridge is of a purely aesthetic nature, due, probably, to the influence of the Beaunier edition and essays by Gilman, Poulet, and Blanchot.[43]

In France, it is possible to identify the continuing influence of Sainte-Beuve in remarks by the Goncourt brothers, Barbey d'Aurevilly, and Jules Lemaître. De Goncourt refers to Joubert in passing as 'le La Bruyère du filigrane'; Barbey d'Aurevilly, the right-wing Catholic, picks up on Sainte-Beuve's reference to Joubert's Platonism and notes 'Regardez bien ce Joubert, et voyez s'il n'est pas Platon, à sa manière; un Platon moderne, chrétien, par conséquent plus Platon, par là, que Platon lui-même.'[44] This little remark is rather important, for it implies that d'Aurevilly saw Joubert as a Christian neo-Platonist, a suggestion first made by Sainte-Beuve which Georges Poulet and Patricia Ward develop in the twentieth century. Lemaître, as we have remarked, made out a case for Joubert as a symbolist with a Baudelairean theory of *correspondances*, and there can be little doubt that the growing perception in France of Joubert, as Ward puts it, as 'an important link with the idealist tradition in aesthetics', influenced critics like Saintsbury, Babbitt and Wellek, although it could not eradicate that of Arnold.[45] Around the turn of the century Richard Arthur provides us with an interesting and amusing example of this. Reacting perhaps to the attitudes of Lemaître, he claimed that Joubert's theory of art was

---

[43] R. Wellek, *A History of Modern Criticism*, ii. *The Romantic Age* (New Haven, Conn., and London, 1955), Patricia Ward's title—*Joseph Joubert and the Critical Tradition*—is misleading, for she remains content in her opening chapters to describe this tradition rather than to analyse it. Ward joins Sainte-Beuve in acknowledging Joubert's Platonism and in dismissing the religious critic, but deviates on to the path initiated by Matthew Arnold with the statement that 'Joubert was largely a generation ahead of his time' and that parallels may be looked for mainly among 'his contemporaries in Germany and England' (p. 11).

[44] E. and J. de Goncourt, *Mémoires de la vie littéraire* (édition définitive publiée sous la direction de l'Académie Goncourt; 9 vols.; Paris, 1935–36), iii. 96. J. Barbey d'Aurevilly, 'Joubert', in *Les Œuvres et les hommes: Les Critiques ou les juges jugés* (Paris, 1885), vi. 192.

More recently, Paul Bénichou has shown how Sainte-Beuve's classification of Joubert among the figures of Chateaubriand's 'groupe littéraire' can still mislead eminent critics. Bénichou, whose treatment of Joubert in *Le Sacre de l'écrivain* (Paris, 1973) is otherwise sensitive, makes the error of assigning him to the generation born around 1770, including, among others, Fiévée, l'abbé de Féletz, the Michaud brothers, Dussault, and Delalot. 'Cette génération est celle de Joubert et de Chateaubriand,' he declares, only a paragraph after noting the outstanding figures of the earlier generation born between 1742 and 1754, including Clément, Geoffroy, Mme de Genlis, Rivarol, La Harpe, Bonald, and Joseph de Maistre. Joubert was born, like Bonald, in 1754, and by no stretch of the imagination can he be considered as 'ayant juste atteint l'âge d'homme en 1789', or as having 'vécu la secousse révolutionnaire à [son] entrée dans la vie' (p. 113).

[45] *Critical Tradition*, 26.

quite opposed to what was later to be the manifesto of the 'art-for-art's-sake' movement. Bowing a fraction to pressure, Arthur admits Joubert's 'vague, mystic, instinctive notions of the unknowable' but brings up an entire battery of Arnoldian epithets to temper his 'aerial flights'. '[Joubert] is emotional, but calmly; enthusiastic but temperately; elated but soberly ... he differed from those of his fellows, the disciples of the Art for Art's sake doctrine, and from those others who profess to follow Art simply for truth's sake, in that for him Beauty and truth were interdependent, reciprocal, inseparable.'[46] This is a statement of marvellously anachronistic nonsense, the term 'art-for-art's sake' being unknown before 1829 at the earliest and not really launched until Gautier's 1835 preface to *Mademoiselle de Maupin*, and its resurgence as a movement in the 1860s.

The publication in 1938 of André Beaunier's edition of the *Carnets* did not necessarily provide, however, an immediate solution to the problems involved in a critical evaluation of Joubert. Indeed the intrinsic flaws of this edition did not help critics who used it to counteract pre-established critical prejudices, and no introduction to a study of Joubert can fail to take them into account.

Marcel Prévost, in a review of the edition in June 1938, was one of the first to voice his bewilderment: 'On conçoit que mille pages in-quarto couvertes—sans ordre prémédité—par des pensées dont le plus grand nombre n'excède pas quelques lignes, découragent à l'avance l'effort qui voudrait les résumer.'[47] Daniel-Rops, also reviewing, had similar reservations and added the valid point that the complete absence of any kind of subject index made the volumes extremely difficult to use:

En publiant les carnets tels qu'ils sont, sans y introduire le classement par titres et paragraphes qu'avait imposé, à la façon d'un carcan, Paul de Raynal, l'éditeur d'aujourd'hui respecte mieux la pensée de l'auteur, mais le lecteur s'y retrouve plus malaisément. Établir des tables méthodiques serait assurément un gros travail: il serait bien souhaitable que quelque jeune candidat à l'agrégation de lettres s'en chargeât.[48]

---

[46] R. Arthur, 'Joseph Joubert', *Westminster Review*, 148 (Nov. 1897), 524–36. Quoted by Ward, *Critical Tradition*, 30.
[47] M. Prévost, 'Les Carnets de Joseph Joubert', in *Marcel Prévost et ses contemporains* (2 vols.; Paris, 1943), i. 135.
[48] H. Daniel-Rops, 'Les Carnets de Joseph Joubert', *La Revue hebdomadaire* (June–July 1938), 104.

Daniel-Rops's condescension is the product of sheer intellectual laziness, demanding his 'Tables analytiques' because reluctant to read all the text, and only willing to make an opinion on the items presented to him for his attention. Needless to say the creation of some form of subject index is necessary, but it cannot be regarded as a mechanical preliminary to the criticism of Joubert. It is sometimes very hard to classify his thoughts under a simple rubric; indeed this would demand a considerable degree of judgement as well as familiarity with the historical and cultural commonplaces of the period. What is more, it is a vital preliminary to any and every study of Joubert that pretends to base its evidence on Beaunier's chronological edition. Nearly all the critics who have written on Joubert since 1938 have felt obliged to use it and, in part, it is this very fact, involving as it does the initial work of classification, that has prevented them from going further than they have done.

Critics of Joubert are further handicapped by other basic faults in this edition. At the back of the second volume an index of names mentioned by Joubert is to be found, but this is lamentably incomplete. According to this table, Plato is mentioned seventy-seven times, whereas in reality he is referred to on more than 120 different occasions. This has led a number of writers into critical inaccuracy and a list of references by Joubert to Plato and the *Dialogues* may be found in an appendix to the present study.

Even more serious is the almost complete lack of scholarly critical apparatus in the form of notes to the text. Beaunier was engaged in this task at the time of his death, but what we have left is inadequate in the extreme. Nineteenth-century critics, relying on Raynal's classification, could write blithely that 'M. Joubert est l'homme du monde qui se passe le mieux de commentaires et d'interprétations',[49] but anyone confronted, for only a few minutes, with Beaunier's twentieth-century edition understands that this is not the case. Examples of such omission include frequent references, throughout the *Carnets*, to books Joubert has read, as well as to particular page numbers and quotations. These are seldom followed up by the editor. Sometimes Beaunier takes the trouble to note that Joubert has written down a list of books in which he has been interested, yet these lists are not always reproduced. Similarly Joubert was in the habit of compiling long lists of quotations from works he had been reading and Beaunier only includes these if

[49] É. Turquety, 'Réponse à un reproche', *Bulletin du bibliophile* (Nov. 1865), 172.

they contain substantial interpolations by Joubert himself. Otherwise they are deemed valueless. Admittedly, Beaunier was faced with producing a marketable text, but it is hard to see why he should have excluded such information, given his readiness to include totally obscure entries that cannot possibly be deciphered or, for example, thermometer readings of the weather which Joubert diligently carried out from time to time.

As indicated, however, such drawbacks have not prevented some good critical essays on Joubert from appearing. Those by Blanchot and Poulet are extremely eloquent analyses of Joubert's appreciation of what might be called the *bearable* lightness of being, his recognition of the illusory opacity of matter and the need to discover 'cette source de l'écriture, cet espace où écrire', an 'espace' creative of the kind of philosophical and poetic discourse irradiated by the divine light which animates the vast spaces of the universe itself.[50] These essays go straight to the heart of Joubert's experience of writing and their testimony will be of considerable relevance at several key points in this study.

Blanchot, in his understandable desire to emphasize the importance of *espace* to Joubert, may, perhaps, be faulted for not giving sufficient attention to his equal interest in 'la ténuité *réelle* de la matière' (C i. 235). Also, both Poulet and Blanchot, obliged by the essay form to draw their conclusions about the nature of Joubert's writing relatively quickly, do not provide a clear picture of the actual content of the *Carnets* and tend to underestimate the influence on Joubert of other writers. As Philippe Garcin writes: 'Chacune des réflexions qu'il énonce porte à la fois le reflet d'un long effort de pensée, la trace d'un vif souci esthétique et déjà la marque d'une ample suite de déductions probables.'[51] Joubert's thoughts so frequently strike us as more than the sum of their parts. They bear the 'reflet' of something that has preceded their final distillation in language. Garcin suggests that this something is 'un long effort de pensée', which is true, but one is tempted to interpolate the words 'sur des textes de base'. One has the notion that these *pensées* emerge ultimately, and sometimes only after some very strange detours, from a sequence of reflections on something quite material, that they do not occur in a vacuum. 'Il faut comprendre Joubert dans l'espace même où sa pensée se constitue,' writes the critic

[50] M. Blanchot, 'Joubert et l'espace', in *Le Livre à venir* (Paris, 1959), 64. Poulet, 'Joubert', in *Mesure de l'instant* (Paris, 1968), 141–55.

[51] P. Garcin, 'Joubert ou la rhétorique efficace', *Critique*, 10 (July–Aug. 1954), 600.

Jean-Louis Chrétien,[52] and that space is not only and not *primarily* the vacant 'zone de recueillement' of which Blanchot speaks so evocatively, but a space full of the porous matter of books read and annotated.[53]

Blanchot is undoubtedly correct when he says that Joubert 'aurait aimé n'être pas de "ces esprits qui s'enfoncent ou pénètrent trop avant dans ce qu'ils pensent"' but the actual content of the *Carnets* shows the vast amount of reading and reflection Joubert had to do before he was able to come to this conclusion. Similarly, Joubert's ultimate goal—'se rendre maître du point d'où lui semblaient sortir tous les livres et qui, une fois trouvé, le dispenserait d'en écrire'—is well defined by Blanchot but can be seen as a better description of what Joubert would have liked to have achieved or did not achieve, than of the actual meditative process to be found in the *Carnets*.[54] Nor can it give us much insight into the *way* Joubert's mind worked in the process of formulating the kind of goals outlined by Poulet and Blanchot. This is partly because many of Joubert's speculations are subtly tangential to those of other writers. Alan Steele puts it well when he says that 'sa pensée frise sans cesse des doctrines et en adopte volontiers les formules, dont cependant elle reste parfaitement distincte'.[55] The reader is constantly stimulated and frequently irritated by echoes and half-echoes of familiar voices caught up in the rhythms of Joubert's thought. Joubert does mention books he has read and occasionally makes helpful references to specific editions and page numbers. They are there to be consulted by those who wish to provide some kind of context for Joubert's thought and believe that it might help them to understand both the workings of his mind and what *he* meant by many of the *pensées*, rather than what they mean to us today. Where these references do not exist, it is possible to bring a general knowledge of literary and philosophical works of the period to bear on the contents of the *Carnets*.

In Joubert's case this approach is rendered more precise by the existence in Paris, Villeneuve-sur-Yonne, and Bussy-le-Repos of a substantial library of books on many subjects collected by him over the

---

[52] J. L. Chrétien, 'Joseph Joubert: Une philosophie à l'état naissant', *La Revue de métaphysique et de morale*, 4, 34 (1979), 467.

[53] M. Blanchot, 'Joubert et Mallarmé', *La Nouvelle Revue française*, 7 (1956), 120; repr. as concluding section in *Le Livre à venir*.

[54] Blanchot, 'Joubert et l'espace', 65, 64.

[55] A. J. Steele, 'La Sagesse de Joubert', in *Studies in Romance Philology and French Literature presented to John Orr* (Manchester, 1953), 284.

course of his life. A number of these have been annotated by Joubert and parallels may be established between passages underlined, marginal comments, and entries in the *Carnets*. Again, such a method does not admit of hard and fast conclusions. There are few occasions when one can point to a particular *pensée* and say that it is a paraphrase or development of a passage in Burke or Montesquieu, but any approach that contributes to the destruction of the myth of a Joubert who lived solely in some kind of rarefied trance, 'trying to feel nothing and think nothing',[56] is worth pursuing.

Indeed, one wonders why the effort to 'contextualize' Joubert has not been made before. The answer may lie simply in the difficulties posed by the Beaunier edition and the possible waning of enthusiasm for the subject after the initial task of classification had been completed and its results analysed. One prefers, however, to conclude that, more recently at least, such a critical approach has been subverted by the conclusions which Poulet and Blanchot reach in their essays and on which we have already touched. Alan Steele entitles his paper 'La Sagesse de Joubert', delineating a philosophy, essentially classical in inspiration, that establishes a dichotomy between mere *knowledge* and divine *sagesse*, *scientia* and *sapientia*. By pursuing the identity of the subtexts to Joubert's thought we fall into the trap that awaited the materialist philosophers of the Enlightenment or the historians of myth like Charles Dupuis or the Baron Sainte-Croix. We are guilty of *libido sciendi*, culpable curiosity. Why can we not accept simply what Joubert gives us?

It is possible to see our refusal to do this as a form of ingratitude. As Blanchot writes of Joubert: 'Il veut que la pensée s'élève au-dessus de la contrainte des raisonnements et des preuves, qu'elle soit pensée finie à partir de l'infini.' He experiences

le désir de substituer à la lecture ordinaire où il faut aller de partie en partie le spectacle d'une parole simultanée où tout serait dit à la fois, sans confusion, dans un 'éclat total, paisible, intime et enfin uniforme'.[57]

Joubert does more than simply experience this desire; he undertakes this hazardous itinerary for us, he reads *for us* or rather for himself, gathering knowledge that is then subjected to a process of necessary purification in a pudic 'distance intérieure' which he tries to put

[56] Mrs Humphrey Ward, 'Preface', in Lyttelton (ed.), *Joubert: A Selection from his Thoughts*, p. xx.
[57] Blanchot, 'Joubert et l'espace', 77, 76.

between him and the fruit of his study, transforming it into 'la sagesse'. The *pensée* that he would then present to us is a miniature 'éclat total', an achieved gift, a moment of 'repos' which he might offer himself and the sympathetic reader. That, at least, Blanchot suggests, may have been the theoretical goal. Whether Joubert actually did wish to achieve this and, if he did, whether he succeeded, remains to be seen.[58]

To examine the sources upon which he operated, from which he drew his inspiration, as this study attempts to do, is to open and drink from a poisoned well that may help us to understand something of the intellectual struggle he underwent but little of the spiritual repose that Joubert claimed as his life's reward. Yet Joubert's fascination lies as much in his incorrigible curiosity about the workings of the human mind, his interest in the process of creativity that lies behind a thought or the expression of a thought, as in the nature of its final form, and he himself gave voice frequently to a dissatisfaction with the literature of maxim and *pensée*: 'Peut être est-il vrai que l'esprit du lecteur aime achever et qu'il ne faut lui donner que ce qu'il faut pour achever facilement et être rappelé de lui-même à l'ouvrage, etc. Je finis trop' (C i. 347). Joubert came to believe that the distinguishing feature of Plato's dialogues was the way they stimulated the reader to think for himself, to come to his own conclusions, and he would not have been entirely disappointed to discover that his own *Carnets* have a similar effect on the modern reader. As Louis van Delft comments, speaking of the competing centrifugal and centripetal rhythms of heuristic discourse:

Ce mouvement qui prête vigueur et vie aux écrits composés de fragments semble bien être le trait le plus original de l'écriture par 'pièces détachées': entre livre et lecteur, celle-ci instaure un rapport d'active connivence. Elle commande une lecture qui soit toute création.[59]

To some extent this study may be seen as a traditional essay in the history of ideas; yet, in so far as Joubert's fragments refer implicitly and explicitly to other texts, to an extent hitherto unexplored, and in the way his language successfully breaks down barriers between vocabularies of different intellectual disciplines, then it bears relation to some of the more fashionable critical methods current today. We shall see how Joubert adopts the language of science and adapts it to metaphysical

---

[58] See Final Profile.
[59] Van Delft, 244.

and aesthetic ends. While examining Joubert, the writer, one is forced to understand him first as reader.

This study of the thought and art of Joseph Joubert is directed specifically, therefore, at the enigma posed by the workings of his mind. It is concerned with what he read, how he read, how this reading influenced his attitude to life and art, how his reading frequently became matter for transformation into the expression of his own thought. It attempts to draw the portrait of a late-eighteenth- and early nineteenth-century French intellectual who is at once representative of his period and contributes something new to it. To do this the original manuscripts have been consulted and a number of significant *Carnet* entries, omitted by Beaunier, restored. Book lists and sheets of quotations compiled by Joubert have also been of considerable help. The books annotated by him which remain in his library have been examined systematically. I have concentrated, particularly, on evidence from the period of his life ranging from 1780 to 1814, firstly, because this is certainly his most fertile and creative period and, secondly, because it is virtually impossible to take account of all nine hundred pages of the fragmentary text as presented by André Beaunier.

In seeking to show how Joubert both belonged to his time and renewed its ideas it has seemed reasonable to choose areas of his thought where these two aspects of his personality are most clearly visible, and demonstrate how questions of language and expression provide a close link between them.

Typical of this dualism are Joubert's speculations on politics, government, and the law. This area is particularly useful, since it provides the opportunity to give the reader a brief biographical sketch while avoiding the tedium of a 'life-and-times' approach. In addition, it helps to combat the pernicious influence of nineteenth- and twentieth-century critics who frequently promote the tired cliché of Joubert the recluse, the other-worldly sage, totally uninterested in the topical scrapes of his friend Chateaubriand. As will become apparent, Joubert wrote vigorously on many political and legal questions. He was frequently scathing about politicians and journalists and undoubtedly preferred the repose of sequestered Villeneuve, but in his time he was an active member of a revolutionary town council, frequented literary salons, and was employed by the Université Impériale as an 'inspecteur général'.

Where he had something new to contribute, or at least something distinctively his own, was in the realm of aesthetics. A major part of this study is devoted to this area of his thought, showing how questions of aesthetics underlie every sphere of debate in which he engaged, including the political and social concerns outlined above. It is necessary, in this context, to re-examine Joubert's alleged Platonism and show to what extent it reflects the birth of an expressive aesthetic that occured during the last twenty to thirty years of the eighteenth century, how it and many other influences contributed to Joubert's attitude to creation, to the role of the imagination, reason, and illusion. Finally, this leads to an understanding of the way Joubert's description of particular art objects doubles, in a sense, as a description of his own fragmentary discourse. Indeed this chapter could well serve as a necessary introduction to a stylistic analysis of the *Carnets*, a study which must, however, fall beyond the scope of the present work. Philippe Garcin writes most interestingly that:

Les puissantes images dont il [Joubert] parsème sa prose, lors même qu'elle se hisse à un haut étage d'abstraction, dénoncent le penchant qui le poussait à joindre aux formes intellectuelles des qualifications sensibles. Tendance qui complique et raffine les pensées qu'il exprime.[60]

A stylistic study of Joubert's language could not do better than to base its initial investigations around this suggestion.

Ultimately the major effect of this study may be simply to have accomplished some, by no means all, of the groundwork necessary to a proper critical edition of the *Carnets*. For this is what is most needed at the moment and what would best do justice to the distinctive genius of Joubert; in so far as an editor annotates another man's work, then Joubert spent his life 'editing' the books in his library, filling the margins with comments and strange signs to which only he knew the key, expanding those blank columns adjacent to spine and edge on to little jotters and strips of paper, themselves resembling detached margins. Joubert's *Carnets*, edited by Beaunier, are the effusive expression of margin become book, of margins that have swollen to invade the space occupied by traditional rhetorical discourse. In this sense perhaps, one at which Mrs Humphrey Ward could never have guessed, Joubert was 'the friend, talker, thinker, the impulse and the critic of other men's lives', one of the purest examples of the instinctive readiness to debate, 'mettre en question', finding, perhaps, in the rhetorical exercises of his schooldays a compulsive source of intellectual pleasure which he was unable, happily, to relinquish.

[60] Garcin, 600–1.

I
The Early Years

(1) Diderot, Rousseau, and a 'Supplément au Voyage de Cook'

While collecting material for his novel, *Bouvard et Pécuchet*, Flaubert made lists of books which might help him to recreate the texture of the period in which he was interested. One of these was *Les Nudités ou les crimes du peuple*, by Chassaignon. Against this entry Flaubert wrote: 'Cataractes de l'imagination, déluge de la Scribomanie, vomissement littéraire, hémorragie encyclopédique, monstre des monstres, etc.'[1] Around the time this book was published, Sébastien Mercier indulged in an orgy of neologism directing his attention to the perpetrators of just this type of literature: 'Folliculaires, Feuillistes, Feuilletonistes, Fréronistes, Mercuriens, gens de l'alphabet, Décadiers, Reviseurs, Jugeurs, Analyseurs, Gâcheux, Sacristains, Sonneurs, tous domiciliés au bourbier du Parnasse.'[2]

Nearly every critic of the work of Joseph Joubert has agreed that it was this plague of *scribomanie* and the bloodthirsty excesses of the Revolution that apparently produced it that confirmed his hatred for journalistic hacks and the entire paraphernalia of revolution. Everywhere we find reproduced his statement: 'La révolution a chassé mon esprit du monde réel en me le rendant trop horrible' (*C* i. 326), while a sonnet by the nineteenth-century poet and critic, Jules Lemaître (from his *Médaillons*), in which Joubert is described in terms of near-Mallarmean idealism, is hailed as the temperate diagnosis of a philosophy of disengagement:

---

[1] J. Neefs, 'Le Volume des livres (Fragments pour *Bouvard*)', *L'Arc: Flaubert*, 79 (Aix-en-Provence, 1980), 87.
[2] L. S. Mercier, *Dictionnaire d'un polygraphe*, *Textes de L. S. Mercier*, ed. G. Bollème (Paris, 1978), 13.

Epicurien angélique
Tu voyais bleu, tout bleu, tout bleu.[3]

A letter of 1817 sent by Joubert to his friend Claussel de Coussergues tends to reinforce this attitude:

Je me suis longtemps, comme un autre, et aussi péniblement, aussi douloureusement, aussi inutilement que qui que ce soit, occupé du monde politique; mais j'ai découvert à la fin que pour conserver un peu de bon sens, un peu de justice habituelle, un peu de bonté d'âme et de droiture de jugement, il fallait en détourner entièrement son attention, et le laisser aller comme il plaît à Dieu et à ses lieutenants sur la terre: je ne lis donc plus aucun journal.[4]

Critics and historians of literature, quite correctly, have preferred to emphasize the latter half of this statement. However, the recent publications by Norbert Alcer and Rémy Tessonneau of hitherto unpublished writings by Joubert, and research among his notes and manuscripts, prove that the author remained interested in politics and history as well as journalism for most of his life.[5]

It is important that attention be paid to this aspect of Joubert's activity, for it helps to counteract the tendency to dismiss him as the philosophic recluse of Villeneuve. Undoubtedly the passivity of Joubert's character can be irritating. He was, as the Scots say, something of an 'auld sweetie-wife', but he had a brilliant mind that was not averse to dealing memorably with issues of political and judicial significance. Even if Joubert's remarks about government or commerce are not always original in the context of his period, the *way* he chose to express himself can be moving and persuasive. He articulates commonplace attitudes succinctly and with verve, sometimes managing to endow them with a poetic resonance that is refreshing for readers familiar with journalism and other ephemeral writings of the period. This enables us to link his social and political concerns to the aesthetic issues that preoccupied him throughout his life.

It is important, firstly, to examine the period up to 1792–3, when Joubert experienced a 'retour aux préjugés', since it is only against this background of *encyclopédisme* that his mature political beliefs may be understood. Until recently it has not been possible to draw any definite conclusions about this period, but the publication, in 1976, of a

---

[3] Quoted by Steele, 282.
[4] *Correspondance*, Raynal, 239.
[5] *Studien* and *E*. See also C. Thévenaz-Schmalenbach, *Joubert: Seine geistige Welt*, for a discussion of his politics and social concerns.

massive thesis by Jean de Viguerie on the Pères de la Doctrine Chrétienne, who educated Joubert in Toulouse, allows us to make a reasonable guess at the nature of the intellectual atmosphere to which he was exposed as a young man.[6]

TOULOUSE

Any student of Joubert's thought and art would be interested in his education by this religious order, from 1768 to 1773, even if he had simply followed the classes of the Esquile, as the school was known, and left after completing his studies, as many of his contemporaries and predecessors had done. But our interest is increased by the fact that Joubert took steps towards becoming a *régent* or teaching member of the school, which necessitated taking holy orders, only to leave the Esquile before doing so. Why did he change his mind? One critic has pointed to the influence of Rousseau and Condillac on the teachings and philosophy of the Order, singling out the Père Navarre, who taught at the Esquile in the wake of the publication of *Émile*, and Pierre Laromiguière, who was appointed to the chair of philosophy in 1785 after having been a pupil and teacher of the Doctrine.[7] Viguerie's thesis confirms this educated guess and reveals the considerable extent to which this order and, in particular, the Esquile de Toulouse, had been penetrated by the spirit of the *Encyclopédie* and modern philosophy in general, while suggesting that Joubert's decision to leave the order was taken not simply on philosophical but also on religious grounds.

The Order of the 'Pères de la Doctrine Chrétienne' was founded by César de Bus in 1607 and from the first its prime function was educational. De Bus was the purveyor of 'une méthode spirituelle, qui conduit les gens du monde et les clercs à la perfection chrétienne, en passant par les étapes classiques de la vie purgative, illuminative et unitive'. Predicative evangelism was shunned, and of every member of the Order it could be said, as it was of the Père du Faur, that 'quoy qu'il eust un don particulier pour la chaire, il a tousiours fait ce qu'il a pu pour se tenir caché et ne point paroistre en public'.[8] From works published by members of the Order it is clear that the kind of

---
[6] J. de Viguerie, *Une œuvre d'éducation sous l'ancien régime: Les Pères de la Doctrine Chrétienne en France et en Italie, 1592–1792* (Paris, 1976).
[7] Tessonneau, *Éducateur*, 11–18.
[8] Viguerie, *Une œuvre d'éducation*, Paris, 397, 398.

spirituality advocated by the *Doctrinaires* in its early days was Augustinian in inspiration.

Around 1660 the Order began to put more emphasis on the 'pratique de la perfection'. As Viguerie interprets it: 'La volonté du Chrétien doit être éclairée et déterminée; elle doit connaître les *motifs* de la pratique du bien, tirer les fruits de la connaissance des vérités de la religion, et surtout, avoir les *moyens* d'accéder à la perfection.' The *Doctrinaires* are at this point 'assez proches de l'école ascétique jésuite', although Viguerie takes care to distinguish this asceticism from that of Nicole in his *Essais de Morale*: 'Tandis que Nicole s'attarde à des considérations souvent ingénieuses, et d'ailleurs destinées à une élite, Doctrinaires et Jésuites se préoccupent d'enseigner à un large public une spiritualité et une moralité simples et pratiques.'[9] As Joubert himself wrote in December 1813 of Nicole's *Essais*: 'La morale de l'Evangile y est peut-être un peu trop raffinée par des raisonnemens subtils' (*C* ii. 770). Despite this, however, nothing could prevent the spirit of Jansenism from penetrating the teachings of the *Doctrinaires* between 1700 and 1750, and it could be argued that, however unconsciously, it was this which lay at the root of Joubert's reluctance to continue his career in Toulouse and that the secular philosophy of the age only confirmed a fundamental dislike for the austerities and subtleties of this form of Catholicism. As Joubert wrote: 'Les philosophes pardonnèrent au jansénisme parce que le jansénisme est une espèce de philosophie' (*C* ii. 839).

It would be possible to argue from hindsight here and quote many more of the extremely hostile remarks Joubert made about Jansenism around the same time as his criticism of Nicole. They are so vituperative in tone that one may be forgiven for seeking to identify personal experience behind them, but this is not really necessary, for Viguerie's summary of the effects of Jansenism on the Order makes it clear that, by the time Rousseau and Condillac were there to be read, the spiritual life of the Order had been so diluted as to be unable to offer much resistance or alternative:

Nos auteurs appellant . . . n'enseignent plus la pratique des vertus chrétiennes, ni les moyens de les pratiquer, ni les profits d'un tel exercice. Certes, il s'agit toujours de la morale chrétienne. Mais les Doctrinaires du siècle précédent complétaient la morale par un ascétisme. Ils indiquaient la méthode à suivre pour se sanctifier. Ce que négligent de faire leurs successeurs . . . Ils prêchent la

---

[9] Ibid. 401, 419. Nicole, *Essais de morale*, (Paris, 1671).

conversion sans en indiquer les moyens ... Le P. Badou donne ... une série d'instructions intitulée: 'Pour faire saintement les actions'. Il y traite de la lecture, des repas, des habits, d'une façon générale de tout ce qui fait le comportement d'un vrai chrétien. Mais lui non plus ne dit rien des vertus ... Leur morale tourne au moralisme parce qu'elle n'est plus animée de la spiritualité des vertus chrétiennes. Il lui manque une vie spirituelle.[10]

During the period 1750-89 only three works were published by the *Doctrinaires*, which, in comparison with previous years, points to a general dissatisfaction on the part of members with their vocation as teachers. One of these was the publication of *Sermons* by le père Anastase Torné in 1765, just two years prior to Joubert's admission to the Esquile, and it is interesting that as much attention is given to the thunder and lightning of the Old Testament as to the New. The God Torné describes is often God in the image of Man, motivated by human sentiments, and, in his 'Sermon sur l'Impénitence Finale', God speaks in tones of anger, spitefulness even, rather than those of Justice:

Je mépriserai vos prières et vos regrets, voluptueux infâmes, qui n'aurez connu que les vices et les plaisirs. J'insulterai à votre malheureuse destinée ô vous qui aurez été les heureux de ce siècle; et je verrai avec un ris moqueur les larmes de pénitence succéder à la folie des joies mondaines ... Votre pénitence imparfaite et tardive ne me touchera pas.[11]

Nor was Jansenism of this calibre confined to Torné. At the time of Joubert's education in Toulouse it was widespread throughout the order, culminating in le père Firmin Lacroix's *Traité de morale, ou des devoirs de l'homme envers Dieu, envers la société et envers lui-même*, published in 1775, in which God's love for Man is absent and where all the author's attention is concentrated on 'La justice, la liberté et la bienfaisance ... les trois principes qui doivent ... régler les rapports des hommes entre eux.'[12] We begin to wonder if it was at all necessary for Joubert to have read any of the *philosophes* publishing at this time in order for him to doubt his religious convictions.

It is inaccurate, therefore, to state that Joubert's 'retour aux préjugés' in later life included a return to the religion of his education in Toulouse. His affection in the *Carnets* goes out almost exclusively to the Jesuits and, when he laments the passing of the *Doctrinaires*, as he

---

[10] Viguerie, 444.

[11] Ibid. 448, quoting père Pierre Anastase Torné, *Sermons prêchés devant le roi pendant le carême de 1764* (3 vols.; Paris, 1765); i. 291-2.

[12] Viguerie, 450, quoting Lacroix, *Traité de morale ou devoirs de l'homme envers Dieu, envers lui-même* (2 vols.; 2nd edn., Toulouse, 1775), 32.

does in a letter to Fontanes,[13] it is an elegy for the *Doctrinaires* of the early seventeenth century as yet untouched by the stain of Jansenism. The only trace we can find in the *Carnets* of the influence of the *Doctrinaires*' religious as distinct from philosophical teaching is, possibly, the infrequency with which Christ is mentioned. As Viguerie points out: 'La personne et les exemples du Christ tiennent beaucoup moins de place dans leur doctrine que dans celle des Jésuites.'[14]

In his *Origines intellectuelles de la Révolution française*, Daniel Mornet dates the 'diffusion générale' of the ideas of the *philosophes* from 1770, some three years after Joubert's entry to the Esquile and an impressionable three years before his decision to leave the Order in 1773.[15] In the two decades leading up to this date the curriculum of the *Doctrinaires*' schools underwent a radical change, with poetics, mythology, geography, history, and natural science being added to the principal subjects, grammar and rhetoric. By the time le père Navarre came to read his prize-winning dissertation, a 'plan d'études', to the provincial chapter of Toulouse in 1762, with its guiding principle that 'Tous les corps qui nous environnent et que nous avons à tout moment sous notre main nous enseignent quelque vérité', much of the preparative groundwork for his reforms had already been done.[16]

The choice of books for the libraries of the schools was frequently influenced by the tastes of the booksellers. The letters of the bookseller Lottin (1768–74) to various members of the Order are highly instructive in this regard, and those to le père Delmas, Curé de St Orens de Villebourbon in Montauban, are particularly interesting. In 1770 he wrote enclosing a volume of the *Encyclopédie* as a present for his client 'et deux brochures nouvelles que je vous prie d'accepter: c'est une plaisanterie contre ceux qui prétendent qu'on peut voir à travers les terres'. The bill he sent Delmas in 1772 is followed by a postscript of the same kind. This time he is asked to accept 'un modèle d'Encyclopédie, un beau frontispice détaché de ce dictionnaire, et une feuille'.[17] Delmas, by way of thanks, tried to procure other colleges belonging to the *Doctrinaires* as clients for Lottin and no doubt continued his philosophic purchases when promoted to the Esquile in 1774.

---

[13] *Correspondance*, Tessonneau, 106.
[14] Viguerie, 453.
[15] D. Mornet, *Les Origines intellectuelles de la Révolution française* (Paris, 1967), 2–3.
[16] Viguerie, 504.
[17] Ibid. 515.

As far as the actual teaching of philosophy was concerned, members of the order did not show themselves backward in adopting avant-garde positions. After a somewhat tardy conversion to Cartesianism around 1711–13, the majority of schools were struggling with some form of Lockean empiricism by 1770. Tessonneau draws attention to the outstanding figure of Laromiguière, yet the activities of a certain Jean Lacroix, teaching at the Esquile in 1772 when he published a *Connaissance analytique de l'homme, de la matière et de Dieu*, are perhaps more contemporary with Joubert's personal crisis.[18] Lacroix's criticism of Descartes is scathing, while his theory of knowledge is a mixture of Condillac and Locke: 'Les sensations', he writes, 'sont de six espèces différentes, et ces six espèces se diversifient de mille manières, selon la nature et la force des impressions que notre corps reçoit.' Like many empiricists he refuses to acknowledge a distinction between 'la connaissance sensible' and 'la connaissance intellectuelle'. 'Il n'existe point en nous ... deux principes, l'un spirituel, l'autre matériel, celui-là pour l'entendement, celui-ci pour les sensations,' and well before Laromiguière, highlights the power of *attention*: 'Par l'attention nous rendons claires et distinctes les connaissances que les sensations nous donnent. L'attention dépend d'une disposition de notre corps. Elle produit la mémoire qui dépend aussi d'une disposition de notre corps.'[19] It is quite possible, therefore, that Joubert was influenced, if not taught, by Lacroix at the Esquile, just as Maine de Biran was influenced by similar currents at the *Doctrinaires*' college in Périgueux, where he was a pupil around the years 1778–80. Such a philosophy, added to the effects of Jansenism on the spiritual resources of the Order and its pupils, was certainly enough to have caused Joubert to think again before committing himself to holy orders.

Equally relevant is the fact that the Collège de l'Esquile had been a part of the University of Toulouse since 1716. According to the letters patent, the students at this college 'jouissent des mêmes avantages que ceux qui estudient au Collège des Pères Jésuites de la même ville', and, in consequence, 'les deux années de philosophie audit College [leur] sont utiles et comptées pour le Quinquennium, commes faites dans un college d'Université'. This meant that the teachers of philosophy at the Collège de l'Esquile could consider themselves 'Agrégés dans la Faculté

---

[18] Tessonneau, *Éducateur*, 11–12.
[19] Viguerie, 562.

des Arts de l'Université de Toulouse'.[20] Without being an integral part of the teaching faculty of the University, they frequently gave courses which students at the University could and did attend, and it is reasonable to assume that Joubert, far from being obliged to choose his friends from among the seminarists of the Esquile, would have had ample opportunity to enjoy the conversation and company of students highly conversant with the most recent developments of modern philosophy and literature and unburdened by the duties of religious vocation.

PARIS

Joubert returned to Montignac in Périgord, the village of his birth, in 1773 and lived there for a period of five years about which we know nothing.[21]

On 5 May 1778, however, François de Paule Latapie passed through the village, in his capacity as 'inspecteur des manufactures', spent the night in the house of Jean Joubert, and noted in his diary: 'Son fils est un jeune homme qui a de l'esprit, de la litterature et du ressort. Il part pour Paris dans le dessein d'y faire fortune; il serait très possible qu'il réussit s'il se livrait à quelque profession lucrative.'[22] The passage is never treated as anything more than a picturesque detail by biographers and critics, but Latapie's identity is important, for he was the son of Pierre Latapie, the intimate friend and adviser of Montesquieu. Born in 1739, he was brought up at La Brède as the close friend and travelling companion of Jean-Baptiste de Secondat and, as the author of the chapter on La Brède in Baurein's *Variétés Bordelaises*, he is one of the earliest authorities on the life of Montesquieu.[23]

These facts transform the rather prosaic nature of Latapie's comments. It is known that Latapie had a tremendous admiration for Montesquieu and it is not unlikely, therefore, that he discussed the President and his work with Joubert. Indeed, in a passage not quoted by Beaunier, following immediately on these remarks, Latapie refers to a conversation on the nature of local customs, a subject relevant to the

---

[20] Ibid. 555.
[21] For speculation as to how Joubert passed these years see A. Beaunier, *La Jeunesse de Joseph Joubert* (Paris, 1918).
[22] F. de P. Latapie, 'L'industrie et le commerce en Guienne sous le règne de Louis XVI' (Journal de tournée de François-de-Paule Latapie en 1778), *Archives historiques du département de la Gironde*, 38 (Paris and Bordeaux, 1893), 321–509 (p. 430).
[23] Baurein (ed.), *Variétés Bordelaises* (4 vols.; Bordeaux, 1876).

spirit of the laws which Montesquieu had tried to describe: 'Il m'a appris quelques détails sur les mœurs du Périgord qu'il prétend, et je crois avec raison, s'être conservées un peu mieux que dans le reste de la Guienne dans leur originalité, quoiqu'elles s'effacent beaucoup depuis vingt ans.'[24] Many years later, in December 1798, Joubert was to write: 'Les premières loix n'ont été que les premières pratiques rendues immuables par l'injonction de l'authorité publique [...] Tout ce qui devint loi, en un mot, avoit d'abord été coutume [...] Les loix de Solon se firent comme la *coutume* de Sens' (C i. 186). Although this remark must be interpreted in the light of a counter-revolutionary campaign against the artificial constitution-making of the 1790s and the 'abstractions' of democracy, it is perhaps permissible to assume that his interest in the customs of his native Périgord was, from the first, something more than the naïve enthusiasm of a local historian. Latapie, indeed, acts as a useful signpost to some of the preoccupations that concerned Joubert in his early years in Paris.

A number of these seem to have been suggested by Diderot, including notes on 'La Bienveillance universelle', an 'éloge' of the sculptor Pigalle, one of the discoverer James Cook, and a series of remarks on 'la peinture à l'encaustique'.[25] All of these show certain affinities with the thought of Diderot, although only the essay on 'La Bienveillance universelle' seems to have been written during the last six years of the *philosophe*'s life, directly at his suggestion.[26]

The parallels with Condillac, however are just as strong, while it is more clearly Rousseau that is behind Joubert's criticism of *le luxe* and *le commerce*. Thus the passage: 'Au sein même de toutes les jouissances du luxe et des arts l'homme ne peut pas se passer de l'homme. Tant la nature nous unit, quand nos institutions nous séparent!' (C i. 45), is a natural preliminary to the bitter expostulation:

Votre commerce n'est qu'une guerre d'argent; votre commerce vous a donné cette avidité qui vous ronge; votre commerce a fait la moitié de vos maux. Et ne vous a fait aucuns biens. O grands hommes et vous parlés des avantages du commerce! c'est que vous conçevés une espèce de commerce bien différente. Le commerce seroit beau, plus beau même que vous ne l'avez conçu, s'il se faisait de peuple à peuple par une seule émulation de générosité et de bienfaisance.

(C i. 47)

---

[24] Latapie, 430.
[25] The fullest versions of these projects may be found in *Studien*. Tessonneau's publication of the same material (*Essais, 1779–1821*) is more easily accessible but more selective in treatment.   [26] See C i. 433.

Here Joubert appears to be making a distinction made frequently by many of the *philosophes* and economists of the day. There is a 'bon' and a 'mauvais luxe'; most could agree on what constituted the latter. Diderot and Rousseau both attacked the 'luxe de magnificence et de vanité' and the 'soif de l'or'—but there were divergences as to what kind might be permitted.[27] Thus Turgot, Dupont de Nemours, and Adam Smith could advocate the pursuit of 'richesses', providing this was translated as the 'esprit d'économie dans une nation',[28] whereas Rousseau naturally rejected any attempt to accumulate capital which could only lead to inequality and unhappiness. He preferred a 'luxe de plaisir et de sensualité sans raffinement ni mollesse', just what was necessary to a certain domestic comfort and local 'bonheur'.[29] He attacked, therefore, those of his contemporaries engaged in the production of luxury goods like wig-makers and embroiderers and it is not surprising to find Joubert subscribing to this polemic, beginning with an image of human industry familiar to readers of Adam Smith's *Wealth of Nations*.[30]

On dit qu'il faut dix mille mains pour former une épingle. Il en est de même de tous les objets de notre luxe. Un pompon occupe presque autant d'hommes qu'en occupa la plus haute pyramide de l'Egypte. Je ne connois pas de réflexion aussi propre à rendre ridicules et mesquins aux ieux d'un homme sensé tout ce qui sert d'ornement à nos maisons ou à nous-mêmes. Oh! que nous sommes loin d'être sensuels, puisque nos sens ont des plaisirs si difficiles et si chers!

(C i. 38)

The last sentence of this entry is an accurate measure of the extent to which Joubert believed his generation to be removed from that of Rousseau's 'natural' man. Undoubtedly the kind of commerce of which he dreams is that of Rousseau, the naturally good man, acting from sentiments of generosity and *bienveillance*. Diderot, who believed in the goodwill commerce might generate some day between nations, was nevertheless convinced of the need and ability of countries to develop and prosper; the 'chasse au bonheur' was everybody's right, and demands for complete equality were incompatible with an am-

---

[27] *Œuvres complètes de Jean-Jacques Rousseau*, ed. B. Gagnebin and M. Raymond (4 vols.; Paris, 1959–69), ii. *La Nouvelle Héloïse*, 531.
[28] *Œuvres de Turgot*, ed. G. Schelle (4 vols.; Paris, 1919), ii. 588.
[29] Rousseau, *Héloïse*, 531.
[30] A. Smith, *The Wealth of Nations*, ed. A. S. Skinner and W. B. Todd (2 vols.; Oxford, 1976), i. 14–15.

biguous programme that was bound to admit the economists' arguments at some level.

The extent of the influence of both Diderot and Rousseau on Joubert, however, centring around topics such as commerce, economic exploitation, property, equality, and religious belief, is most explicit when notes for his 'Éloge de Cook' are compared with entries in the *Carnets*. This reveals both similarities and differences which need to be highlighted since they draw attention to the intellectual conflict Joubert experienced at this stage in his life.

The 'Éloge de Cook'

At the start of their book on the history of *Utopian Thought in the Western World* the Manuels write:

Popular hope literature has not been excluded from this study on principle, or without awareness that a police or other judicial record, or a hospital case book, or a prize essay contest in a provincial French academy might reveal an unnoticed utopian thinker operating in his own world whose dreams could be more representative of large segments of the population than a formally printed utopia. The lines had to be drawn somewhere.[31]

Joubert's depiction of Tahiti in the 'Éloge' forms the central section of an unpublished response to a competition set by the Académie de Marseille, and this 'unnoticed thinker's' utopian dreams are certainly representative of many of his contemporaries (*E* 63). Indeed the majority of themes that may be detached from the body of notes compiled by Joubert in preparation for his 'Éloge' are typical of those being articulated in the exotic travel literature of the day and correspond in varying degrees to many of the beliefs of the major *philosophes*. He may not have spent his entire life reading travel literature, as Rousseau claimed to have done,[32] but he certainly spent a considerable number of years perusing works such as Maupertuis's *Figure de la terre*, Bailly's *Histoire de l'astronomie*, Letourneur's *Voyage au Cap de Bonne Espérance*, and the writings of Bougainville and Amerigo Vespucci, in addition to those by Forster specifically relating to

---

[31] F. E. Manuel and F. P. Manuel, *Utopian Thought in the Western World* (Oxford, 1979), 9.
[32] Rousseau, iv. *Émile*, pt. 5, p. 827.

Captain Cook.[33] Still to be found on the shelves of Joubert's library at Villeneuve is a complete set of the 1780 reprint of the Jesuits' *Lettres édifiantes*. Gilbert Chinard stresses the influence of Jesuit reading on Rousseau, and there is no doubt that the same can be said of Joubert, but it was perhaps less the actual reading of the *Lettres édifiantes* or of Bougainville or Forster than his education by the Pères de la Doctrine Chrétienne that enabled him to spice his perceptions of the South Seas with references to the poets of antiquity and see Cook and the Tahitians as 'descendants des Grecs anciens' (*E* 72).[34]

Like Bougainville, Cook found 'comme partout ailleurs, l'hospitalité des anciens patriarches', and these themes of *bienveillance* and hospitality clearly survived the initial impetus of Diderot's inspiration into the 'Éloge'.[35] On the one hand Cook 'fit du bien à des peuples plus éloignés de l'Amérique que l'Amérique ne l'est de nous' (*E* 70), while, on a more personal level, Joubert thinks Cook would have made an 'ami solide et généreux et lié jusqu'au dévouement par une estime mutuelle' (*E* 73). The Otahitians, for their part, are, above all, the 'peuple ami': 'Il a toute la beauté et la bonté des enfants. Ses légèretés mêmes sont à peine des défauts et parmi ses défauts aucun n'est incompatible avec l'innocence' (*E* 78).

It is specifically in the sections decribing the island of Tahiti that Joubert shows himself representative not only of his age but of the entire Western tradition of paradisiac utopia. 'Le néant est à ses deux bouts, l'âge d'or est dans ses bocages,' he declares. 'Tu es, Otahiti, un lieu de relâche et de radoub pour le navigateur fatigué' with trees 'qui portent le pain', freeing the inhabitants from the curse of toil on the land (*E* 77).[36] Joubert could have found these attributes of his utopia in Bougainville and many other earlier writers. Just as we may call into question the influence of a work like the *Lettres édifiantes* on him, however, so, in this case, we can be confident that it is Virgil and Hesiod themselves that lie behind the imagery of the passage. As Beaunier's edition of the *Carnets* proves, Joubert had started work in 1783 on a translation of Hesiod's *Works and Days*, and it is, perhaps,

[33] For Forster's version of Cook's voyage, see *Voyage au pole austral et autour du monde, écrit par Jacques Cook, commandant de la Résolution, dans lequel on a inséré la relation du Capitaine Furneaux et celle de messieurs Forster. Traduit de l'Anglais* (Paris, 1778).
[34] For the influence of Jesuit reading on Rousseau, see G. Chinard, *L'Amérique et le rêve exotique* (Paris, 1913), 143.
[35] Cook, *Voyage*, i. 382.
[36] See ibid. i. 403-4.

this first-hand knowledge of the golden race that lends his own variation on the theme such an air of charm and freshness.[37]

To what extent, though, may Joubert's 'Éloge' be described as a 'Supplément au voyage de Cook' and more than a collection of utopian commonplaces?[38] Like Diderot, Joubert used his traveller's tale to reflect on issues such as sexual licence, religious superstition, and the evils of European capitalism.

Undoubtedly, Joubert shared Diderot's atheism at this period. If Diderot carefully ignored the various religious cults of the Tahitians precisely in order to highlight the social and intellectual restrictions of European Christianity,[39] Joubert's instinctive reaction to his reading material consisted of mild expressions of disgust when he came upon these 'superstitious' practices:

> Il est resté à ce peuple peu de dogmes de la religion qu'il dut avoir autrefois, mais il lui en reste un abominable usage, celui d'immoler un homme quand il y a quelque guerre redoutable à commencer. Il n'y aurait pas d'air aussi pur que celui de cette île, sans la superstition qui consiste à croire que nous survivrons à la vie.
>
> (E 80–1)

Elsewhere, examining the customs of the inhabitants of Owyhee, he gives a typically rationalist explanation for religious experience: 'A Owyhee on trouve plus d'opinions religieuses. Il faut que les superstitions nous viennent de cette partie du monde' (E 87). In this case, providing Beaunier's dating of these passages is correct, the *Carnets* help to confirm this estimation of Joubert's opinions on religion. While working on 'La Bienveillance universelle' he noted:

> En lisant l'histoire de tous les peuples, on est persuadé qu'ils doivent avoir une origine commune. Leurs erreurs religieuses frappent par leurs ressemblance[s]. Ou c'est un héritage funeste transmis par un peuple premier aux autres peuples ses enfants; ou c'est une contagion apportée de proche en proche par les voyageurs de tous les pais.
>
> (C i. 49)

---

[37] See C i. 36–7.

[38] Tessonneau, *Éducateur*, 31, speculates on whether Joubert had read the *Supplément au voyage de Bougainville* (*Œuvres complètes*, ed. J. Assézat (20 vols.; Paris, 1875), ii. 193–250), or not and concludes that, although this work was not published until 1796, Joubert may have seen one of the copies which Diderot was in the habit of showing to his friends.

[39] For Diderot's attitude to this question, see M. Duchet, 'Le Primitivisme de Diderot', Europe, 405–6 (Jan.-Feb. 1963), 126–37, p. 132.

In 1787, while visiting Saint-Sulpice, he remarked: 'C'est dans de pareils temples que l'homme est religieux et qu'il devient esclave; c'est devant de tels autels qu'il s'instruit à la servitude' (C i. 78). The relative mildness of his reaction to Tahitian religious practices when compared with statements such as these taken from the *Carnets* can only be explained by the general fascination and admiration produced in him by the islanders. He can hardly find it in himself to condemn them for their lack of restraint in sexual matters:

Plaisirs de l'amour. Sont mieux goûtés au fond des bois et sur le rivage des mers et partout où l'homme se voit environné de quelque grande solitude. S'ils aiment le plaisir, ce n'est pas par la corruption de leurs mœurs, mais par l'excellence de leur tempérament.

(E 85)

He also stresses the way in which Cook punished the understandable weakness of his sailors: 'Il fit punir quelques coupables; mais ils le furent mollement' (E 85).

In Diderot's *Supplement au voyage de Bougainville* the character Orou takes a strictly relativist approach to these issues demanding that 'tu n'accuseras pas les mœurs d'Europe par celles de Tahiti, ni par conséquent les mœurs de Tahiti par celles de ton pays',[40] and Joubert was of a similar persuasion. After describing how a native princess introduced *tow-tows* from the Tahitian slave class into her brother's bed, he writes: 'Chez un peuple ou la volupté n'est point un crime, c'était la plus pardonnable de toutes les fautes' (E 80).

If we turn to the *Carnets*, however, to find similar expressions of sexual licence, we are quickly disappointed. As early as 1776 Joubert was writing in praise of 'la chasteté' and in 1783, at the very moment he is supposed to be writing under the influence of Diderot, who describes 'pudeur', 'retenue', and 'bienséance' as 'des vertus et des vices imaginaires',[41] we find the following remark, to the effect that 'Une femme doit avoir de la pudeur, non seulement pour elle-même mais pour tout son sexe [. . .]' (C i. 40).

Despite this, Joubert takes an undeniable pleasure in evoking in his 'Éloge': 'Deux des plus belles et des plus nobles filles de l'île . . . Ce sexe aime le linge. Une d'elles fut frappée par le désir de posséder une paire de draps . . . et peu s'en fallut que, pour l'obtenir elle n'accordât les

---

[40] Diderot, *Supplément*, ii. 233.
[41] Ibid. 243.

dernières faveurs de l'amour' (E 85). Finally, however, he explicitly condemns the kind of prostitution advocated by Orou:

Il paraît que ce peuple eût anciennement des législateurs qui s'occupèrent de sa tranquilité politique. Un de ces génies, plus hardi que tous les autres, introduisit une autre coutume plus révoltante afin de prévenir la multiplication excessive des grands et des puissants: il voulut les engager à renoncer au mariage en établissant une société qui offre tous les plaisirs.

(E 80)

Joubert's attitudes to sexual morality, therefore, are somewhat ambiguous at this period, although it would probably be fair to conclude that any sympathy he shows for the 'licence' of the Tahitians is more a product of his enchantment with the entire myth of Tahiti.

If we return briefly to the passage in which Joubert relates the efforts of Otoo's sister to please her brother by procuring him the favours of a slave girl, we can see how, as in Diderot's *Supplément*, the question of sexual mores leads naturally into matters of an overtly political nature:

Chez un peuple où la volupté n'est pas un crime, c'était la plus pardonnable de toutes les fautes et on n'aurait pas dû la reprocher publiquement à cette fille des rois. Au contraire, N., tu faisais bien. Si le vice même peut être excusé, c'est lorsqu'il ramène parmi les hommes une certaine égalité.

(E 80)

Joubert thus recognizes and implicitly criticizes the class structure prevalent in Tahiti, a fact which Bougainville, at first deceived by the happiness of the natives, stresses, but which Diderot prefers to suppress altogether, seeing it as one of the typical characteristics of the civilized European society from which he wishes to distinguish Tahiti. Elsewhere Joubert is quite open about the nature of the class system: 'Comme la France a eu ses serfs, ce peuple a aussi ses tow-tows... Une inégalité totale ne les afflige point à chaque instant' (E 79). In fact it is an 'inégalité' that is, in its way, 'une *certaine* égalité', and there can be no doubt that this constitutes an ideal for Joubert.[42] In the *Carnets*, around the same time, we find him coming to the conclusion that social inequality is something of an illusion produced by our senses. When describing a deaf-and-dumb man he knew in Paris, Joubert writes: 'Il étoit fort attaché à la subordination. C'est l'opinion qui seule fait l'inégalité... parce qu'il ne pouvait entendre qu'avec ses ieux, il

[42] Cf. Cook, *Voyage*, i. 456: 'La distinction trop manifeste des rangs qui subsiste à Tahiti n'affecte pas autant la félicité du peuple... la simplicité de leur manière de vivre tempère ces distinctions et ramène l'égalité.'

ignorait le malheur des classes inférieures' (C i. 75). Although this observation would have found little favour with the author of the *Lettre sur les aveugles*, had he been questioned more closely on the inequalities visible in Tahiti Diderot would have admitted their inevitability, given the fact that both men believed themselves to be dealing with an 'état social primitif' rather than an illusory 'état de nature'.[43]

Michèle Duchet points to Diderot's implicit reliance on Buffon's definitions '[là] où il est question des rapports de l'homme et de la société', and the short 'éloge de Buffon' produced by Joubert in the course of his work on Cook testifies, despite the rhetorical nature of its expression, to his concern for accuracy and a certain realism in his depiction of the sea captain and his discoveries. Buffon is described as the 'moderne historien de la nature' and 'comme celui que je loue',[44] of whom 'surtout il serait vrai de dire que son histoire est son éloge' (E 69). We have seen already, however, that this quasi-scientific motive is frequently side-tracked by the mirage of the Tahitian 'âge d'or' and it would be true to say that this is what occurs when the vexed question of property arises.

Diderot's various attacks in the *Supplément* on European cupidity and Joubert's own comments in the *Carnets*, which we have already examined, are echoed in the 'Éloge de Cook' with considerable vehemence:

C'est à ses portes que cesse l'empire de la cupidité. On ne trouve pas à dépenser un seul scelin dans les six milles lieues qui forment son étendue. Tout s'y fait par ces échanges mutuels si propres à entretenir l'amitié. Car tout homme qui vend et tout homme qui achète sont dans un état de force.[45]

The issues of commerce and property lead naturally for Joubert, therefore, into those of sovereignty and empire. Like the Rousseau of the *Discours*, who, had he been allowed to choose his place of birth, would have chosen 'une société d'une grandeur bornée...', he believed that happiness depended, partly, on the extent of a nation's territory.[46] The Tahitians, 'bornés dans leurs territoires [...] n'ont rien de mieux à faire que d'y être bons et tranquilles, comme les hommes le sont partout où ils sont indépendants et maîtres souverains d'un pays borné' (E 83).

---

[43] See Duchet, 'Primitivisme', 129.
[44] This is to be found only in Alcer's transcription of the 'Éloge': *Studien*, 369.
[45] *Studien*, 355.
[46] Rousseau, iii. *Discours sur l'origine et les fondemens de l'inégalité*, 111.

1. THE EARLY YEARS

Again, more like Rousseau than Diderot or Marmontel, Joubert's nostalgia for the 'bon sauvage' leads him to remark that: 'peut-être le meilleur des hommes serait-il parmi nous celui qui, à force de philosophie, serait enfin devenu ce qu'est naturellement un jeune Otahitien' (*E* 78), while he concludes with the following fashionable apostrophe: 'O mes concitoyens! plus j'y pense et plus je trouve que nous aurions tous besoin de devenir un peu sauvages' (*E* 79).

Exclamations such as these, however, are almost immediately tempered by passages in which Joubert displays his reluctance to adhere rigidly to the polemics of Diderot and Rousseau, acknowledging the real cruelty of which the 'jeune Otahitien' was capable:

Partout, il y a des jours mauvais: un peuple si bon a ses guerres. On ne peut pas le lui pardonner. Et lorsque, dans la relation, on rencontre tout à coup, au milieu d'un pays si beau, des ossements qui recouvrent la terre, comme les Anglais en rencontrèrent, et lorsqu'on apprend avec eux que ... on s'emporte et l'amitié s'aigrit jusqu'à la colère et jusqu'au mépris.[47]

Here, Joubert has more in common with Bernardin de Saint-Pierre, author of a *Voyage à l'île de France* which the editor of a recent edition describes as an 'anti-voyage'.[48] Bernardin relates, for example, how he happened to meet a group of natives armed with guns:

L'un deux ... menait une femme attachée par le cou à une corde de jonc ... c'était le butin qu'ils avaient fait sur un camp de Noirs marrons qu'ils venaient de dissiper ... La négresse paraissait accablée de douleur ... Elle portait sur le dos un sac de vacoa. Je l'ouvris. Hélas! c'était la tête d'un homme. Le beau paysage disparut, je ne vis plus qu'une terre abominable.[49]

As Yves Bénot puts it in his introduction, Bernardin is 'peu soucieux de retrouver le bon sauvage dans les esclaves de l'île de France'.[50]

It is important, therefore, to register the genuine ambiguity of Joubert's beliefs at this time. As Norbert Alcer points out, we can find, among the short notes entitled 'Systèmes' written during the same period as the 'Éloge de Cook', declarations quite opposed to the Rousseauistic sentiments at which we have been looking.[51] Even among the papers devoted to Cook, Joubert can write: 'Aussi la lecture de leurs voyages contribue à nous rendre plus contents de notre sort.

---

[47] *Studien*, 351.
[48] Bernardin de Saint-Pierre, *Voyage à l'île de France: Un officier du roi à l'île Maurice, 1768-1770* (Paris, 1773), ed. Y. Bénot (Paris, 1983), 13.
[49] Ibid. 161.
[50] Ibid. 18.
[51] *Studien*, 179. See *E* 97-117.

Lisons-les, qui que nous soyons, pour apprendre de combien de maux nous sommes exempts' (*E* 93). We have, therefore, a man, noting with relative impartiality the vagaries of Tahitian sexual licence, while filling his *Carnets* with eulogies of *la pudeur*; attacking the evils of property, while realistically recording the inequality of Tahitian society; sighing after the *âge d'or* inhabited by young savages, as he rubs his hands in front of the Parisian fire denied to the intrepid travellers that form his bedtime reading. It was not until 1791 and his own experience of active politics in Montignac that Joubert had to decide just where he stood on all these matters, and part of the interest of the 'Éloge' is to be found in the sheer muddle of its various intellectual stances, showing us the hesitations of a young man growing up among, and sensitive to, the conflicting criticisms of society as expounded by the major *philosophes*. We are perhaps a little sad when we come to realize that his final ideological position with regard to Tahiti and its inhabitants is best summarized in the words of Louis de Bonald, which Joubert recorded in a small notebook used for noting congenial passages from Bonald's work *Du divorce*:

voyez... (discours préliminaire, pag. XV) ce qu'il dit des louanges prodiguées par la philosophie du dernier siècle aux môeurs et à la vie sauvage:
'... on s'exstasia sur l'industrie de ces hommes qui, la tête dans les deux mains, passent les journées entières sans proférer une parole, accroupis tous nuds dans les cavernes enfumées où ils entrent en rampant...'[52]

Writing in 1801, Joubert does not hesitate to equate 'la philosophie' with '[le] dernier siècle'. It may only just have ended, but a tone of detachment has entered his voice to such an extent that we might be forgiven for believing it to be a country of the past in which he seems, now, never to have lived, much less thought or written. The beautiful Tahitian 'bocages' have given way to smoky caves and the 'bienveillance' of the 'peuple ami' to the innate 'intempérance' of vicious savages.

(II) From Diderot and Rousseau to Maistre, Bonald, and Constant

The area of Joubert's political and social thought which best illustrates the way in which the influence of *philosophes* like Diderot and Rousseau gave way to that of more conservative writers includes entries

---

[52] MSS Bussy. The notebook is entitled 'Bonald I'.

in the *Carnets* on the related themes of liberty, law and order, and religious observance. By tracing the evolution of Joubert's attitude to these concerns and the influence of the various milieux in which he found himself, it is possible to observe how a relatively youthful idealism is replaced by a pragmatic, even sceptical outlook, that does not, however, exclude occasional moments of nostalgia for the type of emotion associated with his early enthusiasms.

Liberty

The following definition of 'la liberté publique', placed among the passages on 'La Bienveillance universelle', is probably the clearest example we have of the direct inspiration of Rousseau, an advocacy of what Benjamin Constant was to call 'la liberté ancienne', and Isaiah Berlin desire for a 'positive' freedom of 'collective self direction'.[53]

La liberté publique ne peut s'établir que par le sacrifice de toutes les libertés particulières sans aucune exception. Dans cette admirable institution, les forts cèdent une partie de leur force, les riches une partie de leurs richesses [. . .] à tous les citoyens qu'ils veulent rendre leurs égaux; et les petits, les faibles, les pauvres cèdent à leur tour une partie de leurs espérances, et de la noblesse, et des richesses, et de la force que le bienfait et l'inconstance du sort toujours variable, pourroit donner soit à eux, soit à leurs descendans.

(C i. 55)

The full extent of Joubert's adherence to a Rousseauist conception of liberty is apparent in a passage that follows naturally from this uncompromising statement and was noted in the *Carnets* on 23 March 1789:

Tout homme est libre et ne peut perdre sa liberté. Il ne peut la perdre par sa volonté car ce seroit une folie, ni par la volonté d'autrui car ce serait une oppression. Quiconque ôte à un homme la liberté pour toute sa vie est digne de mort. La liberté consiste à pouvoir faire et dire tout ce qui n'est pas défendu par la loi.

(C i. 84)

The last sentence is, indeed, strongly reminiscent of statements to be found in the 'Déclaration des droits de l'homme', and the passage as a whole acts as a succinct summary of the 'philosophy' behind the French Revolution. As Bernard Groethuysen remarks, while describing

---

[53] B. Constant, *De la liberté chez les modernes*, ed. M. Gauchet (Paris, 1980). I. Berlin, 'Two Concepts of Liberty', in *Four Essays on Liberty* (Oxford, 1969), 118–72.

the main doctrines: 'Le peuple ... ne peut pas se départir de sa souveraineté. Il ne peut aliéner sa liberté...',[54] and Joubert's statement a few days previous to this entry confirms his enthusiasm for some of the revolutionary ideals emerging from the newly formed 'États généraux': 'La liberté politique pour un peuple consiste à se gouverner comme il veut, sa liberté religieuse à croire ce qu'il veut, sa liberté de commerce à vendre et à acheter comme il lui plaît' (C i. 82).

Notes towards an introduction Joubert wrote in 1790 to a volume, which never appeared, entitled 'Histoire impartiale de France' also give us a clear insight into his opinions on the nature of liberty at this period, suggesting that they held fast for the decade after his arrival in Paris, and testify above all to the ethnological and sociological preoccupations common to writers on the eve of the French Revolution. Easily the most exhilarating and poetic passages of this work occur when he evokes:

les temps anciens [qui] vont revenir, non pas environnés comme autrefois de barbarie et de lumières mais de bonheur et de clarté. L'antique liberté a mis le pied dans nos contrées et la félicité celtique, unie à l'urbanité grecque et romaine, veut se répandre parmi nous. Gardez-vous de lui faire obstacle et de fermer votre pays ou de venir troubler le nôtre. Jetez un pont à la déesse et soyez encore une fois semblable à nous. Acueillez ces grands changemens qu'auraient tant approuvés vos pères et mettez la dernière main à ce que nous avons tenté ... C'est aux législateurs à tout préparer dès ce moment pour hâter ce bienfait des siècles et c'est à nous à l'espérer.

(*E* 150–2)

This work appears to have caused some stir among Joubert's friends, who seem to have read the 'Introduction' in manuscript, for, in a letter to the author, dated 21 February 1791, and later published in his own *Petite histoire de France*, a certain François Marlin or Milran wrote to Joubert in the following ironical vein: 'Je vous ai lu: vous êtes un impie. Vous ne portez aucun respect aux savants discours de M. Moreau sur le despotisme. Vous oseriez bien le taxer d'erreur.'[55] He went on to declare that his work would be consigned 'à l'index dès que MM. Desmeuniers et Mallouet auront rétabli la censure littéraire'.

The Moreau referred to by Milran is almost certainly Jacob Nicolas Moreau, a counter-revolutionary thinker of some importance. Moreau

---

[54] B. Groethuysen, *Philosophie de la Révolution française* (Paris, 1956), 281.
[55] F. Milran, *Petite histoire de France ou revue polémique d'un grand historien* (Paris, 1792), ii. 231. Quoted by Tessonneau, *Éducateur*, 45.

came originally from Burgundy and held the office of 'historiographe de France'. In 1764 the Dauphin asked him for a treatise defending the absolutism of the monarchy and Moreau later developed this into a twenty-one-volume work.[56] His ideas certainly found favour with the royalist movement, for he became for a time principal councillor to the comte de Provence, the future Louis XVIII.

In the 'Introduction' Joubert makes a fierce attack on the absolutism or despotism defended by Moreau, and once again the echoes of Rousseau are not hard to detect:

> C'est par le désir et l'espérance de vivre aux dépens d'autrui que s'établit l'aristocratie ou le gouvernement de ceux qui ont du bien. C'est par l'amour de la conquête et du butin que s'introduit le despotisme ou l'obéissance constitutionnelle à un seul. Le despotisme des peuples fixes n'est que le gouvernement militaire hors de sa place et prolongé au-delà de la durée qu'il doit avoir.
>
> (E 151)

The Testimony of the 1790s

These notes, however, were written on the threshold of a decade that was to witness a profound transformation in Joubert's thinking, as he meditated upon the increasingly terrible course taken by the Revolution in reaction to the outbreak of war. Two events in his life combined at this point to provide him with good practical reasons for a change of heart. These were the year he spent in his home town of Montignac-en-Périgord in 1791–2 as Justice of the Peace, and his marriage to Mlle Moreau in 1793 and subsequent move to her native Burgundian home in Villeneuve-le-Roi.

There is much circumstantial evidence that can be produced to show just how negative an effect the year as Justice of the Peace had on Joubert's republican sentiments, and, although Norbert Alcer has covered much of this ground very thoroughly, there are a number of facts worth noting. Alcer believes, along with Beaunier and Tessonneau, that Joubert returned to Montignac mainly in order to care for his ailing mother after the death of his father in 1789, but adds that Mme Joubert desired his return in order to persuade him back to the religious faith of his childhood.[57] As entries in the *Carnets* of November 1791 reveal, this wish certainly did not bear immediate fruit, but there can be

---

[56] J. N. Moreau, *Principes de morale, de politique et de droit public puisés dans l'histoire de notre monarchie* (21 vols.; Paris, 1771–89).

[57] *Studien*, 230.

no doubt that Joubert's relatives in Montignac, whatever their motives, fought tooth and nail against political opposition to have him elected Justice of the Peace. Joubert's own enthusiasm for the fight seems to have been somewhat lukewarm. Although elected on 28 November 1790, he did not take up his duties until the morning of 7 March 1791. On the 14th someone asked bitterly, in the middle of a session of the Montignac town council: 'Comment se peut-il qu'avant la révolution, vivant comme frères et amis, la révolution nous ait séparés d'intérêts, d'intimité, et de concorde?'[58] which may be construed, not simply as a reflection on the divisive nature of the recent election, but as an accurate measure of general differences of opinion, which frequently made the provinces the site of clashes sharper and more personal than those of the capital.

Some of his *carnet* entries for 1791 show Joubert reacting to developments in Paris. Thus in November he wrote:

On ne tolérera aucune intolérance. Toute doctrine qui ne dit pas que la vertu suffit pour plaire au ciel est d'un méchant ou d'un fanatique, ou d'un hippocrite. Le droit d'aller et de venir ne peut être restreint hors des cas extraordinaires.

(C i. 89)

Here the influence of the reform of the clergy in February, as well as of the war atmosphere created by the growing threat from the Émigrés, is quite clear, and there is no doubt that the disputes which Joubert had to settle in Montignac served to strengthen his growing political conservatism. Most of these disputes were frustratingly petty and had little to do with the judicial process in the wider sense. Rather than multiply the circumstantial details, however, it is more interesting to turn to the resources of Joubert's library, which provide us with evidence far more eloquent and intriguing than the mundanities revealed by archive research in the Dordogne.

On the flyleaf of Burke's *Œuvres posthumes* of 1799 Joubert noted that it contained 'réflections rédigées au mois de décembre 1791 sur la situation et les affaires de la France'. The work was, therefore, exactly contemporary with Joubert's time in Montignac as Justice of the Peace, and it is interesting to find that some of the passages most heavily underlined by him deal with the Revolution as it affected provinces and small communes, like Montignac. Thus we find him underlining the

[58] Ibid. 235.

following remark about the Revolution with thick red crayon: 'Elle tendait à introduire dans tous les pays, des intérêts indépendants de leur localité et de leurs circonstances.'[59] A little further on he was especially impressed by Burke's description: 'de cette espèce de faction, qui détruit la localité des affections publiques, crée des antipathies entre les concitoyens qui diffèrent d'opinions'.[60] Easily the most heavily underlined passage of all, however, is one which constitutes a forceful picture of the spirit of faction and tyranny reigning in the provinces as they attempted to imitate events in Paris:

> A l'imitation du Comité de recherches de l'assemblée, chaque commune a un comité de surveillance; et dans les petits endroits, la tyrannie est si proche des objets, que toutes les actions des individus lui sont promptement connues, et tous les complots étouffés dès leur naissance. Le pouvoir des comités est absolu et irrésistible. Ces municipalités ont si peu de relation entre elles, que la connoissance de ce qui arrive dans l'une, n'excède point ses limites, ou n'est répandue que par l'entremise des clubs qui entretiennent une correspondance très-active et donnent la couleur qu'il leur plaît aux incidents qu'ils jugent à propos d'insérer dans leurs missives. Ils ont tous avec l'autorité centrale, une sorte de communication qu'ils peuvent étendre ou restreindre à leur fantaisie au moyen de quoi les informations étant toutes entre les mains de la faction dominante, les plaintes et les movemens que les vexations produisent dans une municipalité, sont rarement connus des communes qui l'environnent et personne n'ose servir de chef aux mécontens.[61]

Joubert's interest in these passages was certainly coloured by the staunch anti-republican stance he had adopted by 1799, but the fact that he took the trouble to underline them so heavily does suggest that for him, at least, they contained an element of truth and corresponded to his own experience of revolutionary politics in the provinces.

THE MOVE TO VILLENEUVE

While living in Montignac Joubert wrote several letters to a Mlle Moreau of Villeneuve-le-Roi in Burgundy whom he had met in the company of Louis de Fontanes in 1787. In one of these letters he proposed marriage and was accepted.[62] It is difficult to overestimate

---

[59] Burke, *Œuvres posthumes ... sur la Revolution française* (London, 1799), 42. Joubert's copy may be found at M. du Chayla's home in Paris.
[60] Ibid. 46–7.
[61] Ibid. 89–90.
[62] *Correspondance*, Raynal, 11–12. Letter dated 1 May 1793.

the importance of this event in Joubert's life, for it lifted him out of the financially straitened circumstances that had been his lot since youth and enabled him to lead the life of a country gentleman. Joubert married into the Catholic moneyed bourgeoisie; his politics came to reflect this social position and were coloured to some extent by the concerns of the small town in which he spent much of his time.

In biographies of Joubert, Villeneuve-sur-Yonne, as it is now known, is habitually described as a sleepy little town, rather off the beaten track, and as a perfect haven for the meditative philosopher he was to become. The 'Procès-verbaux de l'administration départementale de l'Yonne', however, paint a very different picture and show the struggles of a thriving agrarian community of considerable strategic importance. A report on commerce in the area, drawn up in 1789, demonstrates, as the editor of the documents put it: 'que le sol du département fournit à ses habitants non-seulement toutes les denrées nécessaires à la vie, et à leur consommation, mais encore un superflu qui les met à portée d'en commercer...'.[63] The report continues by listing the forests of Joigny, Othe, Chaumot, and Sens among others, and stresses the paramount importance to Villeneuve of vineyards and tanneries. Villeneuve was in an excellent position to exploit the natural fertility of its soil, for it was a port of some magnitude as well as being on the main highway from Paris to Lyons.

Despite these facts, or perhaps because of them, Villeneuve did not suffer from the fanatical excesses of the Revolution and in this sense could be described as a haven or refuge for the likes of Joubert. The 'Procès-verbaux' of the 1780s show that local government in the area was efficient and actually prepared the way for many of the reforms of the Constituent Assembly. Only one popular revolt was recorded before June 1791, when the *département* gave voice to its concern at the King's flight from Vincennes.[64]

Despite the 'Constitution civile du clergé', and the relative success of the Département in seeing to it that its central premisses were obeyed, 'ces révolutionnaires de fraîche date [étaient] animés d'un profond esprit religieux'. The 'Procès-verbaux' cite the case of a 'frère François de la Maison des Capucins de Saint-Florentin qui désire continuer ses études et prie, étant dépourvu de ressources, le département de vouloir

---

[63] Documents sur la révolution française. Département de l'Yonne, 'Procès-verbaux de l'administration départementale de l'Yonne (7 vols.), de 1790 à 1800 (BL 9225 C. 27) i, p. vii.

[64] Ibid. iii. 135.

bien le placer dans un Séminaire'. The officials involved referred his request to the Assemblée Nationale but in so doing expressed their admiration for 'une vocation décidée pour le Saint ministre'.[65]

If Villeneuve suffered at the hands of revolutionary Paris, it was more a case of economic exploitation than anything else. The capital swallowed up the produce of Villeneuve and its citizens, a state of affairs that was exacerbated by the bad harvests of 1792 and 1793. Yet the town was capable of standing up for itself when it considered that Paris had overstepped the mark. On 13 July 1793 the 'Conseil général de la commune de Villeneuve-sur-Yonne' told the 'Commissaire de recrutement du district de Joigny' that:

la commune a fourni aux précédentes levées 305 hommes, que ce chiffre équivaut au douzième de la population et qu'il lui est impossible de fournir le nouveau contingent de 10 hommes réclamé à la commune; elle fait observer en outre que les hommes de cette levée, destinés d'abord à combattre les rebelles de la Vendée, doivent être affectés à assurer sur la Seine la libre circulation des subsistances...

The 'Directoire' noted that 'quelque soit le nombre que la commune présentera dans les circonstances actuelles, elle aura néanmoins bien mérité de la Patrie'.[66]

A comparison of the 1790 census of the inhabitants of the Département with that taken in 1800 shows that the population actually increased by twenty thousand despite war and famine, so the attitude of measured co-operation adopted by town councils like that of Villeneuve seems to have been successful in the long run.[67] The hard-pressed, industrious bourgeoisie of Villeneuve-sur-Yonne, while remaining loyal to the ideals of 1789, formed a naturally conservative community, far more inclined to worry about its vineyards or temporary lack of grain than indulge in the political antics of its city counterparts. This was the prevalent atmosphere in 1793 when Joubert came to live in his wife's house in the rue du Pont.

At first Joubert seems to have had mixed feelings about his new possessions. Fontanes had written to him in 1785, describing him as 'un grand ennemi du démon de la propriété', and, not without some irony, Joubert himself used identical terms when writing to Madame de Fontanes in 1794. Such idealism, however, was short-lived. Gone were

[65] Ibid. ii. 128.
[66] Ibid. vi. 3.
[67] Ibid. i, p. vii.

the days when he was prepared to spend time taking copious notes from writers such as Lahonton, who had written in the preface to his voyages: 'Il me semble qu'il faut être aveugle pour ne pas voir que la propriété des biens est la seule source de tous les désordres qui troublent la société des européens.'[68] Indeed, Joubert's 1791 entry in the *Carnets* on this subject shows the influence of the bourgeois revolution of 1789 and the attempt of the constitution-makers to restrict suffrage to the property-owning classes:

Si l'on donne quelque exclusion aux hommes sans patrimoine et sans propriété, ce n'est pas qu'on doive penser qu'ils aimeroient moins la patrie ou la vertu. Car ils peuvent aimer l'une et l'autre avec une sorte d'excès, et cette opinion fairoit aux richesses trop d'honneur; mais c'est qu'on sçait et que chacun peut se convaincre par son expérience propre et personnelle, que l'homme en butte aux flots du sort, à la tourmente du hazard est moins le maître de soi-même et n'a pas pour se recueillir et régler ses sentiments et ses pensées assés de calme, de repos, de loisir, de bonheur et risque d'être exagéré. Il est moins sage, non par sa faute, mais par celle de sa position. C'est à ce titre seul qu'on peut, jusqu'à [ce que] cette position soit changée, refuser l'administration des affaires publiques à celui qui n'eut pas d'affaires personnelles à manier.

(C i. 90)

This was an attitude, shared throughout their careers by men whose language was frequently more violent than that of Joubert. In 1774 Marat wrote his first political work in English, *The Chains of Slavery*, which consisted of an address to the British electorate on the eve of the 1774 election, and advised them to choose those 'whom an independent fortune secures from the temptations of poverty'.[69] As Groethuysen writes:

Au début de la Révolution, on s'était demandé si celui qui ne possédait rien n'allait pas tomber dans la dépendance morale de celui qui possédait, et perdre ainsi en partie sa liberté naturelle; s'il pouvait être question d'une égalité de droits entre pauvres et riches.[70]

Certainly Joseph de Maistre, who believed that the 'richesse' of hereditary magistrats guaranteed their independence, did not think so, and the following passage by Joubert is perhaps the logical result of

---

[68] See C i., 71. Beaunier misreads Lahonton for Lahoudan. Joubert quotes from the 1st edn. of 1709, entitling his selections 'Dialogues de Lahontan'. MSS. Bussy.

[69] Quoted by N. Hampson, *Will and Circumstance: Montesquieu, Rousseau and the French Revolution* (London, 1983), 109.

[70] Groethuysen, 240.

remarks made in the context of his notes on 'La Bienveillance universelle', where he had written: 'Ceux qui veulent tout ramener à l'égalité on tort. Il n'y a point d'égalité naturelle. La force, l'industrie, la raison élèvent des différences entre les hommes à chaque pas' (C i. 50–1).[71] As Chateaubriand was to write in the *Mémoires d'outre-tombe*: 'L'égalité complète, qui présuppose la soumission complète, reproduirait la plus dure servitude; elle ferait de l'individu humain une bête de somme, soumise à l'action qui la contraindrait, et obligée de marcher sans fin dans le même sentier.'[72]

In March 1796, after three years of gentle living in the rue du Pont, Joubert noted cryptically in his journal: 'Richesses. Nécessaires. Et comment ne croirais-je pas nécessaire ce qui est inévitable?' (C i. 119). By the end of the year he could express an opinion to which Honoré de Balzac would have been sympathetic: 'La vénalité des charges avoit au moins cet avantage que celui qui achetoit une judicature, n'ayant aucune obligation au pouvoir qui la lui vendoit, il en restoit indépendant dans ses opinions et dans sa conscience' (C i. 130).

The experience of Montignac in 1791 and the move to Villeneuve, therefore, not only provided Joubert with a new realism but encouraged the beginnings of genuinely anti-republican sentiments. During a reading of Plato in December of this year Joubert noted a remark taken from the *Axiochus*, a work attributed to Plato in the 1588 Ficino edition of the dialogues: 'Alors je fus saisi du dégoût de la liberté et je détestai la république. Aucune espèce de gouvernement ne me parut pire et plus dure' (C i. 91). When placed alongside another statement by Plato copied from the Laws, 'D'abord faire des mœurs au lieu de faire des lois' (C i. 92), it is evident that Joubert was beginning to doubt his revolutionary credo. By February 1793 he could write of the course of history: 'Dans les temps qui nous précédèrent j'y vois des libertés d'un jour et des siècles de servitude' (C i. 96). By May, one month after the creation of the Committee for Public Safety, liberty had become a simple question of freedom of movement: 'Liberté d'aller et de venir. Sûreté, propreté, commodité et agrément des chemins, nécessaire à son exercise' (C i. 98), and then reduced to the mere 'indépendance de son corps' (C i. 103). 'Il faut que quelque chose soit sacré' (C i. 97), he wrote with desperation in his voice. By November, with the memory of Montignac still fresh in his mind, he had become convinced that 'il est

---

[71] This is an opinion Joubert shared with Diderot. See Y. Bénot, 'Diderot et le luxe: Jouissances ou égalité', *Europe*, 661 (May 1984), 66.

[72] Chateaubriand, *Mémoires d'outre-tombe*, ii. 27.

impossible de manier les affaires sans se salir de cupidité' (C i. 99). Years later, in a paragraph added to his *Considérations sur la France*, which first appeared in 1797, Joseph de Maistre was to write: 'Il n'y a pas d'homme d'esprit en France qui ne se méprise plus ou moins. L'ignominie nationale pèse sur tous les cœurs.'[73] Joubert would have known exactly what he meant.

By the mid-1790s, therefore, Joubert had come to recognize, much as Rousseau had done earlier, that it was necessary in politics to 'make men positively want what society has decided that they are to be'.[74] In April 1799 he noted 'comment l'ignorance est un lien entre les hommes. La politique doit s'en servir' (C i. 204), and by 1814 he had expanded this into the following kind of advice:

Mettez donc dans les choses ou dans ce qui est semblable aux choses, c'est à dire insensible, impassible et inflexible comme elles (telles que sont ou semblent être la loi, la règle, etc.) les nécessités que vous avez besoin d'imposer aux autres ou à vous-même.

(C ii. 794)

Perhaps the most striking expression of this attitude, however, was recorded in January 1816, when Joubert wrote of: 'La politique, ou l'art (ou le don) de connoître et de mener la multitude ou la pluralité. La gloire de cet art est de mener cette multitude, non pas où elle veut ni où l'on voudroit soi-même, mais où elle doit aller' (C ii. 845).

CONSTITUTION

This kind of thinking, largely the fruit of the 1790s, soon grew into a fully-fledged conservatism, which tends to suggest that Joubert's closest affinities in political matters were with Maistre and Bonald.

The meditation on liberty which played such a considerable role in the early Paris years dwindled to the kind of exasperation surrounding this remark recorded in December 1817: 'Liberté, liberté . . . En toutes choses point de liberté; mais en toutes choses justice; et ce sera assés de liberté' (C ii. 868). The new sense of realism and political expediency came to contaminate his conception of this word, persuading him to write in February 1814, just one month before the capitulation of Paris to the advancing allied armies: 'Etre libre n'est pas faire ce qu'on veut,

---

[73] J. de Maistre, *Considérations sur la France* (Neuchâtel, 1797), ed. J.-L. Darcel (Geneva, 1980), 150.
[74] Hampson, 301.

mais ce qu'on a jugé meilleur et plus convenable' (C ii. 777). Its republican manifestations made it synonymous, ultimately, with the tyranny of the multitude: 'La liberté est un tyran qui est gouverné par ses caprices' (C ii. 909). As David Hume wrote in his *Histoire d'Angleterre*, which Joubert read at some point during the years of the Empire: 'Le principe que tout pouvoir légitime part du peuple est noble et spécieux en lui-même,'[75] and in his copy of Burke's *Œuvres posthumes* Joubert marked carefully a passage dealing with the abuses to which the word 'liberty' had been subjected: 'L'Angleterre est menacée de la contagion par sa proximité, par des relations continuelles, et enfin par le nom de liberté, dont nous sommes jaloux et dont les plus dangereux abus présentent trop souvent des illusions séduisantes.'[76] Democracy, in fact, was just one of these illusions and, in Joubert's opinion, more naturally associated with slavery than with liberty:

La démocratie et l'esclavage inséparables. Pourquoi. La démocratie, telle qu'elle étoit chez les anciens, n'est que le gouvernement d'un nombre d'hommes assés grand pour être appelé peuple. Mais cette dénomination est fausse. Le vrai peuple, dans un tel état, le plus grand nombre, la majorité est dans la classe des esclavages, et l'esclavage s'introduit inévitablement dans un pays ainsi gouverné, parce qu'il est impossible que ceux qui passent leur temps à faire des lois puissent faire des chaussures, des habits, semer, labourer, etc.

(C i. 133)

In France, where slavery theoretically did not exist, democracy, by giving the dreadful responsibility of legislation to the mass of the people, prevented many useful citizens from participating in their usual employment. This is the implication of the above entry and Joubert again found sympathy for his views while reading Burke. In the *Œuvres posthumes* Burke strongly criticizes the wastefulness of democracy for taking active men out of circulation, and Joubert underlined this passage heavily, in red crayon, marking his interest and agreement:

Sept cents cinquante individus, élevés tous les deux ans au pouvoir suprême, ont déjà produit quinze cents politiques actifs et hardis. C'est un nombre très considérable, même dans un pays aussi vaste que la France. Les nouveaux législateurs ne peuvent plus se contenter d'occupations ordinaires, ils ne veulent

---

[75] Quoted by J. de Maistre, *Essai sur le principe générateur des constitutions politiques et les autres institutions humaines* (St Petersburg, 1814), ed. R. Triomphe (Strasburg, 1959), 82, para. XLVII n.
[76] Burke, *Œuvres posthumes*, 80.

plus redescendre à la classe de simple citoyen, ni exercer paisiblement une industrie obscure ou peu importante ...

Ce recrutement périodique du corps qui exerce l'autorité suprême, produira en peu d'années plusieurs milliers d'ex-législateurs, et ce nombre est toutefois fort peu de chose en comparaison de la multitude d'officiers municipaux des districts et des départements, qui après avoir exercé lucrativement une portion du pouvoir, s'agiteront en tout sens, pour rentrer en place.[77]

As Joubert wrote in February 1815, reacting to the constitutional innovations of the Restoration: 'La multitude aime la multitude ou la pluralité dans le gouvernement; les sages y aiment l'unité' (C ii. 817), and that unity could not be achieved through the creation of party politics which would follow inevitably upon the introduction of a representative system of government. The only *corps* or assembly Joubert would admit, therefore, was of the ecclesiastical kind.[78]

A similar train of thought seems to have occurred to Joubert while reading a book entitled *Théorie du monde politique* by Charles His.[79] He took a great many notes from this book, writing that the statement 'la république n'est jamais qu'un état de passage' was 'très digne de remarque', and he copied with care passages expressing the need for a balance between 'la liberté particulière' and 'la liberté publique'. Like Joseph de Maistre and Bonald, Joubert had come to believe that God was the only true creator or, as His put it, 'l'homme est créateur mais à la manière d'une créature'.

This final remark is, indeed, a commonplace articulation of a theme dear to opponents of the Revolution. Maistre gave it its classic expression in his *Considérations sur la France* and *Essai sur le principe générateur des constitutions politiques* where he wrote that:

une des grandes erreurs d'un siècle qui les professa toutes fut de croire qu'une constitution politique pouvait être écrite et créée *a priori*, tandis que la raison et l'expérience se réunissent pour établir qu'une constitution est une œuvre divine, et que ce qu'il y a précisément de plus fondamental et de plus essentiellement constitutionnel dans les lois d'une nation ne saurait être écrit.[80]

This criticism of Man's presumption, his pretension to create or invent what only God can reveal to him, is an obsessive theme of the *Carnets*. It is, more often than not, a case of simple polarity: what is new must

---

[77] Ibid. 87–9.
[78] See C ii. 817.
[79] C. His, *Théorie du monde politique ou de la science du gouvernement considérée comme science exacte* (Paris, 1806).
[80] Maistre, *Essai*, para. I, p.15.

be bad because it is new; what is old must have some good in it because it has stood the test of time:

Lorsque par les réformes que l'on projette on ne cherche à introduire dans les opinions que de la nouveauté, dans les religions que de la variété, dans les loix que des relâchemens, dans les mœurs que de l'isolation (ou de l'isolement) dans les fortunes que de l'agrandissement, et dans les usages que de la commodité, on travaille à tout rendre pire.

(C i. 118)

Laws are laws because they have once been customs, tried by habit and time. 'Les anciens législateurs furent des sages et ne furent pas des inventeurs' (C i. 186), men who merely named and defined what already existed:

Une constitution en effet ne peut être qu'une définition. Or quand on définit l'homme, par exemple, et qu'on parle de son corps et de son âme, on ne les crée pas, on ne les lui donne pas; seulement on les nombre, on les déclare. Que si cette déclaration lui donnoit quatre yeux et trois jambes, il ne les accroît pas pour cela. Il seroit possible à la vérité de faire des règlemens sur l'usage que l'homme peut faire des yeux et des jambes qu'il a, mais non pas les lui donner.

(C ii. 837)

Joubert would have agreed, it appears, with Maistre, who had written:

Non seulement la création n'appartient point à l'homme, mais il ne paraît pas que notre puissance, non assistée, s'étende jusqu'à changer en mieux les institutions établies... Le mot de *réforme*, en lui-même et avant tout examen, sera toujours suspect à la sagesse.[81]

Maistre may well have been influenced by Burke in this criticism of constitutional reform and Joubert himself noted parallels with his own beliefs by underlining the following passage in his copy of the *Œuvres posthumes*:

La réforme tient de très-près à l'innovation... Dans un temps où la réforme, qui comprend l'aveu d'un abus, produit plus de haine contre l'autorité qui l'a souffert, que de reconnaissance pour celui qui cherche à le détruire (et telle est la maladie régnante chez les Français) chaque pas qu'on hazarde hors de la route

---

[81] Ibid., para. XL, pp. 70-2.

ordinaire, devient très critique, et les princes qui, avec des talens médiocres, veulent faire de grandes choses s'exposent à de grands périls.[82]

With Burke, Joubert agreed that 'Jusqu'à cette époque, on n'avait point vu dans ce monde moderne, une faction politique totalement indépendante des opinions religieuses, se généraliser, s'introduire dans tous les pays, et y former un principe de réunion entre ses partisans'. All in all, it was a situation of such gravity that both men believed 'que des causes internes ne suffiront jamais pour opérer en France une contre-révolution.'[83] Not only did Joubert underline this remark, but he favoured it with a large red star, which he placed in the margin, evidently forgetting, in his enthusiasm for the *émigrés*, earlier condemnation of *coups d'état* of any variety.[84]

Of particular interest also is the way Joubert joins Maistre in his use of metaphor drawn from the natural world. Both men shared a preference for what Robert Triomphe has called 'une justification organiciste ... ; la vie de la nature se développe à partir de "germes invisibles"',[85] both subscribing to the venerable idea that nature does not work by leaps and bounds but develops through the slowness of time according to the divine laws of the Creator. 'Toutes les opérations légitimes, de quelque genre qu'elles soient, se font toujours d'une manière insensible,'[86] wrote Maistre, while Joubert remarked in his *Carnet* of 1802 that '[Les] constitutions (vraies) ont été, sont, seront toujours et ne peuvent être que filles du temps' (C i. 335). In 1814, reacting with horror to attempts to create the constitution for a restored monarchy, Joubert used the familiar image of *germe* with vigour:

> On peut plaider les causes, mais il ne faut pas plaider les loix. Plaider publiquement les loix! ... quel abbus! C'est en profaner tous les germes. La source en doit être sacrée, et vous l'exposez au grand air. Quand elles naissent d'une discussion, elles ne viennent plus d'en haut ... quelle horrible profanation! C'est en mettre le germe à nud [...]

(C ii. 789)

Maistre reacted in similar fashion to the same events of 1814: 'Que les racines des constitutions politiques existent avant toute loi écrite,'[87] he

---

[82] Burke, *Œuvres posthumes*, 73.
[83] Ibid. 44–5, 92.
[84] See C i. 110.
[85] Triomphe, in Maistre, *Essai*, 45 n. 1.
[86] Maistre, *Essai*, 45.
[87] Ibid. 26.

wrote, and Robert Triomphe, commenting usefully on this, notes that 'Les *racines* doivent rester "en terre"':

'Il y a des choses qu'on détruit en les montrant'. L'écriture, la définition, représentent une mise à nu, une dénudation ou une levée du 'voile'; cette opération n'est légitime que si elle correspond à la poussée organique d'un 'germe' dont la tige s'échappe de terre tout en restant enracinée dans un sol naturel.[88]

As we shall see over the course of the next few chapters, this metaphor recurs in many of Joubert's speculations on the nature of art and demonstrates that his politics and aesthetics do, indeed, share a common root. To a greater degree than many of his contemporaries, Joubert was sensitive to the way the Revolution and successive attempts to create new constitutions focused attention on the status of the written word as never before. His growing desire for linguistic precision and clarity, which we shall examine shortly, should not be seen simply as the expression of a personal aesthetic preference but as a pragmatic reaction to the political ambiguities of a society that could no longer put its faith in time-honoured, unwritten laws and customs.

[88] Ibid. 26 n. 1.

2
Politics and Aesthetics

THE FAMILY UNIT

One useful way of approaching the aesthetic dimension of Joubert's writing on political matters is to examine his attitude to the family and, in particular, to the role of the father in the family unit. We have examined in some detail the growing pragmatism of his political beliefs but this is complicated by occasional waves of nostalgia for the type of liberty espoused by the ancient Greeks. During the late 1790s and 1800s this is sometimes capable of making Joubert sound like Rousseau or Constant at a time when his politics align him with Bonald and Maistre. It is in examining this apparent paradox that the underlying aesthetic governing Joubert's political preferences becomes clearly visible.

Two of the best examples of Joubert's 'nostalgie de [la] liberté'[1] were written in 1806:

Beaucoup de mots ont changé de sens. Remarquez celui de *Liberté* ches les anciens. Il avoit au fonds le même sens que celui de *dominium*. 'Je veux gouverner ou administrer la cité'; et parmi nous ces mots veulent dire 'je veux être indépendant'. Liberté a chez nous un sens moral et avoit . . .

(C ii. 578)

Joubert breaks off without finishing but it is not difficult for us to imagine how he would have concluded when we compare this passage with the slightly earlier lament for the way in which the word *patrie* had been gutted of all emotional and historical significance:

Le mot *patrie* vouloit dire *la paternelle*. Ce mot a parmi nous un son qui n'a aucun sens pour notre oreille [. . .] ce mot *patrie* ne peut pas exciter dans nous

---
[1] Groethuysen, 176.

les mêmes affections qu'il excitoit dans l'âme des anciens [...] Il avoit pour eux un son qui alloit au cœur [...] Dans nos idiomes actuels, cet adjectif devenu substantif dénomine une chose morale et par conséquent il est froid.

(C ii. 564)

Echoes of Rousseau's evocation of 'ce doux nom de patrie' in the *Discours sur les sciences et les arts* may be detected here,[2] and Joubert's analysis of the history of this word is remarkably similar to that which Constant was to give in his treatise, *De l'esprit de conquête et de l'usurpation*:

Quand Cicéron disoit: 'pro quâ patrîa mori, et cui nos totos dedere et in quâ nostra omnia ponere, et quasi consecrare debemus', c'est que la patrie contenait alors tout ce qu'un homme avait de plus cher. Perdre sa patrie c'était perdre sa femme, ses enfants, ses amis, toutes ses affections et presque toute communication et toute jouissance sociale: l'époque de ce patriotisme est passée. Ce que nous aimons dans la patrie, comme dans la liberté, c'est la propriété de nos biens, la sécurité, la possibilité du repos, de l'activité, de la gloire, de mille genres de bonheur.[3]

This is a passage which, in Joubertian vocabulary, reads as follows:

Les anciens disoient nos ancêtres, nous disons la *postérité*; nous n'aimons pas comme eux la patrie, c'est-à-dire le pays et les loix de nos pères; nous aimons plutôt les loix et les pays de nos enfants; c'est la magie de l'avenir et non pas celle du passé qui nous séduit.

(C i. 137)

But whereas Joubert none the less concluded that 'la première [nos ancêtres] est naturelle, la seconde [la postérité] est artificielle', Constant, wary of what he perceived to be mere sentimentality, faced the future squarely with the dry verdict '[que l']on ne fait pas une monarchie constitutionnelle avec des souvenirs et de la poésie'.[4]

Yet Joubert, along with Bonald and Maistre, was adamant that such 'nostalgia' was far from being misplaced. Behind these etymological investigations into words like *patrie* and *paternelle* is Rousseau's discovery that 'La plus ancienne de toutes les sociétés et la seule naturelle est celle de la famille. La famille est donc, si l'on veut, le

---

[2] Rousseau, *Œuvres complètes*, iii. *Discours sur les sciences et les arts*, 24.
[3] Constant, *De l'esprit de conquête et de l'usurpation*, in *De la liberté*, 107–265, p. 234.
[4] Constant, *Principes de politique*, in *De la liberté*, 265–430, 289.

premier modèle des sociétés politiques'.[5] Joubert and Bonald believed, however, that both Rousseau himself and his interpreters during the Revolution had concentrated too much on the term *modèle* at the expense of the word *famille*. The result had been political and constitutional experiment, with ironic consequences which were to be described by Tocqueville in *L'Ancien régime et la révolution*. Paradoxically, the Revolution which had begun with Rousseau's look at the family unit ended by considering the figure of the citizen:

en dehors de toutes les sociétés particulières, de même que les religions considèrent l'homme en général, indépendamment du pays et du temps. Elle n'a pas recherché seulement quel était le droit particulier du citoyen français, mais quels étaient les droits et les devoirs généraux des hommes en matière politique.[6]

Joubert's hostility towards all the possibilities for constitutional innovation which such a position entailed is best defined by looking more closely at what Constant and Joubert understood by the term *poésie* in a political context. For Constant, writing in 1814 on the eve of the first empire's demise, the 'memories' and 'poetry' associated with old-fashioned understandings of patriotism, loyalty to family and ancestors, were beautiful but inappropriate aids for those concerned with preserving 'la propriété de nos biens'.[7] Joubert would certainly have appreciated Constant's reasoning, if only because he believed that true monarchy, as distinct from the emasculated version Constant promoted, 'est poétique, que les poètes y ont recours' (C i. 222). This has obvious affinities with Maistrean belief in the Divine Right of Kings, in an adherence to the tradition that the first poets were the singing lawgivers of their nations, rare, especially favoured individuals. According to Plato's *Cratylus*, 'de tous les créateurs humains le plus rare, c'est un législateur'.[8] Yet there is a sense in which Joubert's vision of monarchy as an essentially poetic institution is as pragmatic as Constant's rejection of the anachronistic thinking to which he felt his contemporaries fell prey or, indeed, Joubert's own equation of politics with 'l'art de connoître et de mener la multitude ou la pluralité' (C ii. 845). We touch here for the first time on the importance to Joubert of illusion, his belief '[que] c'est une vérité qu'il y a des illusions utiles' (C ii. 608). It

---

[5] Rousseau, *Œuvres complètes*, iii. *Contrat social*, bk. I, ch. II, p. 161.
[6] A. de Tocqueville, *L'Ancien régime et la révolution*, ed. J.-P.Mayer (Paris, 1967), p. 71.
[7] Constant, *De l'esprit de conquête*, 234.
[8] Quoted by Maistre, *Essai*, para. lii, p. 90.

2. POLITICS AND AESTHETICS

was relatively unimportant to him whether the Divine Right of Kings to reign over their subjects was a truth of nature or not. In the final analysis he probably felt that this doctrine was akin to poetic myth and fable in that it reflected in understandable and seductive terms the true nature of God's relationship to man. What mattered was that people should believe it to be true. That way order was established and things were accomplished:

> Il n'importe pas qu'il y ait beaucoup de ce que vous appelez *certitude* dans les choses, pourvu qu'il y en ait beaucoup dans les esprits. La conviction est nécessaire plus que la vérité. C'est par la conviction qu'on se propose un but, qu'on vise, qu'on atteint etc; et qu'on acquiert de la droiture, de l'ordre etc. Qu'importe que le but soit blanc pourvu qu'en l'ajustant on prenne l'habitude de tirer juste?
>
> (C ii. 512–13)

It is Joubert's concern to create the conditions necessary for action to take place that is most striking in this passage. While he remained slightly sceptical of transcendental explanations for absolute monarchy, his experience of republican politics in Montignac made him disinclined to subscribe to any form of government where the legitimacy of debate might bring into question the authority of time-honoured and time-tested laws and customs and paralyse executive power.

The illusion that absolute monarchy is ordained by God is a useful way of preventing its authority from being questioned and Joubert believed that, like the various religious cults themselves, it should clothe itself in mystery and poetry:

> Nota, que ce qui rend le culte utile, c'est sa publicité, sa manifestation extérieure aussi frappante qu'il est possible, son bruit, sa pompe, son fracas et son observance universellement et visiblement insinuée dans tous les détails de la vie publique et de la vie intérieure.
>
> (C i. 141)

As intelligent as the protean Constant, whom he disliked so much,[9] Joubert was aware of the curious paradox at the heart of politics, with its pragmatic reliance on illusion, on fiction, and on poetry to achieve practical ends: 'De la fiction!' he exclaimed in 1807; 'Il en faut partout. La politique elle-même est une espèce de poésie' (C ii. 634).

---

[9] For Joubert's dislike of Constant, see C i., 123.

When the illusions of monarchy failed, however, when the King failed to structure the poem of the state correctly, then the price to be paid was terrible indeed:

> Au quatorzième jour du mois appelé juillet par les hommes et en l'année que nos ères vulgaires et périssables désignent par les quatre chiffres 1789, il y eut dans le ciel un grand bruit. Les immortels s'étoient assis au bord de la matière, en ce point de l'espace par où commence le *lieu* et d'où le *temps* reçoit sa première mesure et le mal son germe premier. L'éternité, l'immensité et le bonheur sont par delà.
>
> Dieu s'étoit retiré en lui et caché dans le sein de sa propre essence, comme notre soleil pour nous quand il s'offusque d'un nuage. Ce soleil des esprits n'étoit plus visible pour eux. Ils n'étoient plus heureux de sa présence, mais de sa seule impression...
>
> Tout à coup il parut devant eux une ombre. Elle avait pour figure ces apparences de son corps qu'une âme emporte de la terre et qu'elle garde jusqu'après son épuration. Elle avait dans ses mains sa tête et sa tête parla. Elle leur dit: 'Hier une paix universelle régnait aux régions d'où je suis venu. Aujourd'hui, mort plein de vie, tué hors de la guerre et frappé par un peuple entier dans les fonctions de ma magistrature, j'arrive avant mon heure, étonné et innocent de ce départ précipité.' Comme il parlait, une infinité d'autres arrivèrent en même temps, tous blessés comme lui et montant de la terre sans relâche et rapidement comme une pluye qui tomberait de bas en haut. — Ils criaient tous: 'Recevez-nous.' Ils étaient tous des ombres d'hommes qu'on avait frappés à leurs postes et qui étaient morts debout ou assis dans leur devoir.
>
> (C i. 102–3)

It is difficult to be certain just how seriously we should take this passage. It has an air of pastiche about it, yet its ironies are not lost on the reader attentive to the demise of Louis XVI's art. What better way could there be of recording for posterity the failing illusions of the *ancien régime* than the preservative structure of poetic myth? As Joseph de Maistre put it, 'la fable bien plus vraie que l'histoire ancienne, pour des yeux préparés' is always at hand to prove that no man can create, or contribute to, a divinely instituted constitution 'à moins qu'il ne s'appuie sur Dieu'.[10] Saint-Martin, in his 'Eclair sur l'association humaine' spoke of the profound truths to be taken from 'des récits mythologiques qui se trouvent envelopper la naissance des nations'.[11] 'C'est toujours un oracle qui fonde les cités,' wrote Maistre, 'c'est toujours un oracle qui annonce la protection divine et les succès du

---

[10] Maistre, *Essai*, para. xxx, pp. 56.
[11] Triomphe, in ibid. 58, n. 1

2. POLITICS AND AESTHETICS

héros fondateur.'[12] Here, somewhat wryly perhaps, Joubert assumes the voice of an oracle in order to relate the destruction of a distant descendant of that hero.

Equally appropriate is the Neoplatonic flavour of the fable, with its references to the Pythagorean plotting of time and eternity and the use of a Ficinian parallel drawn between God and the sun. Myth was important to Joubert and, as we shall see shortly, forms one of the defining characteristics of his Platonism. Even in the realm of politics he was incapable of confining its application to the death of Louis XVI. An entire way of life seemed to end with the King, and the only way to preserve some of the vestiges of his authority was to adopt them into the manageable circle of private family life. This strategy, which involved a weaving of myth around the emotive figure of the father, around Joubert himself, is most clearly visible in his reactions to readings of the Vicomte de Bonald.

Among Joubert's manuscripts may be found several small jotters which he used for taking notes from a number of Bonald's works. While reading the *Recherches philosophiques* of 1818 Joubert noted a passage that has clear echoes in the *Carnets*:

La necessité d'un pouvoir dans un Etat, ou d'un père dans une famille, est une vérité du même ordre que la nécessité d'une cause première dans l'univers, moral ou physique. Cette proposition de philosophie est en même temps un point de croyance religieuse, puisque l'Apôtre nous dit que toute paternité, c'est-à-dire tout pouvoir public ou domestique, tire son nom et son autorité de Dieu: ex quo omnis paternitas in coelis et in terrâ nominatur.[13]

Nevertheless, Joubert must have had real reservations about the way Bonald went about proving his argument. The vicomte uses the family unit as a model on which to base an entire political and metaphysical system in a manner that is not dissimilar—although it is directed towards very different ends—from that adopted by the revolutionary partisans of Rousseau's 'contrat social'.

Because for Bonald 'c'est uniquement dans leur rapport à la société qu'il faut considérer l'homme et ses opinions',[14] the family unit is seen from the very start of the *Recherches philosophiques* as a latent political entity whose individual characteristics may be submerged at

---

[12] Maistre, *Essai*, para. xxx, p. 58.

[13] L. de Bonald, *Recherches philosophiques sur les premiers objets des connaissances morales* (2 vols.; Paris, 1818; 2nd. edn., 1826) (1818 edn.), Joubert's copy may be found at Mme d'Arjuzon's home in Bussy.

[14] Ibid. (1826 edn.), 72–3.

any moment by its symbolic attributes. Thus, in the chapter entitled 'De l'origine du langage', a civilized political constitution blossoms with the minimum of difficulty from a primitive social grouping:

Il faut remarquer avant tout, que la société, considérée dans son essence et sa constitution, a pu, depuis l'origine du genre humain, varier dans ses accidens, c'est-à-dire s'étendre en nombre d'hommes et en espèce de territoire, mais qu'il lui a été impossible de rien ajouter à sa constitution, parce qu'elle a été dès le commencement, comme elle le sera jusqu'à ses derniers jours, composée de trois *personnes nécessaires, père, mère, enfant*, ou en généralisant ces personnes et leurs noms pour en faire une société publique, *pouvoir, ministre, sujet*, dont les rapports sont toute la constitution et toutes les lois politiques de la société.[15]

The single, domestic figure of the father, extrapolated into an abstract symbolic dimension where he becomes *power*, is metamorphosed by Bonald into the acceptable assuring figure of the monarch. Thereafter, references to 'le père' as a 'souverain dans sa maison' are common and may be compared to Joubert's statement:

Dans un état bien ordonné, les rois commandent à des rois; c'est-à-dire, à des pères de famille maîtres chez eux, et qui gouvernent leur maison. Que si quelqu'un gouverne mal la sienne, c'est un grand mal, mais beaucoup moindre que s'il ne la gouvernoit point.

(C ii. 826)

Frequently Joubert lamented that 'les rois ne savent plus régner' (C i. 223) and that 'les esprits propres à gouverner non seulement les villes et les grands états, mais même leurs propres maisons ne se rencontrent presque plus. Aucun temps ne les vit si rares' (C i. 151).

There are more subtle passages in the *Carnets*, however, which do something to suggest just how dissatisfied Joubert may have been with Bonald's later handling of the same group of images. In August 1796 he wrote:

'Il n'est pas honnête de contredire les gens dans leur maison', dit le conte. Ainsi chaque homme a le droit d'être maître absolu dans sa maison, d'y vivre en roi, et d'y être heureux même par son amour propre. C'est là qu'il est comme permis à ses infirmités et à tous ses défauts d'être à l'aise. Il est chez lui. Quiquonque y vient entre dans un empire étranger. Ce sont de tels privilèges qui chez les peuples civilisés rendent la vie domestique délicieuse et préférable à toutes les indépendances de l'homme brute et isolé. Cette vie au surplus a des devoirs qui imposent perpétuellement le sacrifice de ces droits, mais l'abandon qu'on en

---

[15] Ibid. (1826 edn.), 153–4.

fait est volontaire, agréable, généreux, honorable, presque glorieux et devient ainsi une possession, une jouissance et un bien de plus que l'on se donne.

(C i. 127–8)

At first sight, and, indeed, for the duration of the first few sentences, this *seems* like a typical defence of what Isaiah Berlin has called 'negative' liberty: 'a certain minimum area of personal freedom which must on no account be violated', as distinguished from a 'positive' conception of freedom as self mastery, and active participation in the life of government and society, a polarization first brought sharply into focus by Benjamin Constant, in his essay on the 'liberté des anciens et des modernes'.[16] In Joubert's statement we find an insistence on the individual figure of the father and the implication of protective frontiers in the phrase 'un empire étranger'. Unlike Bonald, who uses the domestic family unit only to project it immediately into the public sphere of society and government, Joubert appears to erect a formidable barrier between his private territory and that of society at large.

On the other hand, we could argue that by using words like *maître*, *roi*, and *empire* he actually undermines the privacy he is trying to defend, and thus thrusts the family into a wider public dimension, as Bonald does in the passage quoted from the *Recherches philosophiques*. In fact it is rather more complicated than this. Indeed, if Bonald rather crassly 'nationalizes' the family, in the modern social and economic sense of the word, so Joubert, by using a vocabulary inherited from the *ancien régime*, effectively privatizes the public and the national.

It is as if he had realized, like so many of his contemporaries, in the face of the Terror, that the private sphere of the domestic family circle was the only viable one open to him in which he could act with any authority, and without interference or contradiction from other people and institutions. Yet he was reluctant to abandon that ancient conception of *patrie* and, thus, of active participation in the process of government. The concept of 'positive' liberty still had powerful attractions for him, as we have seen in nostalgic passages on the meanings of words like *liberté* and *patrie*, both contemporary with the one we are examining here. This idea is still prevalent towards the end of the passage, where an isolated family reverts to the status of a tiny participatory collective with its notions of mutual sacrifice and *devoirs* to be performed. These are duties which render its kind of liberty far

---

[16] Berlin, 'Two Concepts of Liberty', 124.

superior to that enjoyed by the 'homme brute et isolé', 'en dehors de toutes les sociétés particulières'.[17]

Because the King has failed in the public domain, Joubert adopts him into the privacy of his own family and resurrects him, in his own person, a person whose status is now secure, because he can be sure that his authority within the family group will not be contested. This, at least, is the illusion he seems to be trying to create by using the tone of voice appropriate to fable and myth. As Jean Starobinski has written of Mozart's Don Giovanni: 'la victoire appartient à l'ordre ancien, au Père offensé. Il était inévitable que s'accentuât, dans la conscience même de ceux qu'entraînait le tourbillon, la figure de ce que l'on s'appliquait à nier si obstinément: le permanent, l'immuable, le transcendant.'[18]

Joubert's insistent elevation of the father, the near mythical transformation of his person into king and pontiff, is, then, both the expression of a social and political 'lieu commun' and, in the wake of its sudden *bouleversement*, a subconscious compensation for the disappearance of a figure that has become central to his conception of morality and politics. There is, about Joubert's portrait of the benevolent, dictatorial father, a warmth and reality entirely missing from the rather stark figure whose sole function, in Bonald's metaphysical system, seems to be to act as the elementary component of an algebraic equation.

The 'Éloge de Cook'

Joubert tells himself a *conte* which inhabits the same aesthetic dimension as the fable of Louis XVI's demise. This aesthetic dimension is, as we have seen, that of creative illusion, of fiction itself, and it is worthwhile illustrating how it controls the successes and failures of the 'Éloge de Cook'. It is in the 'Éloge' that we see clearly, for the first time, how the circumscribed yet curiously liberating topography of *pensée* or note is ideally expressive of this aesthetic of illusion. It is just as appropriate to the discovery of a Tahitian utopia as it is to the vision of the family unit as a tiny paradise with its implicit limitations and well-regulated freedoms.

The poetic nostalgia that surrounds Joubert's evocation of Otahiti has a genuine intensity about it precisely because it does not emerge

---

[17] Tocqueville, *L'Ancien régime et la revolution*, 71.
[18] J. Starobinski, *1789: Les Emblèmes de la raison* (Paris, 1969), 27–8.

from his social conscience or aim at the creation of a traditional utopia. Its source lies much deeper in Joubert's psyche than this. As Jean Starobinski has written:

[Cette] nostalgie se confond avec les motifs néoplatoniciens de la patrie céleste et de l'exil terrestre. L'expérience mortelle de la conscience arrachée à son milieu familier deviendra l'expression métaphorique d'un déchirement plus profond où l'homme se sent séparé de l'idéal.[19]

It is at this juncture, indeed, that Joubert's political and social concerns meet on a subterranean level with his Platonism and it is as well, perhaps, to recall here the terms of his early letter to Fontanes:

Je veux, vous dis-je, être parfait. Il n'y a que cela qui me seye et qui puisse me contenter. Je vais donc me faire une sphère un peu céleste et fort paisible, où tout me plaise et me rappelle, et de qui la capacité, ainsi que la température, se trouve exactement conforme à la nature et l'étendue de mon pauvre petit cerveau ... Quant à ce que l'on nomme force, vigueur, nerf, énergie, élan, je prétends ne plus m'en servir que pour monter dans mon étoile. C'est là que je résiderai, quand je voudrai prendre mon vol.[20]

Joubert's star is the star of Venus, which reigns in the skies above Tahiti guiding the pilot to that island certainly, but also providing him with the glittering image of a heavenly perfection which he may desire yet never attain: 'C'est dans le ciel que le vaisseau trace sa route aux yeux du pilote. Et pour connaître son chemin il faut lire dans les astres. Pour se conduire le nocher ne doit pas regarder à ses pieds mais sur sa tête'(*E* 71).

It is important, too, that the sailor guiding himself by the stars to Tahiti should do so without the aid of a telescope. These tiny fragments, glittering so tenuously between existence and non-existence, figuring forth 'la ténuité réelle de la matière', provide us with a faint glimmer of the 'patrie céleste' evoked by Starobinski, an image of the relationship that exists between spiritual and material realities.[21] As we have already seen, Joubert's reading of His and like-minded writers had confirmed his belief that God was the only true creator, the only true reality. A natural consequence of such a view involved him in an increasingly obsessive attempt to illustrate the essential diaphaneity of

---

[19] J. Starobinski, 'La Nostalgie: Théories médicales et expression littéraire', *Actes du 1er Congrès international des lumières: Studies on Voltaire*, 27 (1963), 1505–18, p. 1518.
[20] *Correspondance*, Tessonneau, 60. Letter of 23 Nov. 1794.
[21] C i. 235: 'Quand je dis "La matière est une apparence", je ne prétends pas contester sa réalité, mais au contraire donner une idée vraie de sa ténuité réelle.'

the physical universe. If man is to attain even a glimpse of spiritual perfection, then he must realize that the material world is nothing more than a 'globe de feu saupoudré', an 'ombre', a 'phantôme', a 'presque rien ou presque néant' whose opacity is a divine illusion (C i. 149). We shall look at Joubert's portrayal of physical illusion in more detail in Chapter 4. For the moment it is sufficient to register his belief that the natural illusions of the universe ought never to be distorted by man-made objects like the telescope and made to adopt a solidity they do not, in fact, possess. There are good illusions and bad illusions as Plato's Sophist pointed out: 'Deux illusions. l'une qui nait de la nature des choses et qui l'ont de △, l'autre qui nait de quelque vice qui se trouve dans notre esprit — dans nos organes ou de quelque opération qui se fait autour de nous.'[22] One kind of illusion destroys another as the telescope brings the tiny prick of incandescent light and its ethereal atmosphere into focus. Its existence as matter, not, in fact, so far removed from that of the earth from which it is viewed, is revealed. Perspective is all important. As Joubert wrote: 'Vérité est en perspective. On ne la voit belle que de chez soi, que de sa fenêtre. C'est à dire, en tenant son esprit dans la disposition et le point fixe où il doit être' (C i. 207). Or, as he emphasized a little later: 'Tout a son point de vue. En deça et au-delà il y a faute et il faut corriger. Il ne suffit pas que l'objet qu'on présente soit lui. Il faut encore qu'il soit éclairé comme il faut et montré à la distance convenable. Tout est tableau et doit être fait et traité comme tableau' (C i. 232).

The *tableaux* of the *ancien régime* had carefully tried to present the illusory authority of the absolute monarch, and rightly so, Joubert believed, for they presented an image of the absolute power and reality of God. We have seen what happened when these illusions were examined in too much detail, and a similar danger lies in store for those who attempt to scrutinize the 'patrie céleste' of Otahiti: 'Les astres plus beaux à l'oeil qu'au téléscope qui les dépouille de leurs illusions' (C i. 168). Tamper with matter in this way, bring it into overpowering close-up, and the results are disastrous for the sailor who needs the perspective of distance to see his route traced clearly in the night skies. And it is a disaster not only for the sailor but for the writer, Joubert, as he maps Captain Cook's voyage to Tahiti.

For, instead of following his captain at a distance, noting and annotating his route mapped according to the pattern of the stars,

---

[22] MSS *Carnets*. This note was omitted by Beaunier in his transcription from the manuscripts of the *Carnets*. It is dated 30 Nov. 1799.

2. POLITICS AND AESTHETICS

Joubert eventually takes a telescope to his hero and brings him into a focus that destroys the writer's ability to remain detached. The result is prose vastly inferior in quality to the notes upon which it is based.

In Cook, Joubert saw an image of the kind of man he would have liked to have been at this stage in his life, one possessed of the 'génie de l'éxécution', who had covered vast distances in a spirit of rigour and dutiful attention to detail, in the way Joubert may have wished at this period to link up his perceptions and bring his articles to a successful conclusion. It is the sheer solidity of Cook's enterprise that fascinates Joubert, a better image for which cannot be found than his admiration for the maps then being printed all over Europe:

Toutes ces mappes où la figure du monde est décrite. On en a tout écrit et jusqu'au sillage invisible de son vaisseau, qui, maintenant, est représenté dans toutes ces cartes et ces mappes, où le globe est décrit par des figures et des lignes tracées.[23]

Diderot had reproached Bougainville with the mass of technical details he inflicted on his readers and the almost mesmerizing effect of his constant plotting of longitudes and latitudes. Joubert, however, seems quite captivated by what the Manuels call the 'necessary pathos of distance',[24] and in the notes he insists on the space that separates Cook from England, partly, of course, because it serves as an accurate measure of his virtue: 'A sept mille lieues de sa patrie, il fut rigide observateur de ses volontés comme si elle eût été présente' (*E* 71). We also get the impression, however, that he likes to dwell on this aspect of Cook's voyage because it induces in him a not unpleasurable feeling of 'vertige', rarely available to the armchair philosopher: 'Cook opéra toujours au-delà du monde,' he intones; 'il fit du bien à des peuples plus éloignés de l'Amérique que l'Amérique ne l'est de nous,' finally turning him into some strange aquatic creature, master of the deep, creator, in some respects, of the new continent and islands that appear beneath Joubert's hand as it traces his route on the map: 'Il habita peu la terre et vécut toujours au milieu des eaux.'[25] The map both increases and reduces to manageable proportions that sense of 'vertige'. On the one hand there is an indelible picture of the *Endeavour* in the left-hand corner and a delicate filigree of lines webbing the South Seas always present for his admiration; but the map may be rolled up and put away:

---

[23] *Studien*, 354.
[24] Manuel and Manuel, 28.
[25] *Studien*, 348.

'Ah! Sachons jouir et goûtons à chaque moment les délices inépuisables de la vie, nous qui vivons en paix sur la terre ferme et songeons quelquefois à ceux qui voguent sur la mer' (*E* 93).

In all the passages where Joubert speculates on Cook himself and his captaincy of the *Endeavour* he returns again and again to the idea that 'il était à sa place'. It is as if Cook fitted his ship exactly, acutely aware of a sense of just limitation imposed on him by the frailty and solitariness of his craft at the mercy of the elements, but also of a power conferred by that very limitation. Unencumbered by too many responsibilities, his ship could slip between the ice floes and penetrate where others could not:

> Cook alla non seulement aussi loin que les glaces purent le lui permettre, mais aussi loin qu'il fut possible en les brisant, en cherchant des ouvertures et des brèches à toutes les hauteurs ... s'il y a la moindre apparence d'issue, on la découvre et on s'y glisse.
>
> (*E* 75)

Similarly Joubert, 'en peu de mots', unencumbered by the responsibilities of continuous narrative, can dart lyrically to the heart of Cook's character and mission, describing the essence of his success. Just as Cook's one vessel has a beneficent effect on all mankind, so Joubert's short paragraphs and notes have an influence and charm that link them together beyond the finality of their periods or the white gaps on the page. They present us with a series of images, of 'prises de vue', of the same small group of objects and people, and form a collage of perceptions that revolve round the central figure of Cook, each one suggesting a slight modification and enrichment of the previous attempt to fix and describe. Language's work is never done; it should be brooding continually over new and better ways to the unattainable perfection of expression and definition, as man should be ever awake to the infinite possibilities of human *bienveillance*:

> Les hommes solitaires s'imaginent que tout est fait, s'ils respirent l'air sans le corrompre et s'ils mangent du pain en le païant. Eh mes amis! tout n'est pas fait, il faut encore remplir sa tâche. 'Mais je fais honnetement mon métier.' Ton métier! Ton métier! est-ce que la nature n'a pas donné pour métier à tous les hommes de se consoler, de s'entraider, de se réjouir les uns les autres.
>
> (C i. 54)

Yet this is an interpretation that can only be imposed on the notes for the 'Éloge' with hindsight, from the vantage-point of the *Carnets* themselves. There comes a stage when Joubert's admiration for Cook becomes a liability, when he seems no longer capable of the 'necessary pathos of distance', and he is sucked into the energetic but obsessive enterprise of a tyrant so single-minded in purpose that no movement of ship or of imagination may deviate from the course he will follow to the bitter end. Cook comes to dominate Joubert's vision of the structure of his 'Éloge', forcing the writer to weave a continuous but unfinished narrative around him that lacks the poetic merits of the preceding notes. Ironically the sense of classical balance, which the 'Éloge' is destined to express, is upset by the very person it is meant to celebrate, and this irony is all the greater in so far as Cook is seen as the paradigm of classical virtue: 'Cet Anglais a vécu de nos jours et on l'honore comme s'il était ancien' (E 69). Joubert is defeated by a necessity to structure imposed not simply by the traditional form of the *éloge* but by the nature of the man he is praising.

At the end of the day, Cook becomes a type, a classical hero as cold, remote, and distant as Bonald's father-figure, their individuality and freedom to manœuvre submerged by the relentless movement forward of argumentative, laudatory prose. We are blinded by the proximity of one particular star, whose place in the pattern made by the heavenly firmament has been lost from sight. Trying to write too continuously or too coherently, as Cook himself did, of his voyage of discovery is like writing out, or up, a constitution for the 'patrie céleste' of family, of South Sea island. We recall Joseph de Maistre's formula: 'ce qu'il y a de plus essentiel, de plus intrinsèquement constitutionnel et de véritablement fondamental n'est jamais écrit, et même ne saurait l'être, sans exposer l'état.'[26] Naturally, he links this attitude to the Platonic theme of the vanity of the written word, which is never capable of anything but the 'apparence de sagesse', a mere shadow of the 'parole divine' it should not even try to express.[27] The laws which govern Tahiti's position in the South Seas are divinely inscrutable. She should appear to sailor and writer alike in the sudden 'éclat total' of a given *pensée* or cry of 'Land Ho!', a note that reproduces the shock of a first glimpse of a tiny corner of an even smaller island. Tahiti, the ideal family, guided by a benevolent dictator, father of his tribe, should come to mind like a thought on which not too much ink has been spilt, so that the unwritten laws of the 'patrie céleste' may guard the secret of their sanctity.

[26] Maistre, *Essai*, para. ix, p. 26.
[27] Ibid., para. xix, p. 40.

Yet even the short *pensées* that attempt to bear witness to this 'parole divine' are doomed to failure, implicated in the travesty of 'un peu de liqueur noire', and we touch here, for the first time, on Joubert's real suspicion of *any* form of writing, of any finished art object, which pretends to express the Ideal.[28] 'La faiblesse et la fragilité d'une constitution sont précisément en raison directe de la multiplicité des articles constitutionnels écrits,' wrote Maistre.[29] Saint-Martin, in his *Nouvel Homme*, asked: 'Quelle plus grande preuve de la faiblesse de l'homme que la multiplicité de ses paroles?'[30]

In this light both the notes for the 'Éloge de Cook' and the *Carnets* may be regarded as the shattered fragments of a 'parole divine' which Joubert would prefer, in part, to have remained unspoken. They exist also, however, as a form of rhetoric whose only excuse may lie in its attempt to tease Joubert himself, or his reader, into the wisdom of Socratic ignorance. The 'Éloge de Cook' presents us with a paradigm of the need to *hesitate*, the intuitive and almost psychically automatic 'pause de réflexion' which both stimulated and plagued Joubert throughout his life. We watch as lyrical note and *pensée*, their discreet, oblique depiction of truth, are tempted fatally into the kind of strenuous witness demanded by continuous discourse, and learn of the extreme vigilance necessary in all who would put pen to paper. We learn for the first time of the pleasures of space between thoughts, of the need for a moment of *repos*, so that the true import of what has just been said may sink in. We learn of the dangers inherent in the rigid imitation of what or who one admires, of the distance, the *perspective* or *point de vue* from which the writer, if he must write, should view his subject.

Like the *Dialogues* of Plato, or rather, as we shall see, in accordance with Joubert's interpretation of them, the *Carnets* orchestrate an attack on Truth from many competing, contradictory points of view, an attack all the more heroic and endearing for the sense of intrinsic indecision which it manages to convey in the process. Almost despite himself, against his better judgement as a Platonist, Joubert remains, with Cook, the archetypal explorer, a seeker after new forms which beauty and truth might take.

---

[28] Ibid., para. xxvi, p. 52. cf. *Correspondance*, Tessonneau, 59: 'Je suis ménager de mon encre, mais je parle tant que l'on veut.'
[29] Maistre, *Essai*, para. ix, p. 26.
[30] Quoted by Triomphe, in ibid. 26.

3

Platonism and Expressive Aesthetics

In the *Mémoires d'outre-tombe* Chateaubriand speaks of Joubert as a 'Platon au cœur de La Fontaine', and since then it has become customary to cite him in critical biographies and literary histories as one of the principal 'Platonists' of his period.[1] Yet the issue of Joubert's 'Platonism' is a complex one which cannot be properly understood except in relation to French knowledge of Plato during the latter half of the eighteenth century. Despite the assurances of literary histories, many of Joubert's friends and contemporaries bore witness to an influence that was by no means confined to German and English writers or to *illuministes* of the 'Martiniste' tradition.[2]

What did Joubert think of Plato? What kind of Platonist was he? There are two ways of answering these questions and both have to be pursued if a complete picture of Joubert's Platonism is to emerge.

The first requires a study of important distinctions made by Joubert himself between the terms *platonique*, *platonisme*, and *platonicien*. This enables us to understand the types of Platonism he was prepared to tolerate and saves the reader of the *Carnets* from much futile speculation about the possible textual sources of many entries.[3] Examination of these distinctions reveals that Joubert's explicit opinion of Plato was typical of seventeenth-century attitudes to the Greek philosopher, although similar sentiments may be found among scholars writing *Mémoires de litérature* for the Académie des Inscriptions et Belles Lettres during the eighteenth century.

---

[1] Chateaubriand, *Mémoires d'outre-tombe*, i. 450.
[2] See *Critical Tradition*, 53.
[3] Ward (ibid. 37) declares that she uses 'the terms "Platonism" and "Platonist" to include both Plato himself and his Neoplatonic and Idealistic successors up through the eighteenth century'.

The other key to his Platonism is provided by the identification and study of editions of the *Dialogues* used by Joubert, and this is partly facilitated by the preliminary examination of the distinctions outlined above. Paul de Raynal, in his introduction to Joubert's correspondence, writes that, on entering his library, 'on y rencontrait ... toutes sortes d'éditions de Platon',[4] and research proves that there is every reason to interpret this statement literally. Joubert was particularly influenced, however, by the polemical commentaries he found in the 1701 edition by André Dacier and the 1588 edition by Ficino. Dacier contributed much to Joubert's 'grand-siècle' attitude to Plato, but Ficino's influence was more subtle and stimulated his growing interest in Renaissance philosophy, poetry, and aesthetics. As we shall see, it is partly to Ficino and to the implicit influence of Renaissance poetry that Joubert's pronouncements on the nature of beauty and the relationship of thought to expression must be traced. Ficino makes Joubert think about the all-important issue of harmony and it is by examining this concept as it emerges from Joubert's constant recourse, throughout the *Carnets*, to musical analogy that the most distinctive characteristics of his Platonic aesthetic become clear.

Platonisme, Platonique, Platonicien

The renewal of interest in Hellenic culture during the second half of the eighteenth century in France has been the subject of a number of books and hardly needs to be discussed in any detail here, yet it is worth noting a dearth of references to a knowledge of Plato.[5] There appears to have been no comprehensive survey made of 'Platonism' during the eighteenth century since the somewhat superficial, but still valuable, study by Charles Huit in the *Annales de la philosophie chrétienne* at the beginning of this century.[6] Huit seems disappointed by the relative

[4] *Correspondance*, Raynal, p. xlv.
[5] See, e.g., E. Egger, *L'Héllénisme en France: Leçons sur l'influence des études grecques dans le développement de la langue et de la littérature française* (Paris, 1869); Ch. Joret, *D'Ansse de Villoison et l'héllénisme en France* (Paris, 1910); M. Badolle, *L'Abbé Jean-Jacques Barthélemy (1716–1795) et l'héllénisme en France dans la seconde moitié du XVIIIe siècle* (Paris, 1926); R. Canat, *La Renaissance de la Grèce antique* (Paris, 1911).
[6] C. Huit, 'Le Platonisme dans la France du XVIIe siècle', *Annales de la philosophie chrétienne*, iv (Apr. 1907), 78–87; 'Le Platonisme dans les temps modernes', *Annales*, iv (Sept. 1907), 627–45; 'Le Platonisme en France au XVIIIe siècle', *Annales*, v (Dec. 1907), 279–95; 'Le Platonisme en France au XVIIIe siècle' (suite), v (Apr. 1908), 50–65; ibid. v (July 1908), 378–93; 'Le Platonisme en France au XVIIIe siècle' (suite et fin), vii (Sept. 1908), 367–78.

lack of interest in Plato on the part of many of the great 'philosophes' and resigns himself to culling the *Mémoires* of the Académie des Inscriptions for studies of Plato. Interestingly, he notes Victor Cousin's important and much neglected remark that:

seule l'Académie des inscriptions et belles-lettres a soutenu en France le culte abandonné de l'antiquité philosophique, puisqu'à parler rigoureusement il n'a pas paru dans notre pays pendant tout le cours du XVIIIe siècle un seul travail un peu remarquable sur la philosophie ancienne en dehors des mémoires de l'Académie.

Nevertheless, he doubts the lasting value of this work.[7] In fact Huit seriously underestimates the influence, if not the intrinsic value, of the studies contained in the *Mémoires*, which bear witness to a lively French interest in Plato that was not necessarily confined to scholars.

These studies, appearing between 1717 and 1790, included dissertations by Fraguier on 'l'ironie de Socrate', by Arnaud on Plato's style, which referred in particular to the *Ion*, translations of the *Criton* and the *Thaetetus*, as well as essays on the first book of the *Republic* by the abbé Sallier. Most important of all, perhaps, were the Académie's researches into the nature and importance of music to the ancient Greeks. Far from being of merely antiquarian interest, these *Mémoires*, when viewed as a whole, put the reader in mind of the aesthetic debates during the Renaissance which led up to Baïf's creation of his Académie de Poésie et de Musique.[8] Joubert was duly grateful and anticipated Cousin's enthusiasm when he wrote that the *Mémoires* were 'seuls irrépréhensibles en ce genre par cela même qu'il y a beaucoup de recherches, peu de systhème et presque rien d'affirmatif. Tout y est proposé d'un ton sage, modéré et seulement comme probable' (C i. 228).

Huit, paraphrasing the historian Egger, is correct, also, to draw attention to the chapter on Plato in the abbé Barthélémy's *Voyage du jeune Anacharsis*.[9] Published in 1788, this book contributed to the growing interest in Hellenic culture and gave impetus to popular

---

[7] Ibid. v (Dec. 1907), 281.
[8] For further details of these works see Académie des Inscriptions et Belles Lettres, *Tableau général* (1791), 49–50. For information on Baïf's Académie, see F. A. Yates, *The French Academies of the Sixteenth Century* (London, 1947), 399.
[9] Huit, v (Dec. 1907), 280.

knowledge of Greek customs and ideas.[10] Significantly, of all Plato's dialogues, it is the *Timaeus* that Barthélémy chooses to dramatize by situating the philosopher's account of the creation of the cosmos in the romantic setting of Cape Sunium. The *Timaeus* has, of course, always been among the most frequently read of Plato's dialogues and to this extent there is nothing very unusual in Barthélémy's choice. Be that as it may, however, the *Timaeus* seems to have taken on increasing significance in the evolution of aesthetic theory as the century drew to a close and is, in fact, the dialogue most frequently referred to throughout the *Carnets*, overt reference to it or its sources occurring on no fewer than nine different occasions.[11]

It was not until the nineteenth century that distinctions between the thought of Plato himself and that of his disciples and successors were made with any regularity. Emeric-David, in the 1830s, was among the first to qualify 'des Platoniciens plus spiritualistes que leur maître' as 'Néoplatoniciens'[12] and this reflected the work of German historians of philosophy such as Brucker, Schleiermacher, and Dietrich Tiedemann, whose commentary on Plato's dialogues Joubert owned and annotated.[13]

In his surveys of Platonism in the seventeenth and eighteenth centuries, however, Huit usefully notes a number of occasions when writers *do* appear to have been aware of such distinctions, few and far between though they were.[14] Thus, in 1700, Leclerc, the author of an *Ars critica*, and known to Joubert, protests at the apparent confusion between Plato's thought and that of the school of Alexandria.[15] Dacier's criticism, typically Christian in bias, of the cabalistic tendencies of Ficino is complemented by D'Aguesseau's more scholarly objections to the Florentine's Latin translation of the *Dialogues*, '[qui] ont besoin d'être retouchés' and his desire for the replacement of Ficino's 'arguments' by

---

[10] It should be noted, however, that Barthélémy's vision of Greece is very biased towards 'Classical' taste and has little in common with the opposing view of Greek civilization that gathered momentum towards the end of the century, best illustrated by the young, vibrant, barbaric antiquity to be found in the poetry of André Chénier. The formalized image was to be upheld by David and neo-classical art.

[11] See appendix.

[12] T.-B. Emeric-David, *Jupiter: Recherches sur ce dieu, sur son culte, et sur les monuments qui le représentent* (2 vols.; Paris, 1833), i, p. xiii.

[13] D. Tiedemann, *Dialogorum Platonis argumenta exposita et illustrata* (Paris, 1786). Joubert's copy may be found at M. du Chayla's home in Paris.

[14] See Huit, iv (Sept. 1907), 630.

[15] Joubert's reference to Leclerc may be found in C ii. 525.

une analyse courte et serrée qui [fasse] sentir toute la méthode et tout l'artifice de la discussion. Enfin, si, de toutes ces analyses particulières, on en pouvait former une générale qui fut comme un tableau de toute la doctrine de Platon, digérée par ordre de matières, je ne verrais rien de plus à désirer pour la satisfaction du public.

By implication Ficino's 'tableau' is found wanting in fidelity.[16]

Huit also notes the distinction made by the *Encyclopédie* between Plato's doctrines and those of his successors which are treated in separate articles, and remarks on Condillac's grudging readiness to acknowledge the difference between *platonisme* and a sect, '[qui] puisait tout à la fois dans Pythagore, qui n'a rien écrit, dans Platon et les cabbalistes'. 'Selon toute vraisemblance,' comments Huit, 'il visait ici Pic de la Mirandole, Reuchlin, Paracelse et leurs partisans.'[17]

Joubert's own desire to make distinctions is not then without precedent, and to some extent he participates in a new historically minded approach to philosophy that gathered momentum towards the end of the century. This awareness is reflected in the 1786 edition of the *Dictionnaire de l'Académie Française*, which takes account of the different nuances between the terms *platonicien*, *platonique* and *platonisme*. Here the definition of *platonique*—'qui a rapport au système de Platon'—is slightly more specific than that of *platonicien*: 'qui suit la philosophie de Platon ou qui y a rapport'. *Platonisme* is defined as the 'système philosophique de Platon'.[18] The fact that these words are admitted to the *Supplément* of the dictionary would suggest, also, that their frequency in conversation and writing of the period prior to 1786 encouraged their inclusion.

Between 1800 and his death in 1824 Joubert returned four times to this subject. On 20 January 1800, while meditating on various methods of approach to metaphysical issues, he wrote:

Il est impossible d'opérer (de procéder) en métaphysique autrement que ne l'ont fait les Platoniciens. Et il vaut mieux parler de leurs idées avec intelligence qu'avec mépris. Il faut convenir aussi que le platonicisme n'est beau que dans Platon.

(C i. 227)

Two years later, however, on 12 February 1802, he revised his opinion quite emphatically, for he recorded that 'il vaut mieux être platonique;

---
[16] Huit, v (Dec. 1907), 286.
[17] Ibid. v (July 1908), 391–2, and vi (Sept. 1908), 380.
[18] *Dictionnaire de L'Académie Française* (new edn., Nismes, 1786), ii. 282, 698.

je ne dis pas platonicien' (C i. 318). On 27 May 1806 he returned once more to the vocabulary of his 1800 entry, writing that: 'le platonisme n'est raisonnable que lorsqu'il est beau, et il n'est beau que dans les esprits qui ressemblent à celui de Platon. C'est à ceux-là seuls qu'il sied bien. Le platonisme sans Platon est insupportable' (C ii. 553). Finally, on 28 July 1813, he took up the tendency visible in the 1800 *pensée* to characterize *platonicien* as a *method* of approach in metaphysics by referring to Porphyry and Iamblichus as

platoniciens de profession, par étude et par volonté. Mais ils ne l'étoient pas par nécessité, par caractère, par nature. Le seul platonicien né dont nous ayons les livres a été moderne et ce fut Marsile Ficin. Mais il eut l'intelligence plus que l'imagination platonicienne.

(C ii. 750)

What is clear from these entries is that Joubert preferred Plato's own writings to those of his successors, whom he describes as 'platoniciens' and to whom we refer as 'Neoplatonists'. This last entry, however, is of particular interest, for it reveals the influence of the two editors who were to have most effect on Joubert's attitude to Plato. Ficino is mentioned overtly as the philosopher closest in spirit to the master, but underlying the criticism of Porphyry and Iamblichus is André Dacier's rejection of pagan interpretations of Plato given by the school of Alexandria. In 1805, Joubert noted: '"La saine antiquité", dit Dacier (vie de Pythagore). Car il y en eut une malade et délirante. Comme celle de Porphyre, de Iamblique' (C ii. 527).[19]

JOUBERT'S EDITIONS OF PLATO

It is at this point, then, that we have to turn to the questions posed by the various editions of Plato used by Joubert in order to clarify further some of the terms used in these definitions and define the true spirit in which they were written.

---

[19] A. Dacier, *La Vie de Pythagore, ses symboles, ses vers dorés* (2 vols.; Paris, 1706). It is worth noting at this point Chateaubriand's reference to Ficino in the *Génie du Christianisme*, where he uses him to establish that the Trinity was known to Pythagorean philosophers (see R. de Chateaubriand, *Essai sur les révolutions, Genie du Christianisme*, ed. M. Regard (Paris, 1978), pt. 1, bk. I, ch. III, p. 476). He describes Ficino as one of the Florentine 'prodiges d'érudition' in the *Essai sur les révolutions* (pt. 2, ch. 23, p. 354). Further, indications of knowledge of Ficino among Joubert's near contemporaries may be taken from Ginguené's biographical remarks about him to be found in his *Histoire littéraire d'Italie* (14 vols.; Paris, 1811–35), iii. 362–6. Here Ginguené criticizes Ficino for relying too heavily on the philosophy of Alexandria.

Joubert liked reading Plato when travelling from Villeneuve to Paris and made use of the two French translations of selected dialogues by André Dacier and Père Grou.[20] A sheet of quotations and page references from the 'Vie de Platon' forming the preface to Dacier's work, which I have discovered among unpublished fragments in Bussy, has established that Joubert possessed the 1701 edition of this work.

In a sense, Dacier's preface provides us with a key to many things Joubert has to say about Plato in the *Carnets*, enabling us to identify them as typical of certain seventeenth-century attitudes to the Greek philosopher. Much in the *Carnets* closely resembles the kind of judgement Dacier makes here: 'Quand la lecture de Platon ne nous rendroit pas plus sçavans, il est certain qu'elle peut nous rendre meilleurs, moins orgueilleux et plus sages ...'. While reading Plato, Dacier remarked, 'on peut y former son jugement et y acquérir la justesse d'esprit',[21] and it is quite legitimate to relate statements like these to Joubert's own worries, frequently articulated throughout the *Carnets*, about how *literally* Plato should be interpreted.[22] As Joubert wrote in December 1791, in the context of a reading of the *Cratylus*: 'La lecture de Platon est comme l'air des montagnes. Elle ne nourrit pas, mais elle aiguise nos organes et donne le goût des bon alimens' (C i. 90). In August 1800 he returned to this idea and refined it a little:

Platon ne nourrit pas l'esprit, mais il le dispose à se nourrir. Il ne fait rien voir, mais il éclaire. Il met de la lumière dans nos yeux et place en nous une clarté dont ensuite tous les objets deviennent illuminés. Il n'aprend [*sic*] rien mais il aprend. Il nous dresse, il nous façonne, il nous rend propres à tout sçavoir. Sa

---

[20] A. Dacier, *Les Œuvres de Platon* (2 vols.; Paris, 1701). Le père Grou, *Dialogues de Platon* (2 vols.; Amsterdam, 1770). According to Tessonneau, the Grou edition with annotations and underlinings by Joubert is still extant, but, as neither I, Dr Alcer, nor Patricia Ward has been able to locate it in Paris or Villeneuve, I conclude that it belongs to M. Tessonneau himself. The Grou edition, according to Gérando among others, is particularly notable for the fidelity of its translation from the Greek, as well as for making the *Ion* more widely available than Arnaud had been able to do in his version. See J. M. baron de Gérando, 'Plato', in Michaud (ed.), *Biographie universelle*, xxxi (Paris, 1843), 495–505, p. 504. Arnaud, 'Mémoire sur le style de Platon en général et en particulier sur l'objet que ce philosophe s'est proposé dans son dialogue *Ion*', in Académie des Inscriptions, *Mémoires de littérature*, xxxi (Paris, 1769). Huit (v. 282) draws attention to the increasing enthusiasm for the *Ion* and mentions, in addition to Arnaud's *Mémoire*, which was supplemented in 1771 by his translation of the dialogue itself (*Mémoires*, xxxix), another translation by the abbé de Faramont, published in *Mémoires*, xxix.

[21] Dacier, *Œuvres*, 230.

[22] See C i. 120, 125, ii. 478, 492, 495, 524, 640, 641, 754, 808.

lecture (on ne sçait comment) augmente en nous notre susceptibilité à distinguer et à admettre toutes les belles vérités qui pourront se présenter.

(C i. 266)

Three verbs—*aiguiser, se nourrir, distinguer*—emerge from these passages as succinct encapsulations of the effect produced by Plato's dialectic on the reader, and they were almost certainly stimulated by the similar vision of the *Dialogues* communicated in Dacier's preface. There, Dacier notes the sharpening, defining effects of a method of reasoning by means of which:

> la vérité y sort peu à peu du sein de la dispute mesme, comme quand on déroule des tableaux et on voit les personnages s'élever peu à peu, et paroistre enfin tout entiers... Or une vérité que notre esprit a devinée, nous plaist bien autrement qu'une vérité qu'on nous a prouvée.[23]

A little later, quoting Plato's own explanation of his veiled approach to divine mysteries, Dacier translates a passage that reminds us strongly of the way Joubert read the Greek philosopher and of the type of inspiration he drew from him:

> Ce ne sont pas les livres, disoit-il, qui donnent ces grandes connoissances: il faut les apprendre par une profonde méditation, et en y puisant soy-mesme ce feu celeste dans sa véritable source. Car de cette union avec son object, une flamme divine venant à s'allumer tout d'un coup comme un feu qui s'élance, éclaire l'ame, *s'y nourrit* et s'y entretient elle-mesme. C'est pourquoy je n'ay jamais écrit, et n'écriray jamais sur ces matières. C'est à dire pour les expliquer d'une manière claire et intelligible.[24]

As Joubert wrote: 'Platon. Une lumière diffuse. Il éclaire et ne fait rien voir si ce n'est lentement et à la longue quand ce grand jour est dissipé' (C i. 120). Much later, perhaps thinking of Dacier again, but possibly also with Sebillet's metaphor for poetic madness in mind,[25] he noted:

> Il y a dans cet homme une lumière qui est toujours prête à se montrer et qui ne se montre jamais. On la voit dans ses veines comme dans celles d'un caillou. Il faudroit frotter ses pensées et les heurter pour l'en faire jaillir. Il amoncèle des nuées qui recèlent un feu céleste. Ce feu céleste attend le choc.

(C ii. 720)

Plato's art is that of the kindler, his dialogues 'aiguise[nt] nos organes' until they strike the fire of revelation from the mind of the reader who then begins to learn from himself: 'Platon. C'est un auteur dont on ne

---

[23] Dacier, *Œuvres*, preliminary 'Discours' (no page numbers given).
[24] Ibid. 77.   [25] See T. Sebillet, *Art poétique françois* (Paris, 1548), 29.

comprend les idées que lorsqu'elles sont devenuës les nôtres' (C i. 125). As indicated earlier in this study, such a view of Plato is in accord with Joubert's attitude to his own type of rhetorical discourse, leaving the reader to finish what the author has begun.[26]

Above all, therefore, Joubert sees in Plato's dialogues 'une manière d'opérer en métaphysique', a method, an approach, and, what is perhaps even more important, he believes Plato regarded them in the same light. This is evident from what Joubert has to say in one, crucial, passage about the doctrine of Ideas, crucial for it also clarifies his attitude to the question of innate ideas, a subject to which we shall return at a later stage.

In August 1799, Joubert devoted a number of paragraphs to a comparison of Aristotle and Plato, noting the former's unfortunate tendency 'de vouloir que dans ses livres tout fût doctrinal ... ne songeant qu'il y a des vérités, et les plus belles peut-être, qu'on peut seulement faire imaginer' (C i. 211). This, writes Joubert, is precisely what Plato is about: 'Sa doctrine sur les idées expliquoit à l'esprit la formation du monde et ses rapports avec Dieu. C'étoit assés. Aristote en attaquant comme un point dogmatique ce que Platon n'enseigna que comme un moyen explicatif ne fit pas montre de sagesse' (C i. 211-2).[27] It is Joubert's insistence on the status of the doctrine of Ideas as 'un moyen explicatif', characterized by the powers of the imagination, that needs to be emphasized here. Nor can this be regarded as atypical of Joubert's understanding of this doctrine. While reading Malebranche, in April 1804, he used exactly the same expression:

Ah! Voilà Malebranche qui fait des idées 'des êtres réels' et positivement existans. Platon à qui on l'a tant reproché n'avoit pas à beaucoup près été si hardi. Ce qu'il ne donnoit que comme une manière d'expliquer, celui-ci l'affirme comme une vérité indubitable.

(C i. 438)

It is possible to relate this phrase 'une manière d'expliquer' to a translation of a famous passage in the *Republic* concerning the doctrine of Ideas and the mysteries of dialectic, given by Jules Brody in a

[26] See above, Introduction.
[27] This attitude of Joubert to Plato is not without *some* relation to the article 'Platonisme', in *Encyclopédie* (Paris, 1751-65), and even to the opinions of Voltaire. Robert Triomphe, who gathers together usefully diverse testimonies to the influence and place of Plato, quotes a paragraph from the *Encyclopédie* that may well have appealed to Joubert. It notes the prevailing atmosphere of scepticism in the dialogues '[qui] en ressemblent d'autant plus à la conversation' (R. Triomphe, *Joseph de Maistre: Étude sur la vie et sur la doctrine d'un matérialiste mystique* (Geneva, 1968), 462).

3. PLATONISM AND EXPRESSIVE AESTHETICS

fascinating article entitled 'Platonisme et classicisme'.[28] Glaucon asks Socrates about the nature of 'la dialectique' and how it leads to the 'but où nous trouverons, comme des gens de voyage, le repos et le terme de notre course'. Socrates replies:

> Tu ne pourrais plus me suivre, cher Glaucon ... car, pour moi, j'ai toute la bonne volonté possible, mais alors ce ne serait plus l'image du Bien que tu verrais, mais le vrai Bien lui-même; s'il est réellement tel ou non [i.e. tel que l'image que je t'en ai fait voir] ce n'est pas le moment de le démontrer, mais on peut affirmer, n'est-ce pas, que c'est quelque chose d'approchant *qu'il s'agit de voir*.

Brody italicizes these final words, and, in a note, declares them to be a more complete translation of the original Greek than that given in the Chambry edition, remarking that:

> Cette tournure est assez révélatrice. Elle nous invite à croire, comme le fait l'ensemble de la réponse de Socrate, que pour Platon ces Idées du Juste et du Bien, ces essences lumineuses et parfaites, furent, non pas le terme ultime d'une longue enquête philosophique, mais bien plutôt un point de départ, un premier principe, dont le soi-disant 'système philosophique' de Platon, fabriqué, lui, après coup et de toutes pièces, n'aurait été que l'élaboration nécessaire.[29]

This is a translation and interpretation to which Joubert would have been sympathetic. Plato's Ideas represent for him an imaginative point of departure, a guiding 'premier principe', a *way* of explaining. Like the dialogues as a whole, they are meant not to indoctrinate, to teach no stable or fully coherent philosophy, but to stimulate us as *dialectic* to our own discoveries of what constitutes moral life, divine wisdom— 'un long préparatif à une lumineuse intuition', as Brody puts it.[30] Aristotle and, if we recall the terms of Joubert's distinctions between various types of platonic thinkers, Porphyry and Iamblichus, deviate from the true spirit of Plato's method precisely because they fail to recognize it as a method, preferring to see it as a doctrine, a *profession*, a matter for *étude* and explication.

This attitude has something in common with Joseph de Maistre's evangelically inspired condemnation of 'l'esprit de division' which he found to be typical of the Greek mind. The Hellenic peoples, living in the first centuries after Christ, 'armés d'une dialectique insensée [...]

---

[28] J. Brody, 'Platonisme et Classicisme', in J. Brody (ed.), *French Classicism: A Critical Miscellany* (Englewood Cliffs, NT, 1966), 186–207.
[29] Ibid. 189.
[30] Ibid. 190.

3. PLATONISM AND EXPRESSIVE AESTHETICS

veulent diviser l'indivisible, pénétrer l'impénétrable; ils ne savent pas supposer le vague divin de certaines expressions qu'une docte humilité prend comme elles sont.'[31] Without, perhaps, feeling the need to subscribe to Maistre's Christian polemic, Joubert would, nevertheless, have been attracted by his understanding of the essentially inexpressible nature of much spiritual thought.

Much the same kind of thinking can be found in the abbé Fleury's *Discours sur Platon* of 1686, published at the end of the *Traité du choix et de la méthode des études*,[32] and it is reasonable to suppose that Joubert read this as well, given the fact that he noted Dacier's own references to Fleury on the sheet of quotations mentioned earlier.[33] Speaking of the *Parmenides*, Fleury notes that:

il est intitulé des idées: et toutefois je n'y ai point trouvé, ni en aucun autre, cette doctrine des idées séparées de Dieu, que l'on attribue à Platon. Mais j'ai vu en plusieurs endroits de ses écrits, que l'objet de la véritable science est, non pas la chose singulière et périssable que nous voyons, comme un homme, une maison, un triangle, mais l'original immatériel et éternel, sur lequel chaque chose a été faite: ce qui n'est en effet que la connaissance divine, première cause des créatures.[34]

For Fleury too, Plato provided a philosophical method: 'On y peut voir la fin pour laquelle on doit étudier, la *manière* de la faire solidement, et de se servir de ses études', and he attacked Ficino and other Platonists for seeking everywhere in Plato 'mystères' and 'allégories' which ought not to be interpreted 'à la lettre'.[35]

As Dacier pointed out, Plato himself 'ne veut pas qu'on écrive sur les mystères de la Religion et de la Nature'.[36] 'Peut-être mesme que ce n'est qu'un langage poétique,' he added a little later,[37] and Joubert, quoting Plutarch, was to agree: 'Il vaut mieux dire poétiquement comme

---

[31] Triomphe, *Joseph de Maistre*, 397.
[32] C. Fleury, *Traité de choix et de la méthode des études* (includes the *Discours sur Platon*) (Paris, 1686).
[33] Joubert writes: 'vid: denis d'halycarnasse—traité de la composition, fleury—traité des études' (MSS Bussy).
[34] Fleury, *Discours sur Platon*, 320.
[35] Ibid. 341, 296. It is worth noting here that this attitude to Plato is a development of Ficino's own belief that Plato was fully aware of the figurative nature of much of what he was writing and that he never intended to reveal publicly his inmost thoughts on theological matters.
[36] Dacier, *Œuvres*, 78.
[37] Ibid. 129.

Platon' (C i. 389–90).[38] Plato's mistake, which Joubert noted on his sheet of quotations from Dacier, was to have encouraged allegorical interpretation through recourse to 'métaphores dures et excessives ... C'est un défaut qu'il auroit évité, comme dit Demetrius, s'il avoit employé plus souvent les images que les métaphores.'[39]

Nor were these kinds of argument confined to Fleury, Dacier, and Joubert. In 1761 J.-J. Garnier inserted a dissertation on 'l'Usage que Platon a fait des fables' into the *Mémoires* of the Académie des Inscriptions, in which he reminded those shocked by the 'mélange impur de superstitions grossières et absurdes' that Plato 'comme écrivain ... a voulu orner son discours de fictions propres à délasser l'esprit et à réjouir l'imagination: je les nommerai fables poétiques, parce qu'elles semblent appartenir d'avantage à la poésie'. They offer 'à un esprit attentif une *explication probable* de quelque difficulté' and Garnier stresses that it is 'la différence entre *la méthode de philosophie* dont il s'est servi et celle qu'ont employé presque tous les autres philosophes'.[40] The *Encyclopédie* pointed in the same direction, noting that 'il est souvent obscur, et peut-être moins à lire pour les choses qu'il dit que pour la *manière* de les dire'.[41]

Fable and Myth

In January 1800 Joubert began to read *L'Origine de tous les cultes* by Dupuis,[42] and it is interesting to note that his revulsion at what he read there stems to a considerable degree from the attitudes to Plato at which we have been looking. Undoubtedly Joubert would have disliked Dupuis's vituperative attack on Christianity, his praise of the French Revolution, but what he singles out for attack is just the same corrosive attempt to explain ancient fable and myth, to systematize what ought not by its very nature to be treated so, which he had criticized by implication in *platoniciens* like Porphyry and Iamblichus. Dupuis, Joubert felt, was guilty of an assault upon a type of poetic discourse which, as we have seen, he himself was interested in using to

---

[38] Joubert is referring to a quotation from Plutarch, cited by the abbé Batteux in his commentary to his translation of Timaeus Locrus' treatise on the nature of the universe (see Académie des Inscriptions, Mémoires, xxxii (1768), 45).
[39] Dacier, *Œuvres*, 218–19.
[40] Quoted by Huit, v. 55–7.
[41] Huit, v. 391.
[42] Ch. Dupuis, *Origine de tous les cultes* (4 vols.; Paris, 1795).

3. PLATONISM AND EXPRESSIVE AESTHETICS 83

preserve the political and social status quo.[43] Again, with Maistre he could have written: 'Chez toutes les nations du monde, avant que le raisonneur tristement s'accréditât, on a aimé donner à l'instruction une forme dramatique.'[44]

It is, in fact, in the context of reading Dupuis that Joubert remarks that 'le platonicisme n'est beau que dans Platon', and then goes on, the following day, to attack Dupuis's massive display of erudition for its own sake: 'Le sçavoir étoit fou (par le vuide); vous l'avez abruti (par le plein)' (C i. 227). A day or so later, he noted:

> L'érudition a autant d'obscurités que la métaphysique. Ses vérités sont moins certaines et surtout moins satisfaisantes. Le livre de Dupuis prouve mieux que tout autre les incertitudes de cette partie de nos vaines études... Il n'y a de bon à chercher dans l'érudition que les traits: les traits de mœurs, les traits d'imagination etc. Vouloir retrouver l'ensemble de ces antiquités rompuës est une entreprise inutile. Je m'y suis plongé, je m'y suis mouillé, je m'y suis noyé.
>
> (C i. 228)

Like Plato, '[qui] plane toujours ... ne perche jamais, ne prend pas pied' (C ii. 642):

> Il faudroit traiter ces abymes comme l'hirondelle traite les eaux. Elle les raze, elle s'y joue, elle s'y trempe, mais seulement au bout des ailes... Prétendre à reconstruire et à réintégrer tant de débris, c'est se condamner à perdre son esprit ... Quand on s'est complettement fait illusion, on achève d'arranger son système, on l'étale, on le publie. On est content comme Dupuis.
>
> (C i. 228)

A few days later he added: 'Antiquité. J'en aime mieux les ruines que les reconstructions' (C i. 230), forgetting, perhaps, how much Volney's *Les Ruines, ou Méditations sur les Révolutions des Empires* of 1791 owed to the inspiration of Dupuis.[45]

A note in Beaunier's edition of the *Carnets* suggests fairly conclusively that Joubert met the great Hellenic scholar, Ansse de Villoison, in

---

[43] See above, Ch. 2.
[44] Quoted by Triomphe, *Joseph de Maistre*, 452–3.
[45] It is interesting to compare Joubert's opinion of Dupuis with that of Emeric-David in *Jupiter*. In his introductory chapter, 'à l'étude de la mythologie', Emeric-David notes how Dupuis 'trompé par son érudition ... a rassemblé et confondu ensemble, dans son savant ouvrage, presque tous les systèmes, l'évhémérisme seul excepté', and writes of the need to remove from his work 'tout ce qui appartient au néoplatonisme, au néopythagorisme, tout ce qui le surcharge, en un mot, sans utilité', before its merits as 'le traité le plus lumineux qui ait été composé sur la mythologie' are made manifest (pp. lxiv–lxv).

September 1801, although he may well have known him since the 1780s, when Villoison was an assiduous attender of many Parisian salons, including those of Mme de Chénier.[46] Their conversation, evidently dealing with various aspects of Greek culture and Villoison's own travels in Greece, is not of outstanding interest, but his connection with the scholar does merit some attention, since it highlights certain parallels in their attitude to the various systems of ancient Greek philosophy.

Villoison was a close friend and collaborator of the scholar Clermont-Lodève de Sainte-Croix, author of *Recherches historiques et critiques sur les mystères du paganisme*.[47] This book had originated in a *mémoire* submitted in competition for one of the yearly prizes of the Académie des Inscriptions. Villoison had also competed for this prize and lost out to his friend, whose work was honoured by the Académie. Sainte-Croix, living in the provinces, left the publication of his work to the care of his friend, who, in a remarkable fit of academic pique, spitefully published a short Latin dissertation of his own, entitled *De triplici theologia mysteriisque veterum commentatio*, as the centrepiece of Sainte-Croix's work.[48]

Sainte-Croix, displaying just the kind of erudition that so irritated Joubert while reading Dupuis, set out to prove that most of the modern writers who had investigated the religious mysteries of Paganism and found them to have been 'constamment la même dans tous les temps' were wrong. '[Si] l'on remonte à l'origine des mystères, on sera convaincu de la fausseté de cette opinion.'[49]

Villoison's dissertation struck with an equal display of erudition at the very heart of Sainte-Croix's thesis, criticizing his attempts to make capital out of the contradictory nature of ancient philosophy and religion.[50] His objections are, in fact, best articulated in a letter to Moulines quoted by Villoison's biographer Joret, and we need only think of Joubert's reaction to Dupuis or his sympathetic readings of

---

[46] See C i. 299 n. 1.
[47] G. de Clermont-Lodève, baron de Sainte-Croix, *Mémoires pour servir à l'histoire de la religion secrète des anciens peuples; ou Recherches historiques et critiques sur les mystères du paganisme* (Paris, 1784).
[48] See Sainte-Croix, *Recherches historiques et critiques sur les mystères du paganisme*, 2nd edn., ed. S. de Saci (2 vols.; Paris, 1817); Villoison's insertion is at ii. 3–111.
[49] Ibid. i. 400–1.
[50] It is worth noting, however, le bon Joseph Dacier's similar criticism of Villoison himself in a *Notice sur M. de Villoison* (Paris, 1806).

3. PLATONISM AND EXPRESSIVE AESTHETICS

Dacier and Fleury to see to what extent he would have been able to subscribe to Villoison's approach. Citing Cicero:

[qui] a fait lui-même cette remarque importante qui doit nous diriger dans l'étude de la philosophie ancienne et qui a été malheureusement trop peu suivie ... Il faut embrasser tout ensemble, pour pouvoir saisir le moindre détail, et alors on *sauve* une foule de contradictions apparentes que l'ignorance fait remarquer dans les écrits des anciens philosophes ... on a souvent bâti des systèmes sur des morceaux détachés dont on ne sentoit pas la liaison et l'enchaînement avec ce qui précède et ce qui suit.[51]

Dupuis had turned 'ruines' into 'reconstructions'; Sainte-Croix had turned 'morceaux' into 'systèmes'. As Joubert wrote: 'Des fables qui se font croire. Il n'y a qu'un certain nombre d'images, de formes, de distributions sous lesquelles l'esprit humain puisse concevoir quelque nature que ce soit' (C i. 230), and any attempt to increase that number, or systematize too rigidly those already in operation, would fall into the same trap as those philosophers who belonged to 'l'antiquité délirante'. It is worth noting in passing that it is this same disparagement of the mystical and systematic excesses of pagan Neoplatonism that is behind Joubert's witty denunciation of another contemporary, the *illuministe* Louis Claude de Saint-Martin, 'un homme qui s'élève aux choses divines avec des ailes de chauve-souris' (C ii. 580).

Emeric-David later accused Sainte-Croix of being himself a Neoplatonist,[52] and this is evident in so far as Sainte-Croix believed that: 'les philosophes éclectiques parvinrent sans doute aussi à faire passer leur spiritualisme dans l'enseignement des mystères ... [qu'ils] cherch[oient] dans la mythologie ... l'histoire des âmes humaines avant leur union avec la matière'.[53] Significantly, Villoison singled out this belief for refutation, quoting Warburton, who wrote in his *Dissertations sur l'union de la religion, de la morale et de la politique* that:

Le secret des grands mystères ne consistoit pas dans des spéculations métaphysiques des philosophes sur la nature de la Divinité et de l'âme humaine. Ce seroit supposer que les doctrines cachées des écoles de la philosophie, et les mystères de la religion, étoient la même chose: ce qui est impossible, puisque leur but étoit différent; celui de la philosophie étant la vérité seulement et celui de la religion païenne, l'utilité.[54]

---

[51] Joret, 135.
[52] Emeric-David, p. xlvi.
[53] Sainte-Croix, ed. de Saci, i. 430–3.
[54] Villoison, *De triplici*, 16.

This remark about the utility of pagan religion is particularly appropriate, for it recalls the pragmatic exasperation of Joubert with contemporary enthusiasm for the meaning and origin of fable and cult.[55]

Qu'importe qu'un vieux récit contienne un événement fabuleux ou un événement réel, si la même authorité qui nous l'a fait adopter en l'inculcant dans notre esprit y implique une moralité qui contient des maximes vraies, utiles, nécessaires, indispensables?

(C i. 229–30)

As Auguste Viatte pointed out usefully, while stressing the differences between the 'Platonism' of Joubert and that of Saint-Martin, 'pour lui [Joubert] "la religion n'est ni une théologie ni une théosophie, elle est plus que tout cela: c'est une discipline"'.[56]

The appreciation of the distinctive philosophic imagination of Plato is evident also in other important entries in the *Carnets* that critics seem to have thought unworthy of remark. In September 1805 Joubert noted that one should read the *Dialogues* 'en sorte que les comédies de Platon ne sont pas seulement celles de Platon le comique. Le philosophe eut sa Thalie, ses masques et son brodequin' (C ii. 513), and this is echoed in his exclamation: 'Platon. Oh le bon comique!' (C ii. 491). These remain enigmatic only if we fail to take Chateaubriand's description of Joubert as a 'Platon, au cœur de La Fontaine' seriously, and prove that Joubert had read La Fontaine's preface to Maucroix's 1685 translations of a number of the dialogues.[57] There, he would have read that, if we put ourselves in the position of ancient Greeks:

ce sera d'excellentes comédies que ce philosophe nous aura données . . . Il faut . . . s'en divertir et considérer Euthydemus et Dionysodore comme le docteur de la Comédie . . . C'est le père de l'ironie . . . Les circonstances du Dialogue, les caractères des personnages, les interlocutions et les bienséances, le stile élégant et noble et qui tient en quelque façon de la poésie . . . n'a plus rien qui choque.[58]

Along with La Fontaine and Racine, Joubert was ready to appreciate 'la raillerie fine de Socrate', but again we must take note of his penchant for making distinctions, at least in the 1805 entry.[59] There, we

---

[55] See above, ch. 2.
[56] A. Viatte, *Les Sources occultes du romantisme français, illuminisme, théosophie, 1770–1820* (2 vols.; Paris, 1928), ii. 24.
[57] *Œuvres de prose et de poësie des sieurs de Maucroix et de la Fontaine* (Paris, 1685), cited by F. Gohin, *La Fontaine, études et recherches* (Paris, 1937), 41.
[58] Gohin, 42–3.
[59] Ibid. 39.

are subtly reminded, as when watching Molière's greatest dramas, that there is more to comedy than *le comique*; there is *le masque* that points a moral, that stimulates reflection.

All of this is indicative of what Thérèse Goyet defines as the typical attitude of 'grand-siècle' writers to Plato: 'Le grand mérite de Platon est d'être aussi agréable qu'il est solide', she writes,[60] and this helps to clarify the meaning of Joubert's distinctions between *platonisme*, *platonique*, and *platonicien*, the former two relating to Plato's own thought and to that of his interpreter Plutarch, one of the few successors of Plato to escape complete condemnation. *Platonicien* is reserved mainly for the 'delirious dreams' of Neoplatonists like Porphyry and Iamblichus and probably covers their schematic interpretation of Platonic ideas in general.

FICINO AND RENAISSANCE PLATONISM

What, though, of the influence of Renaissance Platonism on Joubert? While reading Dacier on Plato, Joubert undoubtedly came across the reference to Antiphanes' comparison of Plato's writings 'à une ville où les paroles se geloient en l'air dès qu'elles étoient prononcées'. Not until the following summer do these frozen words thaw out and the inhabitants of the town become able to hear 'ce qui avait esté dit l'hyver; car les discours de Platon pour estre entendus doivent être échauffez, et comme fondus par les rayons d'une intelligence bien exercée'.[61]

Joubert does not mention this particular aspect of the story, which may be found in Plutarch, but it may have been Dacier's reference that reminded him of Rabelais's version to be found in the *Quart Livre*.[62] On 13 May 1797 Joubert wrote:

O mon cher ami, ils disent de même que la parole, en formant dans l'air des caractères qui imitent ses figures, acquiert quelque durée et subsiste assés pour parvenir à des oreilles éloignées et en être ouïe, de même nos pensées, se revêtant du corps de je ne sçais quelles vapeurs, subsistent après que nous les

---

[60] T. Goyet, 'Présence de Platon dans le classicisme français', *Congrès de Tours et Poitiers, Association Guillaume Budé* (Poitiers, 1953), 369.

[61] Dacier, *Œuvres*, 79. The story originates in Plutarch, *Œuvres morales*, trans J. Amyot (8 vols.; Paris, 1574), i. 142E.

[62] F. Rabelais, *Quart Livre*, in *Œuvres complètes*, ed. P. Jourda (2 vols.; Paris, Garnier, 1962), ii. 203–8.

avons conçues, s'exhalent dans les airs, y montent, y arrivent à la région supérieure de l'athmosphère et que là elles surnagent, subsistant comme ces écumes légères qui couvrent nos mers, et exposées à l'attention des esprits célestes qui en contemplent la difformité ou la beauté et qui scavent ainsi tout ce que les hommes projettent, imaginent, désirent, espèrent et forgent en un mot de plus intime et de plus secret. Ces paroles gelées dont on dit que notre Rabelais a fait le conte peuvent vous aider à concevoir aisément leur idée: mais cette idée-ci, mon cher ami, a je ne scais quoi d'entéléchique et de poétiquement moral qui mérite qu'on la rapporte et qu'on lui donne de l'attention.

Mais, de même que des paroles balbutiées et qui n'ont pas été duement formées de toute la force de la langue font un bruit qui n'est pas distinct et ne peuvent pas être: de même, disent-ils encore, celles de nos pensées auxquelles la volonté n'a pas concouru et n'a pas imprimé sa force n'ont pas de forme décidée, ne produisent qu'une fumée et ne peuvent pas être vues, pas plus qu'elles ne le sont . . .

(C i. 145)

Comparison of this passage with the various sources which lie behind it—Plutarch, Rabelais, Dacier—shows that Joubert was not accurately recalling any one text in particular. Here he seems concerned to create his own myth about the relationship between thought and its expression in language. The glancing reference to Rabelais, however, should not be overlooked. In the first place, it reminds us that Renaissance Platonic aesthetics in general lie behind many other *Carnet* entries which deal with this issue. Secondly, Rabelais's version of the story may be related not only to this particular entry but to the form of the *Carnets* as a whole, as was discussed at the end of Chapter 2. I shall return to this aspect later.

It is to Joubert's knowledge of Ficino and Ronsard that we have to turn if we wish to understand his frequent attempts to define what constitutes expressive harmonious discourse and the relationship of that discourse to thought.

Joubert, as I have already stated, was aware of Ficino's shortcomings. In his copy of Tiedemann's commentary on the *Dialogues* he underlined a passage, at the very start of the preface, in which Ficino is accused of shedding little light on their obscurities, of abandoning the thought of Plato himself for the 'dreams' of the school of Alexandria and the Cabalists. It is only Ficino's 'intelligence' and not his 'imagination' that can be described as Platonic. Nevertheless, as a number of page references to an edition of Plato prove, Joubert was using the 1588 edition of the Latin translation of the *Dialogues* by

3. PLATONISM AND EXPRESSIVE AESTHETICS

Ficino from the early 1780s on, and could not fail to have been influenced by the Florentine Neoplatonist's commentaries.[63]

In addition, Joubert refers overtly to Florentine commentaries on the *Symposium*,[64] and, as we shall see, his reading of Plato through Ficinian spectacles amply bears out André Chastel's thesis that 'l'inflexion la plus originale du néo-Platonisme florentin ait justement été une insistance nouvelle sur l'émotion esthétique et sur l'attitude privilégiée de l'artiste'.[65]

The greatest privilege that the artist or, more specifically, the poet enjoys is his receptivity to that 'estincelle du feu divin', or 'feu céleste' as Joubert preferred to call it (C ii. 720). Undoubtedly Joubert was interested in the idea of poetic fury, as his identification of it in Plato testifies, and it played an important role in his growing appreciation of the expressive power of music and of harmony in general which may be found scattered throughout the first few hundred pages of the *Carnets*. Joubert may have come across the doctrine of poetic madness in Ficino's translations of the *Ion* and *Phaedrus* and in the brief essays that prefaced them. Ficino had, of course, an immense influence on the poets and theorists of the French Renaissance, so it is equally possible that Joubert encountered expressions of the theory while reading Ronsard's *Odes* in 1790.[66] Ronsard was, as Festugière puts it, 'le plus fidèle disciple de Ficin en France au XVIᵉ siècle'[67] and in the great 'Ode à Michel de l'Hospital' Joubert would have noted the way poetry in the person of the Muses attempts to raise the soul to the highest sphere by pre-empting for itself the offices of the other three types of inspiration outlined by Ficino in the *Commentarium in convivium* and in his introduction to the *Ion*.

Four years later in 1794, in the letter to Fontanes quoted earlier, Joubert described this 'sphère un peu céleste', this 'étoile', in language which bears the mark of his familiarity with Ficinian ideas, and which glances humorously, perhaps, at Diotima's comparison of the search for the Idea of Beauty with the climbing of a staircase:[68]

---

[63] Plato, *Divini Platonis opera omnia, Marsilio Ficino interprete. Accesserunt sex Platonis dialogi, nuper a Sebastiano Conrado tralati: Apud Nathanaelem Vicentium: Lugduni, 1588*.
[64] See C ii. 748.
[65] A. Chastel, *Marsile Ficin et l'art* (Geneva, 1954), 32.
[66] See C i. 86.
[67] J. Festugière, *La Philosophie de l'amour de Marsile Ficin* (Paris, 1941), 139.
[68] For Diotima's comparison, see Plato, *Collected Dialogues*, ed. Cairns, *Symposium*, 526–74, paras. 210–12.

C'est là que je résiderai, quand je voudrai prendre mon vol; et lorsque j'en redescendrai pour converser avec les hommes, pied à pied et de gré à gré, je ne prendrai jamais le peine de savoir ce que je dirai, comme je fais en ce moment où je vous souhaite le bonjour.[69]

The tone of this is amused and amusing and Joubert abjures most of the *force, vigueur, nerf,* and *énergie* necessary to the actual ascent as it is described by Ficino, or, for that matter, by Joubert's contemporary, André Chénier. Nevertheless their feet are on the same ladder and they both climb 'pied à pied et de gré à gré'. A history of the earth narrating 'les époques de la nature' in Chénier's neoplatonically inspired poem 'L'Invention', gives way in his poem 'L'Amérique' to an epic account of Man's discoveries, religious, social, historical, all of which are animated and inspired by the spiritual *élan* provided by the divine 'enthusiasm' described in Plato's *Ion*. This allows the poet to progress up through the different orders of knowledge until, with one foot on the chain of Being, he may cry out in Ficinian ecstasy, perhaps with memories of Ronsard's Sonnet CLXXII in mind:

Que je m'élève au ciel comme une flamme ardente!
Déjà ce corps pesant se détache de moi.
Adieu, tombeau de chair, je ne suis plus à toi.
Terre, fuis sous mes pas! L'éther où le ciel nage
M'aspire. Je parcours l'océan sans rivage.
Plus de nuit. Je n'ai plus d'un globe opaque et dur
Entre le jour et moi l'impénétrable mur.
Plus de nuit, et mon œil et se perd et se mêle
Dans les torrents profonds de lumière éternelle.[70]

This was exactly the kind of poetry that seemed to prove that it was the product of an elevating fury. Indeed, it implied that it was itself the first and greatest fury of them all, just as Ficino had thought: 'Poetico ergo furore primum opus est', he had written in his *Commentarium in convivium*. Even more significant for Chénier, Joubert, and many of their contemporaries, however, was Ficino's emphasis upon music and its harmonies as the element of poetic fury that does most to recover and unify the soul: 'Poetico ergo furore primum opus est', he wrote, 'qui

---

[69] *Correspondance*, Tessonneau, 60. Letter of 23 Nov. 1794.
[70] A. Chénier, *Œuvres complètes*, ed. P. Dimoff (3 vols.; Paris, 1910), ii. 105–6; this passage is from 'L'Amérique', chant III, pt. 4. See also Ronsard, *Les Amours*, ed. A. M. Schmidt and F. Joukovsky (Paris, 1974), Sonnet CLXXII, p. 113.

per musicos tonos quae torpent suscitet; per harmonicam suavitatem quae turbantur, mulceat.'[71]

It is not entirely surprising, therefore, to find that music and its expressive power became one of the chief topics of research and conversation among cultured French society of the late eighteenth century and it is worth examining this background if only to show that Joubert's interest in Renaissance philosophy and poetry was by no means eccentric and helps to explain the nature of his own pronouncements on harmony and mimesis.

The remarkable number of dissertations by French scholars to be found in the *Mémoires of the Académie des Inscriptions* between 1717 and 1793 on the nature and function of Ancient Greek music should not be regarded, as I have already suggested, simply as a by-product of the renewal of interest in the Hellenic world. Rather they may be seen as an echo and continuation of the researches undertaken by the Renaissance poet Baïf's Académie de Musique. His aim had been to 'remettre en usage la Musique selon sa perfection, qui est de représenter la parole en chant accomply de son harmonie et mélodie', and the explosion of opera, hymns, cantatas, 'opéra-comiques', and 'romances' which occurred in France at the beginning of the nineteenth century may be viewed in the context of a revival of interest in the spiritual power of the human voice.[72] As we shall see, most of Joubert's references to music are concerned with *le chant*, while to Chateaubriand's ear the murmur of nature reminded him of Gregorian chant, which, in his opinion, descended directly from the Ancient Greek scale.[73]

As Marie Naudin has written: 'la pensée se renouvelle en se retrempant aux sources—oubliées à l'époque précédente—des théories pythagoriciennes, platoniciennes et néo-platoniciennes, mettant en valeur la portée métaphysique de la musique';[74] yet the beginnings of this process may be dated back quite accurately to the early 1770s. Père Grou published his translation of the *Ion* in 1770 and it is, perhaps, no coincidence that the Académie des Inscriptions took as the subject of a *concours* of 1773 'La Métaphysique de la musique et son union avec la

---

[71] Ficino, *Commentarium*, VII, xiv. Ficino's commentary on the *Symposium* may be consulted in any of the great sixteenth-century editions of Plato's work by means of the same references to *oratio* and *caput*.

[72] J.-A. de Baïf, *Statuts de l'Académie*, quoted extensively by Yates, 320.

[73] R. de Chateaubriand, *Génie du Christianisme* (Paris, 1930), 119–21.

[74] M. Naudin, *Evolution parallèle de la poésie et de la musique en France: Rôle unificateur de la chanson* (Paris, 1968), 169.

poésie'.[75] One book, in particular, frequently reads as if it were a direct result of this competition and was written by the author in whom Florentine ideas are most visible. Villoteau's *Recherches sur l'analogie de la musique avec les arts qui ont pour objet l'imitation du langage* was published as late as 1807 but it had been gestating for many years and refers to a number of other earlier works on music that seem to have both Platonic dialogue and Académie *concours* as their backdrop. Villoteau frequently quotes from Grou's translation of the *Dialogues*, using, in particular, his version of the *Philebus* and its refutation of the claim that our notions of Beauty in art are dictated by the sensible pleasure it evokes in us.[76] But he uses, also, Ficino's testimony to the unity of the arts by adhering to his interpretation of the significance of the Muses, follows the Florentine Academy's rejection of mimesis as the guiding principle in Art, saves the Poet from Plato's censure in the *Republic* by referring us to the *Ion*, which he calls his 'Traité de l'inspiration poétique',[77] and defines *le beau* in terms which relate to Ficino's own conception of 'la beauté [qui] appartient en propre aux réalités parfaitement pures'. For Ficino, beauty consisted of 'lumière, grâce, proportion, nombre et mesure'[78] and Villoteau wrote of it as 'une harmonie inaltérable de toutes les parties qui constituent un ensemble parfait'.[79] The pleasure music gave must be:

pur et parfait, c'est-à-dire, sans aucun mélange de quoi que ce soit qui puisse jamais causer le moindre désordre dans le cœur et dans l'âme; qu'il doit avoir sa source dans ce qui est réellement *beau* et aussi parfaitement *bien* qu'il peut l'être sous tous ses rapports et dans toutes ses parties ... il doit enfin élever et ennoblir notre âme en épurant et fortifiant notre raison.[80]

Villoteau's book sets out to prove that, in Ancient Greece, poetry and music were one, that this unity was sacred and governed by strict laws which enabled legislators like Orpheus and Solon to rule over a people united in their respect for this principle. In so far as the alliance of 'poésie, chant, musique' formed a 'science encyclopédique de l'homme

---

[75] There are no references to this *concours* in the 'Rapports' of the Académie. The only overt mention of it is to be found in a letter from Turgot to Caillard of 1773 (*Œuvres de Turgot*, iii. 646).
[76] G. Villoteau, *Recherches sur l'analogie de la musique avec les arts qui ont pour objet l'imitation du langage pour servir d'introduction à l'étude des principes naturels de cet art* (Paris, 1807; repr. 2 vols.; Geneva, 1970), i, pp. xxv–xxviii.
[77] Ibid. 104.
[78] Chastel, 88, 87.
[79] Villoteau, *Recherches*, i, p. xxix.
[80] Ibid., p. xxxvii.

3. PLATONISM AND EXPRESSIVE AESTHETICS 93

[qui] ne se borne pas aux seuls plaisirs de l'imagination et des sens mais ... nous [rappelle] la mémoire des faits instructifs ... [inspirent] des vertus sociales et ... [renouvèlent] dans le cœur l'impression des sentiments dont elle imite le langage', then Villoteau recommends it to the poets of his time.[81] Like Fabre d'Olivet, who, in his 'Discours sur l'essence et la forme de la poésie', regrets that Man has lost sight of this important distinction and has frequently mistaken mere form for essence,[82] Villoteau appeals to the ideas of Plato's *Ion* and recommends 'une prose expressive—on pourrait dire presque incantatoire—afin de s'adresser directement sans l'intermédiaire de la raison, au souvenir, aux sentiments, aux fibres du cœur'.[83] As Fabre d'Olivet interprets, the essence of poetry is 'une inspiration divine', by means of which 'on revêt d'un langage humain et ... l'on transmet aux hommes les idées des Dieux'.[84]

The same reprise of Renaissance metaphysics may be found in the work of Chabanon. Chabanon frequently read *Mémoires* to the Académie des Inscriptions on the technicalities of Greek music and in 1779 wrote a brief series of *Observations sur la musique*, which, he comments, 'portent essentiellement sur la Métaphysique de l'Art, partie qui nous a semblé neuve, que personne n'a jusqu'à présent approfondie'.[85] These observations were expanded at greater length in 1785, when he published *De la musique considérée en elle-même et dans ses rapports avec la parole, les langues, la poésie et le théâtre*. Here we find that music, 'rangée sous le domaine de l'esprit, s'associe aussitôt la parole; on peut regarder même cette association comme émanée de l'instinct, et antérieure aux combinaisons de l'esprit'.[86] A comprehensive attack follows on the application of mimesis to the musical arts and on Aristotle, the originator of this doctrine, 'celui de tous les philosophes qui s'est le moins livré aux prestiges de l'imagination'.[87] Imitation, Chabanon declares, 'a bien peu de part au plaisir que la musique procure' and, if we must paint nature, then 'supprimez tous

---

[81] B. Juden, *Traditions orphiques et tendances mystiques dans le Romantisme français (1800–1855)* (Paris, 1971), 302.

[82] Fabre d'Olivet, 'Discours sur l'essence et la forme de la poésie', in *Les Vers dorés (de Pythagore) expliqués* (Paris, 1813).

[83] See Juden, *Traditions orphiques*, 303.

[84] Fabre d'Olivet, 'Discours', 12–13.

[85] M. P. G. de Chabanon, *Observations sur la musique et principalement sur la métaphysique de l'art* (Paris, 1779), p. ii.

[86] *De la musique considérée en elle-même et dans ses rapports avec la parole, les langues, la poésie et le théâtre* (Paris, 1785), 5.

[87] Ibid. 39.

ces tableaux de détail qui ne peignent rien, peignez en masse'. 'Peindre n'est que le second de ses devoirs; chanter est le premier.'[88] We find, in Chabanon, a refreshing attention to the expressive function of art: 'La peinture des effets soumis à nos sens, s'appelle imitation; la peinture de nos sentiments s'appelle expression,' while lyric poetry 'enivre pour ainsi dire la raison', its poets, as Plato put it in the *Ion*, 'des Corybantes qui dansent avec un esprit égaré'.[89] 'Le mot *émouvoir* est donc pour la Poésie et la Musique le seul mot de ralliement,' Chabanon concluded, and recommended a reading of Ronsard:

La langue de Ronsard fut-elle plus stérile que la nôtre? Elle eut peut-être plus d'abondance. Fut-elle obscure? Ronsard fut entendu de tout son siècle, puisqu'il en fut admiré. Fut-elle timide? Nous pourrions lui envier son énergie et sa franchise.[90]

Chabanon was not the only writer to react against mimesis and the stagnation of aesthetic theory in general. He himself refers to 'une brochure de M. l'abbé Morellet publiée il y a huit ou dix ans, une de M. Boyé, plus récente', these being 'les seuls écrits où nous ayons trouvé des opinions conformes aux notres'.[91] Boyé's work *L'Expression musicale mise au rang des chimères*, published in 1779, takes a swipe at imitation in much the same way as Chabanon does, but the attack is better orchestrated by Morellet, whose 'De l'expression en musique et de l'imitation dans les arts' was reprinted in the *Mélanges* of 1818. 'Je regarde comme synonymes,' he told his reader, 'au moins dans la question présente, les termes *exprimer* et *peindre*', and went on to base an examination of 'cette correspondance de différens organes qui autorise la musique à peindre, par les sons qui semblent n'affecter que l'ouie, des impressions faites sur d'autres sens' on the familiar model of the 'squelette anatomifié', common to Diderot, Joubert, Chabanon, and many of their contemporaries.[92] At the heart of this mystery, as

[88] Ibid. 49, 59, 62.
[89] Ibid. 233.
[90] Ibid. 231, 454. Cf. La Harpe's dislike of contemporary Pindars: 'Nos odes ... n'étant pas faites pour être chantées, ne doivent pas ressembler aux odes grecques et latines. La plupart, au contraire, sont des discours en vers à peu-près aussi suivis, aussi bien liés qu'ils le seraient en prose. Je ne dis pas qu'il faille nous en blâmer absolument, mais ne seraient-elles pas susceptibles d'un peu plus d'enthousiasme et de rapidité qu'on n'en remarque, même dans nos plus belles?', *Lycée: Cours de littérature ancienne et moderne* (16 vols.; Paris, 1821–2), ii. 165.
[91] Chabanon, *De la musique*, 11.
[92] A. Morellet, 'De l'expression en musique et de l'imitation dans les arts', *Mélanges de littérature et de philosophie du xviii*^{e} *siècle* (4 vols.; Paris, 1818), iv. 376. For Joubert's version of the 'squelette', see C i. 66–7.

always, there were 'les fibres qui reçoivent ... ces ... sortes d'impressions [et] voisines les unes des autres, se communiquent réciproquement leurs ébranlemens [et] aboutissent à un centre commun'.[93]

Least satisfactory of all for Morellet was the strict application of mimesis to music: 'L'imitation à laquelle la musique travaille ... est sans doute bien imparfaite,' he wrote. What is more, it must be so by its very nature 'et différente de la nature par quelque côté, sous peine de perdre une partie de ses droits sur notre âme, et le pouvoir de produire en nous les impressions qu'elle veut obtenir'.[94]

In 1780 La Borde published an *Essai sur la musique ancienne et moderne* and he was of the opinion that it was quite impossible 'qu'un musicien ... peigne par les seuls sons d'un instrument, un ordre ou une prière, un consentement ou un refus', and went so far as to declare that even 'dans la Poésie, qui est autrement imitative que la Musique, il y a bien des momens sans imitation et qui n'en sont pas moins, pour cela, de la bonne Poésie'. He concluded that 'c'est l'expression qui doit être le but de tous les compositeurs ... ce sentiment délicat qui ne tient point aux yeux, mais à l'âme'.[95]

Lacépède's *Poétique de la musique* of 1785, despite its description by an anonymous reviewer in the *Année littéraire* as 'un poème plein d'imagination',[96] is in some ways a more conservative document than any mentioned so far. Like La Borde and Morellet, however, he is chary of using the term *peindre* to describe the operative techniques of poetry and music, preferring to substitute the word *représenter*: 'La Poésie ne peint rien, au moins à la rigueur, et en ce sens qu'elle ne montre rien de ce qu'elle cherche à peindre; mais elle *représente* tout de telle sorte qu'on croit le voir ou l'entendre.'[97]

The advantage that music has over 'plusieurs arts d'imitation' is that 'elle peut, quand elle veut, exprimer à la fois plusieurs choses différentes, sans même que ces expressions dissemblables se nuisent beaucoup, et qu'il soit difficile de les distinguer'.[98] Later, Joubert was to demand a similarly enriching experience from metaphorical language. Perhaps more familiar than these works on music is Marmontel's *Éléments de littérature*, where the articles on 'Imitation', 'Analogie',

---

[93] Morellet, 'De l'expression', iv. 375.
[94] Ibid. 390, 391.
[95] J.-B. de La Borde, *Essai sur la musique ancienne et moderne* (4 vols.; Paris, 1780), i, pp. xi, 51.
[96] *Année littéraire* (Paris [Amsterdam], 1785), iii. 113.
[97] B.-G.-E. de la Ville Lacépède, *La Poétique de la musique* (2 vols.; Paris, 1785), i. 78.
[98] Ibid. 130.

and 'Poésie' all express equivalent sentiments. In the second of these, Marmontel joins Morellet in an analysis of the suggestive reciprocity of different sensations and demands a 'style qui peint, non pas le bruit ou le mouvement, mais le caractère idéal ou sensible de son objet'. This type of analogy consists, not simply in harmony, 'mais surtout dans le coloris', and recalls Du Bos's concern for the image. Then, Marmontel writes, 'le style n'est pas l'écho, mais l'image de la nature'.[99] If the imitation of a writer, orator, or poet is in order, then it must not be a question of servile copying: 'C'est dans le sens le plus étroit, se pénétrer de sa pensée et la rendre avec liberté.'[100] Poetry, Marmontel declared, 'demande une langue figurée, mélodieuse, riche, abondante, variée et habile à tout exprimer',[101] or, as La Harpe put it in an uncharacteristic moment, 'mouvements, images, sentiments, figures, voilà sans contredit, l'essence de toute poésie!'[102] La Harpe went on to demand a greater role for the imagination in preference to *la raison* in the formulation of 'un précepte de goût', and in his hands the lyrical poet of the Ancient Greeks became a 'chanteur ... un oracle, un prophète ... il transporte et il est transporté; il semble maîtrisé par une puissance étrangère qui le fatigue et l'accable; il halète sous le dieu qui le remplit'. Undeniably, 'il n'y a pas du chant à la mesure des paroles'.[103]

Possibly the best example, however, of the dynamic aesthetics to which all these men contributed can be found in Fabre d'Olivet's *La Musique expliquée comme science et comme art et considérée dans ses rapports analogiques avec les mystères religieux, la mythologie ancienne et l'histoire de la Terre*. This work first became known through extracts published in *La France musicale* in 1802 and illustrates admirably the clumsy mesh of scientific, spiritual, and artistic obsessions typical of the period, while giving an account of the energizing creative principle at work in this art. The lengthy etymological analysis of the word 'music' is typical in this respect:

Le mot musique nous est venu du grec, *mousikè*, par le latin, *musica*. Il est formé, en grec, du mot, *mousa*, le muse, qui vient de l'égyptien, et de la terminaison grecque *ikè*, dérivée du celte. Le mot égyptien *mas* ou *mous* signifie proprement la génération, la production ou le développement extérieur d'un

---

[99] J. B. du Bos, *Réflexions critiques sur la poésie et sur la peinture* (3 vols.; Dresden, 1760); Marmontel, *Éléments de littérature* (3 vols.; Paris, 1879), i. 150–1.
[100] Ibid. ii. 284.
[101] Ibid. iii. 140.
[102] La Harpe, ii. 279.
[103] Ibid. ii. 137, 148.

principe; c'est-à-dire la manifestation formelle, ou le passage en acte de ce qui était en puissance. Il se compose de la racine *âsh*, qui caractérise le principe universel primordial, et de la racine *mâ*, qui exprime tout ce qui se génère, se développe, s'accroit, prend une forme à l'extérieur. *As* signifie, dans une infinité de langues, l'unité, l'être unique, Dieu, et *mâ* s'applique à tout ce qui est fécond, formateur, générateur; il veut dire proprement *une mère*.

Ainsi le mot grec *mousa* (muse) s'est appliqué dans son origine, à tout développement de principe, à toute sphère d'activité où l'esprit passe de puissance en acte et se revêt d'une forme sensible . . . La terminaison *ikè* (ique) indiquait qu'une chose était rapportée à une autre par similitude, ou qu'elle était une dépendance, une émanation.[104]

Here is another autopsy, and, as in other cases, the patient remains alive, well, and singing. There is little need to point to the compulsive repetition of verbs of growth, generation, and energetic activity and how they are directed towards the sensible, formal manifestation of *esprit*, of intellect—a goal that was of central importance both to Fabre d'Olivet and, as we shall discover shortly, to Joubert himself.

Joubert could not have been insensitive to the change in atmosphere created by these works and it is not in the least surprising that his own opposition to 'ut pictura poesis' and his concern for the expressivity of music and art in general should be most strikingly formulated in an entry of 1802 which attacks the poverty of imagination displayed in much ecclesiastical decoration:

Pourquoi les instrumens que les peintres ont mis quelquefois dans les mains des anges sont ridicules. 1ᵉ c'est que le son en est connu. 2ᵉ c'est que dans l'imperfection terrestre de nos voix mêmes, nous n'en usons que pour en tirer des effets propres à nous donner une idée . . .

1ment Une bouche entrouverte avec une certaine rondeur dans un visage où est dépeinte l'expression qui est propre au chant fait imaginer une voix. Mais un clavier d'orgue sous des doigts, un violon entre des mains, une flûte sous une bouche, ne fait point du tout imaginer des sons.

2ment Nos instrumens dont l'effet est connu, déterminé, fixe, invariable ne prêtent point à l'idéal.

3ment Nous n'usons de ces instrumens dans notre imperfection terrestre que pour en tirer des effets propres à nous donner l'idée d'une harmonie supérieure telle que nous pouvons aisément nous figurer des voix célestes.

Peintres, faites chanter les anges, mais ne les faites pas jouer du luth, et encore moins de la basse. Il est ridicule de mettre un pareil orchestre ou dans les

---

[104] Fabre d'Olivet, *La Musique expliquée comme science et comme art et considérée dans ses rapports analogiques avec les mystères religieux, la mythologie ancienne et l'histoire de la Terre* (Paris, 1896), 46–8 (BN V 26798).

airs ou dans les cieux. Et Raphaël lui-même eut tort lorsque dans la Sainte Cécile . . .

On peint une bouche qui chante, parce qu'il y a là de la vie. Mais on ne peut en aucune manière peindre un instrument qui résonne parce qu'il est de bois et qu'il n'a point de visage qui puisse en exprimer.

En tout, il ne s'agit pas tant de peindre quoi que ce soit que d'en donner l'idée. Mais on ne parvient jamais à donner l'idée d'une chose qu'en peignant avec vérité ce qui se trouve propre à la donner.

(C i. 320)[105]

This rejection of the dead hand of orchestral instrumentation and the preference for an expressive face with a mouth which sings is quite typical of his period. What is needed, he wrote earlier, is 'un opéra sans orchestre, un chant sans accompagnement', 'Il faut un style aérien et qui ne touche pas la terre', a formula reminiscent of that used to describe Plato's style: '[qui] plane toujours [. . .] ne perche jamais, ne prend pas pied' (C ii. 642).

Like Mme de Staël, who turned to the harp and the piano in *Delphine* and to the lyre in *Corinne*—all instruments used to accompany the human voice and much in vogue in the salons of the early 1800s—Joubert preferred to describe himself:

Comme un solo suivi d'un orchestre. Ignorants qui ne connoissez que vos clavecins et vos orgues! Je jouë de la lyre antique, de la lyre à trois ou à cinq cordes, de la lyre d'Orphée, non de celle de Timothée. Je jouë de la harpe ou du basson quand ils accompagnent la voix. Instrumens (s'il faut vous le dire) qui causent autant de plaisir à celui qui les tient qu'à ceux qui les regardent; car il s'entend, il se juge, il est retenu dans son air, il est forcé de s'écouter. Il se charme lui-même et ne reçoit pas tout son plaisir des applaudissemens qui sont indispensables à vos concerts bruyans, comme un accompagnement sans lequel le nombre de leurs accords multipliés ne seroit pas complet.

(C i. 399)

This lyre is like the Ficinian 'lyra orphica' present in countless Renaissance and seventeeth-century texts as the instrument best qualified for accompanying choral music of ancient Greek origin. What is most important about Joubert's reference, however, is his insistence upon the interior harmony which the music of the lyre instils in the soul of the player: 'il s'entend, il se juge, il est retenu dans son air'. As

---

[105] Cf. C ii. 472. Readers of Blanchot's comparison of Joubert with Mallarmé will be eager to find in the last paragraph of this entry an anticipation of Mallarmé's famous dictum: 'peindre non pas la chose mais l'effet qu'elle produit'.

Mersenne had written in his *Harmonie universelle* of 1636, 'le son de la lyre est fort languissant et propre pour exciter à la dévotion, et pour faire rentrer l'esprit dans soy-mesme'.[106]

Ficino and his disciples, including Ronsard and other poets of the French Renaissance, had subscribed to the views of Pythagoras and Plato, according to whom musical harmonies, like the structure of the universe itself, were founded upon numerical proportions. Receptivity to music thus necessarily re-established the harmony of the human soul with the cosmos and with God, who was the origin of the proportions underlying both music and the universe. As Ronsard wrote, the music of the lyre was but a 'petite partie de celle qui si armonieusement (comme dit Platon) agitte tout ce grand univers'.[107] Playing upon their lyres or harps, listening to the *Lieder* of the early nineteenth century, Joubert, Mme de Staël, Sénancour, and Chateaubriand attune their souls to the harmonies of the cosmos; microcosm responds to and attempts to reflect in art the beauty of the macrocosm.[108]

To Ronsard's mind the spiritual harmony achieved by music was intimately related to poetic fury. Like poetry, music was a gift from heaven, and, shortly after his description of the effects of music on the universe quoted above, he went on to state that 'les divines fureurs de Musique, de Poësie et de Paincture ne viennent pas par degrés en perfection comme les autres sciences mais par boufées et comme esclairs de feu'.[109]

For Joubert, too, the inspired fury of the poet and the notion of harmony were never far apart. In the following passage, poetic fury is seen as a form of physical and psychological imbalance, a form of illness: 'Tout grand talent vient d'une maladie,' he writes, 'maladie animale, mais force et santé de l'esprit.' But it must be tempered: 'Cette prédomination a ses règles et ses mesures [. . .] Je dis donc que la raison du poète est une raison supérieure, incapable de réflexion quand il opère. Demeurer en harmonie en excédent [sic], voilà la condition indispensable' (C i. 303). This last sentence reads as a perfect motto for the aspiring yet disciplined souls of Ficino, Ronsard, and Chénier, but it is also an appropriate description of the type of harmony which Joubert sought for in the *pensées* of his *Carnets*. It seems unlikely that this 'harmonie' was ever a question of producing perfectly expressed,

---

[106] Le père Marin Mersenne, *Harmonie universelle* (Paris, 1636), IV. x. 206.
[107] Quoted by T. Cave, *Ronsard the Poet* (London, 1973), 140.
[108] See Naudin, 183.
[109] See Cave, 140.

self-sufficient *maximes* destined for a traditional *recueil*. Joubert's conception of harmony went far deeper than this and involved an appreciation of the various ways a human being might respond to the divine harmonies of the cosmos. Above all, Joubert's *harmonie* was a question of noticing and then expressing the *connections*, however tenuous, between one idea and another, one emotion and another, but it was an *harmonie* as respectful of the creative silences that linked these experiences as of their expression in language.

Ever since the early 1780s Joubert had been at pains to discover the nature of the harmonious relationship that ought to exist between thought, expression, and emotion: 'Je chercherai les rapports des mots aux pensées et des périodes à la succession harmonique de nos affections' (C i. 44), he wrote, and this was a project at once moral, aesthetic, and metaphysical which derived much inspiration from the philosophy of Renaissance thinkers and poets. So familiar, indeed, did they become to Joubert, that he rarely has to mention them by name, but there can be no doubt that it is the numerical analogies so characteristic of Renaissance Neoplatonism that lie behind Joubert's continual attempts to describe the perfectly organized human being and the perfect structure that regulates the expression of his thought. In September 1805 he wrote:

De ceux qui sont organisés, où dans lesquels chaque point de leur surface est une touche, chaque fibre une corde, en harmonie avec leur âme; chaque capacité un vuide, un espace retentissant.—dont les actions et les paroles sont les notes d'une musique; dont la vie enfin est un air (dorien dans les uns, ionien dans les autres).

(C ii. 513)

It is only the man, the poet, who has attuned his soul to the harmony of the spheres, that is capable of attempting to articulate beauty. Strikingly, this attempt is one that eschews the restrictive medium of 'des paroles mesurées'. In the following passage, written in 1815, the soul's harmonious discourse derives from the suggestive relationship that exists between the images and expressions which it uses to articulate beauty:

Naturellement l'âme se chante à elle-même tout ce qui est beau, ou tout ce qui semble tel. Et, elle ne se le chante pas toujours avec des vers ou des paroles mesurées, mais avec des expressions et des images où il y a un certain sens, un certain sentiment, une certaine forme et une certaine couleur qui ont une certaine harmonie l'une avec l'autre et chacune en soi.

Quand il arrive à l'âme de procéder ainsi, on sent que les fibres se montent et se mettent toutes d'accord. Elles résonnent d'elles-mêmes et malgré l'auteur, dont tout le travail consiste alors à s'écouter, à remonter la corde qu'il entend se relâcher et à détendre celle qui rend des sons trop haut, comme sont contraints de le faire ceux qui ont l'oreille délicate quand ils jouent de quelque harpe. Ceux qui ont produit quelque pièce de ce genre m'entendront bien et avoueront que pour écrire et composer ainsi, il faut jouër et que, pour jouër de la sorte, il faut d'abord faire de soi ou devenir à chaque ouvrage un instrument organisé.

Et, en ce genre, le diapazon, hors duquel il n'y a plus de chant, mais du bruit, ou tout au plus un gazouillement. Et à chaque air, l'exécution sur une clef déterminée qu'il faut garder jusqu'à la fin sans en changer un seul instant.

(C ii. 822)

Joubert was not alone in his opinion, however, as he was aware. In May 1807 he had written: 'Une certaine "musique intérieure" (pour parler comme Mme de Staël) nous ravit, quand notre âme est en harmonie. Car notre âme est un instrument qui jouit de son propre accord, comme il souffre de son désaccord' (C ii. 619). The reference to Mme de Staël is particularly interesting, for it reminds the reader of a significant passage in *Corinne* that deals specifically with the relationship of *âme* to *parole* and *musique*. Moreover, Mme de Staël employs a Neoplatonic metaphor which Joubert also found especially congenial. Corinne goes to the opera in Rome one evening and is moved by the arias she hears. She concludes that:

les paroles que l'on chante ne sont pour rien dans cette émotion; à peine quelques mots et d'amour et de mort dirigent-ils de temps en temps la réflexion, mais plus souvent le vague de la musique se prête à tous les mouvements de l'âme, et chacun croit retrouver dans cette mélodie, comme dans l'astre pur et tranquille de la nuit, l'image de ce qu'il souhaite sur la terre.[110]

The point of contact between Joubert and Mme de Staël lies, of course, in the image of the star, encountered earlier in Joubert's letter to Fontanes and in the 'Éloge de Cook'.[111] It is the star whose heavenly music echoes and is echoed by the human melody of the singer. But here the similarity ends, for Joubert would certainly not have subscribed to Mme de Staël's dismissal, in this context, of *la parole* in the communication of emotion.

On the contrary, Joubert uses the musical pattern made by the night stars as an aesthetic and metaphysical model on which the relationship

[110] Quoted by Naudin, 184. Mme de Staël, *Corinne ou l'Italie* (Paris, 1875), 193.
[111] See above, ch. 2.

of *la parole* to *la pensée* might be based. As in a much later entry of February 1815, quoted above, in which Joubert describes the 'âme [qui] se chante à elle-même', an important entry of August 1800 perfectly defines the clear yet uninsistent nature of the harmony that should govern expression. Here Joubert paints a night sky in which the independence of his stars is never compromised by their proximity to one another and where this proximity may be translated as the distance or *espace* necessary for them to shine upon and illuminate each other:

1er août (insomni nocte).

Je voudrois que les pensées se succédassent dans un livre comme les astres dans le ciel, avec ordre, avec harmonie, mais à l'aise et à intervalles, sans se toucher, sans se confondre; et non pas pourtant sans se suivre, sans s'accorder, sans s'assortir. Oui, je voudrois qu'elles roulassent sans s'accrocher et se tenir, en sorte que chacune d'elles put subsister indépendante. Point de cohésion trop stricte; mais aussi point d'incohérences: la plus légère est monstrueuse.

(C i. 263)

A little lower down the same page of his *Carnet* he wrote 'perles défilées' and this image was included in a later formulation of the same thought which follows immediately upon the long passage, quoted earlier, critical of the unimaginative, cluttered detail of ecclesiastical art: 'Il faut que les pensées s'entresuivent et se lient, comme les sons dans la musique, par leur seul rapport—harmonie—et non comme les chaînons d'une chaîne, comme des perles enfilées' (C i. 320). The good writer was the man who had learnt to 'espacer ses mots, ses phrases, ses pensées ...' (C i. 321), and learnt the need for perspective and illusion which he first encountered in the 'Éloge de Cook'.[112]

Les autres écrivains placent leurs pensées devant notre attention. Ceux-ci gravent les leurs dans notre souvenir. Ils ont un langage qui est souverainement ami de la mémoire. Et ce n'est pas par un méchanisme, mais si j'ose ainsi dire par sa spiritualité. Les mots, les choses: il sort pour eux des figures des uns, des autres des images.

Une image s'élève de toutes les réalités.

A leurs yeux, les mots ont une figure, des couleurs. Une harmonie en appelle une autre. Cette séparation qui [est] entre leurs paroles est entre leurs pensées. Leur idées ne s'enchaînent pas, elles se mettent en rapport comme les astres du ciel.

(C ii. 480)

---

[112] See above, ch. 2.

3. PLATONISM AND EXPRESSIVE AESTHETICS

Harmful writers—and Joubert included Mme de Staël among them—were guilty of:

> Effusions d'esprit. Otent à nos pensées du poids et de l'authorité. Pourquoi. L'effusion convient au cœur et à lui seul. L'imagination même doit parler à mots séparés et par figures détachées. Elle n'a rien à épancher. Une palette est dans ses mains; et l'esprit tient une balance. Les pensées doivent se suivre, le sentiment seul doit couler.
>
> Les hommes ont été exacts, pénétrans et profonds dans les images premières qu'ils se sont faites de toutes choses. Remontons à ces 'prime intenzione'.
>
> (C i. 263)

Joubert found an ally for this point of view in Longinus, although he found his chapter titles more suggestive than their actual content:

> Le chapitre de Longin qui a pour titre 'que les figures ont besoin de sublime'. Les figures ont besoin du sublime, comme le feu a besoin de l'air, comme l'air a besoin de l'espace. Il n'est peut être pas vrai que les figures ont besoin de sublime précisément; mais elles ont au moins besoin de l'idéal, d'un certain vaste dans les idées. Sans cela, elles n'ont pas de lieu, de place convenable. On les met dans le plein, où rien ne les dessine et ne les fait valoir, où elles sont pour ainsi dire un trop. Quand donc vous voulez employer une figure, faites lui et préparez lui d'abord une région. Région est le mot convenable ici.
>
> Au reste je soupçonne que le titre de Longin est plus ample et meilleur que son chapitre. Je vais le voir.
>
> P.S. Le chapitre n'est pas mauvais, mais le titre vaut mieux.
>
> (C ii. 499)

Again there is the same insistence on the need for a type of discourse that will have room to breathe, to suggest: 'il ne s'agit pas tant de peindre quoi que ce soit que d'en donner l'idée' (C i. 320), Joubert had written earlier, in the passage attacking Church art, and he extends this principle to all the arts: 'Comme, dans la musique, le plaisir naît du mélange des sons et des silences, des repos et du bruit, de même il naît dans l'architecture, du mélange bien disposé des vuides et des pleins, des intervalles et des masses' (C i. 83).[113]
It is not difficult to see how these entries may be read as implicit comments on the type of writing which Joubert himself tries to practise in the *Carnets* and return us to the conclusions of Chapter 2 and the figure of Captain Cook: 'Il faut laisser la part du ciel, comme il y a dans

---

[113] Cf. C i. 63: 'Tout son dans la musique doit avoir un écho; toute figure doit avoir un ciel dans la peinture; et nous qui chantons avec des pensées et peignons avec des paroles, toute phrase et chaque mot devrait aussi dans nos écrits avoir son horizon et son écho.'

la navigation la part du vent,' he wrote. 'Ils construisent des pleins sans vide: leur vaisseau ne peut pas voguer' (C i. 197). Instead of a tightly constructed philosophical treatise, Joubert's *Carnets* present us with a musical score where the rests are as important as the notes, and the moments of silence as evocative as the brief effusions of articulated thought which dazzle us like the brilliant stars they faintly hope to reflect.

Joubert's poetic fury is concentrated into 'Des pensées détachées: élans de l'âme' (C ii. 824). These are thoughts 'qui s'exhalent' and Joubert's use of the verb *s'exhaler* recalls those other thoughts which have to take on some measure of form before climbing up into 'la région supérieure de l'atmosphère', reminding him of Rabelais's account of the 'paroles gelées'. I stated earlier that Joubert's reference to this episode betrays no deep familiarity with Rabelais's text, yet the way Joubert ends this entry has particularly suggestive implications for the form of the *Carnets* as a whole when related to an important interpretation of Rabelais's story by the critic Michel Jeanneret.[114]

It is striking that, after referring to the tale of the 'paroles gelées', Joubert immediately draws a distinction between perfectly expressed thoughts that rise towards heaven and those which do not because not enough care has been lavished upon them:

Mais, de même que des paroles balbutiées et qui n'ont pas été duement formées de toute la force de la langue font un bruit qui n'est pas distinct et ne peuvent pas être: de même, disent-ils encore, celles de nos pensées aux-quelles la volonté n'a pas concouru et n'a pas imprimé sa force n'ont pas de forme décidée, ne produisent qu'une fumée et ne peuvent pas être vues [...]

(C i. 145)

In nearly all the *pensées* quoted over the last few pages, Joubert's concern for clarity of expression has been obvious. Yet, if he returns again and again to the notion of 'Des pensées légères, nettes, distinctes, achevées; et des paroles qui ressemblent à leurs pensées',[115] it is again so that these *pensées* may communicate more naturally with one another. Thoughts which are not of this nature or treated in this way do not contribute to the creation of harmonious discourse and turn out in the

---

[114] M. Jeanneret, 'Les Paroles dégelées, Rabelais, *Quart Livre*, 48–65', *Littérature*, 17 (1975), 14–30. Rabelais, *Quart Livre*, ch. LV, pp. 203–8.

[115] Cf. C ii. 478: 'Que chaque mot ait un son et un sens tellement net que l'attention s'y arrête avec plaisir et s'en détache avec facilité pour passer aux mots qui suivent et où un autre plaisir l'attend.'

end to be mere noise. It is interesting, therefore, to discover that Rabelais makes a similar distinction in his story. When Pantagruel hears the strange sounds coming from some invisible source, he stops to listen, he pauses, and then he gives four possible accounts for what he names 'des paroles dégelées'. Perhaps they come from some transcendent 'manoir de Vérité' where all the Platonic Ideas have their being; perhaps they are the after-life of Homer's words, 'voltigeantes, volantes, moventes et par conséquent animées'; perhaps they are Plato's difficult words, maturing in the upper atmosphere until they are ready to be decanted into our understanding; or perhaps they are the posthumous song of Orpheus' lyre. The important point Jeanneret makes is that Pantagruel does not claim priority for any one interpretation; the tense used is the conditional, his analysis is considered, 'doué d'une légèreté aérienne'.[116]

Pantagruel's comrades, however, rush in where angels fear to tread and immediately identify the sounds as 'paroles gelées', as physical phenomena. What they hear are Joubert's 'paroles balbutiées', noise not words: 'Ce sont, par Dieu! coups de canon', exclaims Panurge, and Pantagruel's stimulating hypotheses are reduced to a story about a war: 'Icy est le confin de la mer glaciale, sus laquelle feut, au commencement de l'hyver dernier passé grosse et félonne bataille entre les Avismapiens et les Nephelibates. Lors gelèrent en l'air ...'[117] Shortly after this Alcofribas Nasier decides he should like to gather up the thawing cacophony of this battle and make provision of 'quelques motz de gueule'. Pantagruel opposes him in this, 'disant estre follie faire réserve de ce dont jamais l'on n'a faulte et que toujours on a en main, comme sont motz de gueule entre tous bons et joyeulx Pantagruelistes'. As Jeanneret interprets:

Alcofribas Nasier voudrait faire provision de paroles: réflexe d'écrivain qui pense à la fabrication de son livre. Mais le livre, insinue Pantagruel, est un tombeau pétrifié, où les signes menacent de s'immobiliser et, abandonnés à des lecteurs indolents, de se recroqueviller en significations simplistes ... A l'inverse, les Pantagruélistes sont, depuis toujours, ceux qui écoutent et qui parlent: ceux qui, à l'écart de l'échange littéraire, perméables au monde et à autrui, réinventent leur langage ... La rigoureuse binarité du thème se précise: camarades—gel—perceptions sensuelles—significations univoques—voir—écrit—littéraire. Pantagruel—dégel—perception étagée—significations plurielles—écouter—oral—vécu. Du reste, dès le début de leur histoire, les géants

---

[116] Jeanneret, 17–18.
[117] Ibid. 19. Rabelais, *Quart Livre*, ii. 203, 206.

érodent de l'intérieur le livre qui les porte favorisant un mode de communication a-littéraire, la conversation, fonction sociale et humaine, alimentée par l'actualité, en opposition systématique à l'artifice de l'écrit.[118]

Jeanneret's analysis of this episode is extremely persuasive, but if I quote from it at such length it is because the 'binarité du thème' which he identifies in Rabelais resembles that which lies at the heart of Joubert's *Carnets*. For in them we discover a writer working 'à l'écart de l'échange littéraire', constantly proclaiming the subversive power of 'pensées détachées', some of which betray their origin in conversation of the salon society which Joubert frequented. As he grew older, Joubert rejected his friends' exhortations to produce a book of *maximes*, and, in their constant openness to new perspectives, to fresh flashes of wit, or simply to the need to hesitate outlined in the conclusion to Chapter 2, his *Carnets* erode the narrative pretensions of writers like Chateaubriand and Mme de Staël. Joubert remained slightly suspicious of Chateaubriand's lyrical effusions throughout his life, and 'le tombeau pétrifié' of the *Génie du Christianisme* or the prose passages of his own 'Éloge de Cook' were probably not far from his mind when he wrote in 1805: 'F.V. l'a fort bien dit, "le style descriptif n'est qu'une nomenclature", aride chez les uns, peinte et ampoulée chez les autres' (C ii. 476). Only a very fine line divided such productions from 'paroles balbutiées' or 'coups de canon'. Preferable by far was the 'perception étagée' provided by thoughts 'qui s'exhalent dans les airs'. As Joubert wrote while thinking about Gluck:

> Toutes les émotions qu'on n'exprime que pour les exhaler et se rendre soi-même plus calme, n'admettent l'air périodique qu'autant qu'il est court et brisé comme l'air fameux *Che faro senza Euridice*.
> Les plus beaux sons, les plus beaux mots sont absolus et ont entre eux des intervalles naturels qu'il faut observer en les prononçant. Quand on les presse et qu'on les joint, on les rend semblables à ces globules diaphanes qui s'aplatissent sitôt qu'ils se touchent, perdent leur transparence en se collant les uns aux autres et ne forment plus qu'un corps pâteux quand ils sont ainsi réduits en masse.
> Chantez sans intervalles *Objet de mon amour*, prononcez sans intervalles *Il était jour*, etc.
>
> (C i. 66)

Jeanneret describes Rabelais's language and that of Pantagruel in the episode of the 'paroles gelées' as 'un langage mobile', and the same

---

[118] Rabelais, *Quart Livre*, ii. 207. Jeanneret, 20.

3. PLATONISM AND EXPRESSIVE AESTHETICS 107

may be said of Joubert's, as one thought displaces another, as one *pensée* jostles with its predecessor, multiplying the perspectives on a Truth which remains elusive.[119] It is significant that very early on in the *Carnets* Joubert should take his stand against the doctrine of mimesis in terms which imply an openness to the polysemy of art in general:

> Quand ils disent que l'art est une *imitation*, ils le définissent par son procédé ou sa manière d'opérer et non par son objet. J'aimerais encore mieux dire que l'art est une *multiplication* car alors je le définirois par son effet et son utilité. L'art en effet n'existe que pour multiplier les choses qui émeuvent nos sens en nous les représentant, et il n'est utile qu'en multipliant autour de nous les belles choses, c'est-à-dire les choses qui nous émeuvent agréablement, utilement, délicieusement et de manière à nous rendre heureux.

(C i. 56)[120]

The constant desire articulated throughout the *Carnets* is for an *espace*, a *lieu* where art will have the freedom to move, to multiply, to provide a range of perspectives that will not stifle our own creative response but increase our ability to understand and see with the eyes of the soul.[121] As Joubert wrote on 24 November 1805:

I. Un meilleur langage a de meilleures opinions.—Et toutes mes étoiles dans un ciel.—Tout l'espace est ma toile.
II. Il me tombe des étoiles de l'esprit

(C ii. 525).

We catch these stars as they fall from the canvas of Joubert's mind and seem able to read them easily, aware of their location in the firmament,

---

[119] Jeanneret, 21.
[120] Cf. C i. 43: 'Le poète s'interroge, le philosophe se regarde. La réflexion produit les passions parce qu'elle est une contemplation réitérée d'un objet.'
[121] It is not entirely fanciful, indeed, to hear an echo, in Joubert's use of the term *multiplication* of a significant passage from Ficino's commentary on the *Symposium*. In the translation by Guy Le Fèvre de la Boderie, which Joubert may have known, 'le désir d'amplifier la propre perfection est un certain Amour. La souveraine perfection est en la souveraine puissance de Dieu. Icelle est contemplée de l'intelligence divine: et d'icy la divine volonté entend produire hors de soy, par lequel amour de multiplier toutes choses de luy créées ... Le mesme instinct de multiplier est infus en tous de l'amour supreme.'
The artistic analogue to the divine multiplication described here becomes more and more evident as Ficino's discussion of love and its relation to beauty continues. In his copy of Tiedemann's commentary on this very passage, Joubert indicated his interest by noting cryptically in the margin 'Que le monde est plein de germes', a statement whose significance will become fully apparent, shortly, in our discussion of his obsessive interest in the production and reproduction of physical being. See M. Ficino, *Discours de l'honnête amour sur le Banquet de Platon*, trans. from the Tuscan by G. le Fèvre de la Boderie (Paris, 1578) 81–2, and see below, ch. 4.

attuned to the measured pace of their music. A day later, however, Joubert hesitated again: 'Etoiles sans scintillation. Et en effet, la vérité est très cachée; il faut fouiller pour la trouver' (C ii. 525). The difference between these two thoughts—and it is but the difference of a day—is a measure of the alternating beat, the systole and diastole which regulate the *Carnets* themselves. On the one hand, 'il me tombe des étoiles de l'esprit' and the illumination is instant: truth is revealed, the philosophical source of Joubert's *pensée* is clear. But then the star ceases to shine, the truth is obscured, the reader of the *Carnets* searches in vain for a clue, an echo of some other writer that will enable him to understand: 'En musique "l'art de l'augmentation et de la diminution du bruit"—d'en marquer, d'en faire sentir les gradations et les dégradations par nuances et demi-tons—véritable art du clair-obscur' (C i. 321).

It is likely, therefore, that Joubert's reading of Plato's doctrine of Ideas, and indeed of his philosophy in general, as a poetic fable or as imaginative dialectic designed to stimulate the reader to think for himself, was either the result of, or the necessary preliminary to, his interest in Renaissance Neoplatonism, with its belief in the privileged status and power of the artist.

There are many passages in the *Carnets* which, at first sight, seem to express an interest in the creation of certain types of literary harmony. On further investigation, however, it becomes clear that it is the spiritual harmonies of the inspired 'lyra orphica' that regulate the ideal form of discourse, enabling it to aspire beyond the limits of the merely literary. Joubert's 'pensées détachées' are also to be seen as 'élans de l'âme' and his *Carnets* to be read as the record of a spiritual process. Indeed, we shall have cause to return time and again to this word 'process', which takes us to the heart of Joubert's enterprise. His interest in the way one *pensée* relates to another, his concern for the 'espace retentissant' between thoughts, demonstrates that, ultimately, what mattered most to him was not the creation of a style, a book, or contribution to a particular genre, but the articulation of a spiritual energy which may be seized *in the process of moving* from one word to another, one thought to another. It is the interior harmony produced by this process that is of paramount importance, a 'chant de l'âme' which echoes the divine harmony of the cosmos.

The evidence gathered in the course of this chapter suggests that Joubert had little difficulty co-ordinating the results of his Platonic and Neoplatonic studies. Our next chapter will demonstrate, however, that this is far from being the case. In Chapter 2 we touched on Joubert's sensitivity to the traditional Platonic hostility to art, his awareness of the vanity of the written word, and this is a problem that never ceased to trouble him. Joubert's refusal to create or publish a book may thus be as much a result of the Platonic scorn evoked by 'un peu de liqueur noire' as a reaction to the Neoplatonic vision of the *Carnets* as the inspired articulation of a spiritual process.

As we shall see, Joubert's belief in the power of expressive language to talk about the nature of the universe and Man's relationship to God was not easily come by and comes to fruition in the context of reading works by writers more immediately interested in the material universe.

4
The Status of Art in the Carnets

Joubert's frequent use of musical analogy and his interest in the concept of harmony must be seen to some extent in the context of a renewed enthusiasm for Pythagorism, which enjoyed tremendous popularity among the Empire's intellectuals. August Viatte and Léon Cellier have charted its various manifestations in the work of Dutoit, Sylvain Maréchal, Restif de la Bretonne, Maurice Quai, Gleizes, and Delisle de Sales, through Dupont de Nemours's *La Philosophie de l'Univers* to Nodier's *Apothéoses et imprécations de Pythagore*, and Fabre d'Olivet's *Les Vers dorés de Pythagore*.[1] Few of the principal writers of the 1790s and early 1800s were immune to aspects of this influence. André Chénier, for example, was attracted by the theme of metempsychosis and Chateaubriand wrote favourably of it in the *Essai sur les révolutions*. Brian Juden has traced the aesthetic implications of interest shown in the Pythagorean concept of harmony by such writers as Saint-Martin, Fabre d'Olivet, Senancour, Mme de Staël, and Ballanche.[2] Even the creator of Figaro had translated 'Les Vers dorés'.[3] It is not surprising, therefore, to find traces of Pythagorism in Joubert, and yet it is important to emphasize that there were limits to his readiness to sympathize with the mystical excesses of this philosophy. His reaction to Bernardin de Saint-Pierre's *Harmonies de la nature* is instructive in this regard and reminds one strongly of his aversion to Alexandrian

---

[1] See L. Cellier, *Fabre d'Olivet: Contribution à l'étude des aspects religieux du Romantisme* (Paris, 1953), 202–5.

[2] B. Juden, 'L'Esthétique: "L'Harmonie immense qui dit tout"', *Romantisme*, 5 (1973), 4–17.

[3] Cellier, 204 n. 1.

4. THE STATUS OF ART IN THE CARNETS

Neoplatonism. Chateaubriand had noted, in his *Essai sur les révolutions*, affinities between Bernardin's harmonies and those of Pythagoras.[4] The same assumption seems to be implicit in Joubert's passing reference to Bernardin in an attack on Buffon '[dont le style] flatte la matière et le monde' (C ii. 675). As Joubert wrote later:

Ses *Harmonies* nous font aimer les dissonances qu'il bannissoit du monde et qu'on y trouve à chaque pas. La nature a bien sa musique, mais elle est rare heureusement. Si la réalité offroit les mélodies que ces messieurs trouvent partout, on vivroit dans une langueur extatique, on mourroit d'assoupissement.

(C ii. 807)

It was just such bracing scepticism, just this refusal to be blinded by any one particular philosophy, no matter how seductive he may have felt it to be, that allowed Joubert to benefit aesthetically from the insights of thinkers towards whom he might otherwise have been completely hostile. Fabre d'Olivet's work on music, to which we have already referred, presents us with another example which nicely illustrates how difficult it is to categorize Joubert.

D'Olivet's treatise contains a biting attack on 'cet Aristoxène, disciple d'Aristote et par conséquent ennemi de Platon', who had developed a purely mechanical theory of the art. Again, the comparison of human body to musical instrument occurs, this time with unfavourable overtones: 'Il disait que, comme le chant est dans les instruments, la proportion fait l'harmonie, de même toutes les parties du corps sont tellement disposées, que, du rapport qu'elles ont les unes avec les autres l'âme en résulte.'[5] Fabre d'Olivet immediately links this idea to those of Cabanis, one of the most influential of the *idéologues*. This is an idea Cabanis has 'trop éloquemment développée, en présentant, ainsi qu'Aristoxène, l'âme comme une faculté du corps'. D'Olivet's hostility to this idea is absolute and there can be no doubt that Joubert was equally opposed to such materialism.

Nevertheless, as this chapter will seek to demonstrate, Joubert was not content with simple, explicit refutation, but preferred the more devious strategy of using the vocabulary of writers like Cabanis and Charles Bonnet to reinforce a spiritual view of the cosmos. His growing concern with matter, body, and the extension of the physical universe is motivated by the desire to situate such phenomena in the context of

---

[4] Chateaubriand, *Essai sur les révolutions*, pt. 1, ch. xli, p. 177.
[5] Fabre d'Olivet, *La Musique expliquée*, 33.

divine creation and leads him ultimately into an attempt to determine the ontological status of human creativity and art.

As one might expect, such an approach is fraught with unforeseen complexities and is productive of irony: Joubert's defence of the Platonic world view with enemy weapons backfires, as a growing Platonic suspicion of art is undercut by quite distinctive enthusiasm for the creative process itself, which may be related to the Neoplatonic aesthetic examined in Chapter 3.

The Influence of Charles Bonnet

Joubert's first mention of Bonnet is interesting precisely because it outlines the ambiguity that characterizes his use of the Swiss thinker during the closing years of the eighteenth century:

Bonnet s'écrie: 'Nos yeux seront alors des télescopes et des microscopes!' Il n'imagine pas dans le ciel d'autre bonheur que celui du savant.
Œuvres de Bonnet: la matière y vaut mieux que l'ouvrage.

(C i. 126)

The perspective is exactly that from which Joubert viewed the work of Dupuis, but there is a clear hint that, despite Bonnet's pretentious erudition, Joubert will find some use for him.

In fact Bonnet's *Œuvres d'histoire naturelle et de philosophie*, which appeared from Neuchâtel in 1779, are one of the major sources of Joubertian imagery during the 1780s and 1790s. The first two hundred pages of the *Carnets* are alive with the energetic, fragile activity of insects as diverse as the 'chenille', the 'araignée', the 'limaçon', the 'papillon', and the 'abeille',[6] all of which emerge from volumes iii and iv of the Swiss thinker's collected works.[7] These volumes contain Bonnet's *Considérations sur les corps organisés* and the *Contemplation de la nature*. There the 'abeille qui ne se nourrit que du suc le plus délicat des fleurs', and whose government 'tient plus du monarchique que du républicain', can be found next to its more democratic neighbours, 'des chenilles qui vivent en société et se construisent des nids qu'on pourroit nommer en pendeloques dans lesquels elles passent l'Hiver'.[8] Other chapters include one on 'Le Fourmilion et en particulier

---

[6] See C i. 125, 146, 157.
[7] Ch. Bonnet, *Œuvres d'histoire naturelle et de philosophie* (7 vols.; Neuchâtel, 1779).
[8] Ibid. iii. 69, iv, pt. II, 258, 237.

4. THE STATUS OF ART IN THE CARNETS

sur sa structure' and it was there Joubert found his 'Fourmilière. Ville à cent portes. Hecatonpylos' (C i. 125).

The relationship of much of the information provided by Bonnet to the general tenor of many of Joubert's remarks between 1796 and 1800 will be obvious to readers browsing among the early pages of the Beaunier edition of the *Carnets*. Just as Pascal had been stimulated, while meditating on the vexed relationship between microcosm and macrocosm, by the scientific investigations of Hobbes, Fontana, and Pierre Borel, so Joubert, a century later, became fascinated by Bonnet's microscopic discoveries and his analysis of 'les infiniment petits abîmés les uns dans les autres'.[9] Around the same period Joubert's friend, the poet Chênedollé, was moved by André Chénier's attempt in his poem 'L'Invention' to fuse the contemporary discoveries of Buffon and Bailly with a Neoplatonic chain of Being, and Chênedollé's own long poem, *Le Génie de l'homme*, embarked on a similar description:

Tout se tient, tout s'unit; un lien mystérieux
Joint le ver et l'Homme et la Terre et les Cieux,
L'Éternel dans ses mains tient cette chaîne immense
Que termine l'insecte et que l'homme commence.[10]

Brian Juden has written of this poet's desire 'de concilier Platon et Pythagore, Pascal et Buffon'.[11] Joubert was provided with some of the theories and imagery necessary to a similar eclecticism by Charles Bonnet and the German scientist, Albrecht von Haller. In the works of these thinkers he discovered graphic descriptions of the diaphanous nature of the physical world. Bonnet and Haller provided him with illustrations of its illusory solidity while simultaneously directing his attention to the immaterial spiritual principle that animates the universe.

Joubert's interest in Bonnet's descriptions of human and animal nerve systems are a good example of this. Thus on the same day that he reflected poetically on Bonnet's 'Fourmilion', he noted '[que] si l'âme habite le cerveau (pour parler comme ces modernes) elle est absolument logée comme l'araigné je veux dire au centre d'une toile où mille fils (appelés nerfs) vont aboutir' (C i. 125). This is a fairly obvious conflation of Bonnet's remark that 'la découverte de l'origine des nerfs a donné lieu de placer l'Ame dans le cerveau' and his reference to these

---
[9] B. Pascal, *Pensées*, ed. M. Le Guern (2 vols.; Paris, 1977), 300 n. 10.
[10] C.-P. de Chênedollé, *Le Génie de l'homme*, chant III, p. 74.
[11] Juden, *Traditions orphiques*, 253.

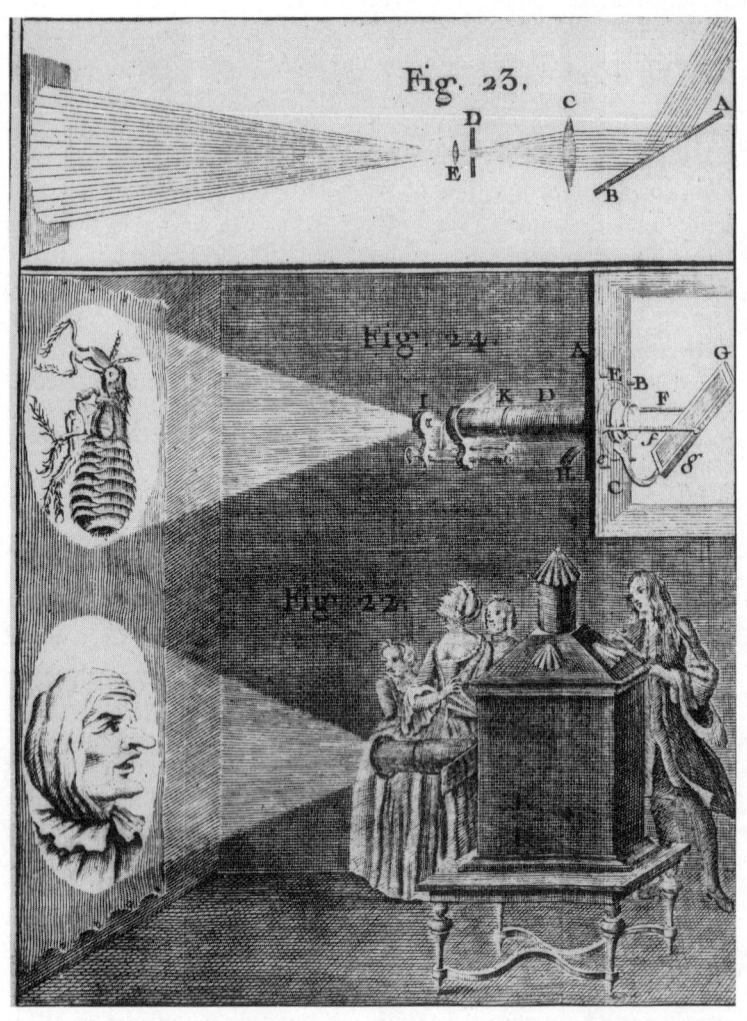

1. Experiments in magnification and refraction: an illustration from J. A. Nollet, *Leçons de physique expérimentale* (6 vols.; Paris, Guérin, 1764)

4. THE STATUS OF ART IN THE CARNETS

nerves as 'une espèce de réseau semblable aux toiles d'Araignée'.[12] Bonnet's spider is still at the centre of Joubert's thoughts in 1797, as the world is compared to

> la toile d'araignée. Dieu l'a tirée de son sein et sa volonté l'a filé, l'a déroulé et l'a tendu. Ce que nous nommons le néant est sa plénitude invisible, sa puissance est un pelotton, mais un pelotton substantiel, contenant tout, inépuisable, qui se dévide à chaque instant en demeurant toujours le même, c'est-à-dire toujours entier.
>
> (C i. 146)

Here, Joubert seizes upon Bonnet's analogy between human nerve system and spider's web, with the soul at its still centre, and extends it to provide a poetic account of the creation of the macrocosm. In the following fragment he adopts another image used by the Swiss thinker to focus upon the indestructible spiritual core of the human microcosm. This time it is the image of 'le noyau de l'amande'[13] that provides Joubert with the relevant metaphors:

> Notre chair n'est que notre pulpe. Nos os, nos membranes, nos nerfs ne sont que comme une charpente du noyau où nous sommes renfermés comme en un étui. C'est par exfoliations que cette enveloppe corporelle se dissipe, mais l'amande qu'elle contient, l'être invisible qu'elle enserre reste entier, est indestructible.
>
> (C i. 143)

This passage introduces us to a number of *pensées* in which the workings of the human mind are explained in terms of the energetic activity of bodily juices: 'Quand nous réfléchissons, il se fait matériellement dans nos organes des plis, des déplis, des replis qui vont jusques au froncement si la réflexion est profonde' (C i. 141). These reflections take place in the context of 'sucs', 'eaux chaudes', 'vapeurs', 'légèretés' (C i. 173), all constituting a necessary 'fluide subtil' characterized principally by 'des excrétions et des sécrétions' (C i. 191). 'Quand on exprime ce que je pense,' Joubert wrote, 'il se fait une espèce de sécrétion agréable et quand on pense ce qu'il faut une nutrition s'opère' (C i. 111).

This last remark, indeed, sounds much more like the *idéologue* Cabanis, to whom Fabre d'Olivet had been so hostile. In the 'Histoire physiologique des sensations' by Cabanis we find un paragraphe whose

---

[12] Bonnet, iii. 276, 112.
[13] Ibid. 123.

main concern is to establish how ideas may be transformed by means of 'les signes de la parole et de l'écriture', and thus manifested 'au dehors'. Cabanis concludes that 'le cerveau digère en quelque sorte les impressions, qu'il fait organiquement la sécrétion de la pensée', a remark Maine de Biran criticized for its naïve materialism.[14]

It is possible, of course, to relate these metaphors to Joubert's reading of Plato's *Timaeus*, but this does not constitute a sufficiently accurate analysis of what is happening, particularly in the lengthier thoughts quoted above. The real source—or rather one of the real sources—is Bonnet, but the reason they also sound as if they might come from a study of the *Timaeus* is because Joubert is using Bonnet's biological investigations, much as Plato used Timaeus Locrus, to provide analogical models on which to base metaphysical and epistemological discussion. Joubert is evidently fascinated by Bonnet's descriptions of the ever-changing nature of the physical world and seems to have been quite familiar with contemporary materialist enthusiasm for 'les fibres du corps', but he sees these descriptions primarily as an ideal opportunity to draw attention to the status of the material universe as mere 'enveloppe corporelle' which encloses an indestructible spiritual reality, an 'être invisible', 'le noyau de l'amande'. As he wrote in November 1799: 'Tout ce qu'on voit, tout ce qu'on touche, n'est que la peau, le cuir, l'écorce, enfin la dernière surface d'une autre matière impalpable, invisible, intérieure' (C i. 217). It is not surprising, therefore, to find Joubert turning again to Bonnet when he attempts to work out the nature and status of human art forms that must, of necessity, work with such illusions in relation to this spiritual reality.

As he read through Bonnet's early works he would not have failed to be struck by the remarkable degree of influence given to seminal liquid, not just in the creation but in the development of organic life, and Joubert seems to have recognized in the stimulating activity of this 'liqueur transparente, presque sans couleur' an analogy for the creation of a type of ideal poetry whose rhythms and diaphanous textures

[14] H. Gouhier, *Les Conversions de Maine de Biran* (Paris, 1937), 112, quoting P.J.C. Cabanis, 'Histoire physiologique des sensations', *Mémoires de l'Institut* (1798), i. 147–8. What makes this similarity particularly interesting is that Cabanis did not begin to read his work at the Institut until January 1796, a whole year after Joubert made this entry in his journal, and that the text of these lectures was not published until July and August 1798. Rather than conclude, however, that such a coincidence of thought has its origins in a personal conversation between Joubert and Cabanis prior to 1795—which is always possible—it is perhaps more reasonable to assume that both men were reading Charles Bonnet at roughly the same time. See also Cabanis, *Rapports du physique et du moral de l'homme*, ed. L. Peisse (Paris, 1844), 138.

4. THE STATUS OF ART IN THE CARNETS

rearticulate the divine creation of the cosmos.[15] In February 1802 Joubert wrote: 'La transparence, le diaphane, le peu de pâte, le magique; l'imitation du divin qui a fait toutes choses avec si peu et, pour ainsi dire, avec rien; voilà un des caractères essentiels de la poésie' (C i. 319). When he comes to add detail to this definition in January 1805, the constituent elements of his ideal poetry participate, to some extent, in the states of transition and metamorphosis which Bonnet excelled at describing. On the 20th of the month he wrote:

Poësie. Ce qui la fait. Claires pensées, paroles d'air et lumineuses. Or, perles, fleurs et diamans. Ce qui est terreux—peu de matières—un esprit pur qui nomme tout. Rien ne presse le poète. Il ne s'agit pas là des nécessités de la vie. Son art est fait pour nos plaisirs et non pour nos besoins ... comme une suite de mots lumineux et diversement colorés.—ampoules d'encre et bulles de savon.

(C ii. 477)

The following day, returning at even greater length to this subject, he concluded: 'Le poète a un souffle qui enfle les mots, les rend légers et leur donne de la couleur: une teinture, une liqueur, comme ce nectar de l'abeille qui change en miel la poussière des fleurs. Faire voltiger les mots' (C ii. 478). Here poetry is born from the vivifying breath of the inspired poet, who injects into the clear, luminous words at his disposal a persuasive honey. He inseminates language so that words begin to flutter like butterflies. The analogy is not unjustified, for, as the Hellenist Ansse de Villoison reminds us in an article devoted to Greek inscriptions on marble, the butterfly is traditionally a symbol for the soul.[16] Joubert's poetry will be, therefore, instinct with soul, a fluid necklace of words, each bead like a curious pearl whose milky substance enshrines the perfect alliance between transparency and opacity.[17]

This entry is, indeed, a remarkable example of Joubert's ability to awaken multiple associations within the reader's mind, linking past,

---

[15] Compare, also, similar analogues provided by the abbé J. A. Nollet, *Leçons de physique expérimentale* (6 vols.; Paris, 1764). See, e.g., i. 52: 'La transparence du sable blanc le rend propre à d'autres usages: il est la base de tous les ouvrages de verre; le mélange de quelques sels, et l'action d'un feu très violent qui le divise et qui en sépare les saletés, met ses parties en état de se lier et de former une pâte susceptible de toutes sortes de formes, et qui en se refroidissant, prend de la consistance, sans cesser d'être diaphane.'

[16] *Remarques de J. B. Ansse de Villoison, sur quelques inscriptions grecques de marbres antiques et de pierres gravées, principalement sur celles qui sont en forme de dialogue* (s.a.) (BN: 8° Zz 3965). In Greek the butterfly is 'psyché' (Aristotle, *Historia animalium*, iv. 7, v. 19).

[17] Cf. C i. 66: 'Les plus beaux sons ...'

present, and future poetic theory together in one pregnant whole. For here, apart from the hovering presence of Bonnet, we can find echoes of the *Ion*'s comparison of poets to bees gathering honey, of Renaissance poetic fury in the notion of an inspired *souffle*, of La Fontaine's Platonic description of himself in the 'Épitre à Mme de la Sablière' as 'Papillon du Parnasse et semblable aux abeilles', a clear anticipation of Vigny's vision of poetry as 'perle de la pensée', as well as of Gautier's appreciation of 'des mots diamants, saphir, rubis, émeraude, d'autres qui luisent comme du phosphore quand on les frotte'.[18]

Poetry, for Joubert, has the metamorphosing, preserving powers of the bee, but, crucially, it must also remind us of 'bulles de savon', the fragility of human life which he found so persuasively described in Bonnet, the 'ténuité réelle' of earthly matter that exists merely as a shadow cast by the divine 'esprit pur qui nomme tout'. Here, indeed, we catch a first glimpse of the paradox outlined in the introduction to this chapter. For Bonnet's 'matter', which Joubert would like to use simply as a means of illustrating the transcendant reality of the divine, as a way of measuring the distance that separates *le ver* from God, ends by becoming caught up in the inevitable aspiration of all created things towards the divine. The *souffle* of the inspired poet is identified in Joubert's mind with Bonnet's life-giving *liqueur* and with the creative activity of his tiny insects. It is likely, indeed, that Joubert partially recognizes this when he writes cryptically in his journal: '"les âmes des brutes" dit Marcile Ficin, "exercent les arts". En effet, l'araignée ourdit, l'hirondelle maçonne, le ver à soie file' (C ii. 694).[19] Shining through the Platonic shadows of mimetic art is a Neoplatonic energy and faith in the power of the inspired artist.

Joubert's butterflies emerge from the cocoon of Bonnet's *observations* and the inspired atmosphere of Plato's *Ion* to flutter musically about the white pages of the *Carnets*, pausing momentarily here and there, leaving a brief trace of their passage. White page becomes night sky and their secretions glow brilliantly like stars, faint reflections of

---

[18] *Ion*, 534b. La Fontaine's poem was published in 1684; cf. C ii., 867. A. de Vigny, 'La Maison du Berger', from *Les Destinées*, ed. V. L. Saulnier (Geneva, 1967), 47; see also Saulnier's commentary on this theme, pp. 37–8. Th. Gautier, *Souvenirs romantiques*, ed. A. Boschot (Paris, 1929), 316.

[19] The 'ver à soye' could also have come from Nollet, i. 41. Indeed Nollet's comparison of the art of 'filant ... les métaux' to that of the silkworm demonstrates clearly that the various insects to be found in the *Carnets* and the 'grain d'or' (C i. 146), 'grain de métal applati' (C i. 147), form a coherent network of images of dematerialization in Joubert's mind.

4. THE STATUS OF ART IN THE CARNETS

that heavenly sphere to which the poet must ultimately aspire. And it is here that we must locate the tension that cuts across the *Carnets* in their attempt to come to grips with the ontological status of art. On the one hand we have Joubert's genuine interest in Bonnet's depiction of the ceaseless activity and beauty of the physical world; on the other we register his belief that this world is but a faint reflection of a divine reality, an 'être invisible'. Joubert's recipe for ideal poetry tries to combine aspects of both the diaphanous shadow and the 'esprit pur', advocating a language that is transparent rather than opaque, one that does not pretend to the self-sufficient wisdom of the aphorist but allows an element of the divine to show through. In a sense these passages on 'ideal' poetry articulate a compromise between Joubert's awareness of the human need to create and his realization that God is the only true Creator. As such they constitute privileged moments in a continuing struggle to define the nature of art and the conditions appropriate to its creation.

In the remaining pages of this chapter we shall see how this paradox relentlessly pursued Joubert during the early years of the Empire. In general his dilemma was that of a man confronted everywhere by the energies of the physical universe but unsure if, and in what way, it might be possible to use them to give satisfactory expression to the immaterial principle that lay behind their changing forms.

THE ROLE OF ANALOGY

In his eagerness to confront the phenomenon of creativity head on, Joubert turned from one source to another, ceaselessly comparing, noting, matching one version of it with another. As one would expect with a private journal, Joubert never explicitly says that this is what he is doing, but it is possible to deduce his intentions by following the tenuous threads of argument through juxtaposed entries in the notebooks.

It is clear, for example, from a number of passages that Joubert again found stimulation for his reflections on the nature of human creation in Bonnet's writings on the immortality of the soul. These writings emerge logically from the Swiss thinker's study of *développement*, an investigation of 'les différens ordres d'infiniment petits abîmés les uns dans les autres', a process Bonnet also refers to as 'emboîtement'.[20] This is a process originating in 'la préexistence des germes'. Unlike Buffon, who

---

[20] Bonnet, iii. 2.

adhered to a limited and rather idiosyncratic form of epigenesis, Bonnet believed that 'rien ne peut se développer qui n'ait été préformé.'[21] This conclusion is based largely upon Leibniz's monadology and on a study of the chicken in the egg, one that Bonnet considered vital to a correct understanding of all forms of genesis, both animal and human. As Bonnet wrote:

Je suis donc ramené plus fortement que jamais au grand principe dont je suis parti, en commençant cet ouvrage; c'est qu'il n'est point dans la Nature de véritable *génération*, le commencement d'un développement qui nous rend visible ce que nous ne pouvions auparavant appercevoir. Les reins nous paroissent engendrés au moment qu'ils tombent sous nos sens; ils séparoient pourtant l'urine lorsque nous ne doutions pas le moins du monde de leur existence.[22]

This passage explains quite clearly a fragment Joubert noted in his journal on 9 December 1798:

Mon ancien mot 'une feuille qui tombe remuë le monde'. Et les mouvemens qui se font en nous quoi qu'ils soient grands, quoi qu'ils soient forts, ne nous remuent pas toujours nous-mêmes. De même qu'il y a dans l'économie animale des vaisseaux qui sont absorbans de même il pourroit y avoir dans la nature des moyens inconnus de dégorgement, des réservoirs, des réceptacles d'absorption, de cohibition [*sic*], d'anéantissement.

(C i. 184)

---

[21] It is interesting to note at this point how Joubert's general interest in Bonnet and, in particular, his theory of *germes* sets him distinctly apart from a writer such as Chénier. Joubert would have disagreed with Chénier's *éloge* of Buffon in his poem, 'Invention', inspired, according to Dimoff, by an engraving to be found in the first edition of *La Théorie de la terre*. There we see 'la terre entr'ouvrant son sein pour permettre à un génie ailé qui vole au-dessus d'elle d'apercevoir, par une large crevasse, les mystères qu'elle recèle' (P. Dimoff, *La Vie et l'œuvre d'André Chénier, jusqu'à la Révolution française, 1762–1790* (2 vols.; Paris, 1936), ii. 57). This description is strikingly similar in conception to that noted by Joubert while reading Winckelmann on allegory: 'Platon représenté avec des ailes de papillon (à la tête) parce qu'il avoit le premier parlé de l'âme et de son immortalité (Vid. Win sur l'allegor. pag 143)' (C i. 347). Here were two winged genii in direct competition with each other; if Chénier believed they were conciliable, Joubert preferred to replace Buffon with Bonnet. Reading Buffon was like reading Dupuis: 'Quand on a lu Mr de Buffon on se croit sçavant' (C i. 200). He had sung of 'le chaos' (C ii. 750), a man: '[qui] attribuoit en secret une toute puissance à cette ombre, à ce phénomène, à ce phantôme, à ce presque rien ou presque néant que nous appelons la matière, le grand tout' (C ii. 906). He magnified everything, while Bonnet seemed to be engaged in a process of rarefaction quite opposed to this. The mysteries Buffon discovered while gazing down into that 'large crevasse' were almost exclusively of a material nature, whereas Bonnet's saving grace was that his microscopic investigations led him eventually, like Plato, to theories of immortality and palingenesis.

[22] Bonnet, iii. 135.

4. THE STATUS OF ART IN THE CARNETS

Joubert does not comment immediately on Bonnet's point about *génération* but seems more concerned here simply to gather further evidence for his belief, noted while reading the abbé Nollet, that 'vie et mouvement sont deux idées associées, inséparables' (C i. 237). The reference to 'imperceptible' movements within the human body looks back to Leibniz, but the more immediate source appears to be Bonnet's observation of the discreet motions of his kidneys. Further evidence of this link is provided by the fact that this passage comes directly after the passage cited below, and both contribute to the understanding of an extremely important diagram drawn by Joubert in the *Carnets* at this point:

Au delà des corps, au delà des mondes, au delà du tout—au delà et autour des corps, au delà et autour des mondes, au delà et autour de tout, il y a la lumière et l'esprit. Sans l'esprit, je dis l'esprit élémentaire, tout seroit plein et rien ne seroit pénétrable; il n'y auroit ni mouvement, ni circulation, ni vie.

(C i. 183–4)

Joubert illustrated this *pensée* by drawing in his *Carnet* a sun, next to which he placed the earth. Around these globes he wrote the word 'air' several times, which he enclosed in turn within circles made out of the words 'les mondes'. Another circle, lower down, is formed by 'la lumière', which is repeated several times. After this he wrote 'l'esprit'. Finally he noted: 'Le mot de Platon que tout est génération. (Peut-être faut-il dire germination). Avoir d'Haller le traité du poulet' (C i. 184 n. 1). In the light of a reading of Bonnet we can begin to see, perhaps, how Swiss thinker and ancient Greek complemented each other in their influence on Joubert. Plato's *mot* can be found in both the *Timaeus* and the *Cratylus*, but the word *germination* derives from Haller's 'traité du poulet' and Bonnet's own subsequent concentration on the properties and potential of *germes*.

Instead of seeing Joubert's diagram, then, purely as a Joubertian version of Platonic or Neoplatonic metaphysics, which is how it has been regarded until now, it seems possible to regard it also as a metaphysical application of, or commentary on, Haller's and Bonnet's theories of *emboîtement*. Joubert's *pensée* and diagram reflect Bonnet's Chinese box mentality and relate to the latter's desire to reduce everything to a pre-existent *germe*, an essential 'esprit élémentaire', without which there would be 'ni mouvement, ni circulation, ni vie'. 'Tout est sans cesse germant ou germinant' (C i. 411), Joubert wrote and, as Bonnet had shown him, he understood that 'tout corps épais

2. An extract from the manuscripts of Joubert's *Carnets* (C i. 183–4)

4. THE STATUS OF ART IN THE CARNETS 123

n'est qu'un carton divisible par exfoliation en une infinité de couches plus minces encore que l'on ne peut l'imaginer' (C i. 236). Ultimately, however, they did not believe that matter was itself infinitely divisible:

> Toute portion, toute partie de matière, quelque petite qu'on veuille la supposer, doit être matière, c'est à dire susceptible de longueur, largeur et profondeur. Par conséquent si la matière étoit divisible à l'infini comme on le prétend, elle pourroit cesser d'être matière en demeurant matière, ce qui est absurde.
>
> (C i. 229)

Much more in keeping with Joubert's fidelity to a spiritual higher reality of which all else is but an infinitely complex shadow were Bonnet's *germes*, Leibniz's *monades*, and Democritus'

> Atomes, particules de matière qu'on déclaroit insécables, indivisibles [...] pour arrêter l'imagination. Tant il faut à l'homme une cause première, un point fixe d'où il puisse s'élancer par la pensée, une vérité convenue ... antérieure à toute opération de son esprit affin que son esprit puisse opérer.
>
> (C i. 150)

The importance of Bonnet's theories for an understanding of Joubert's diagram is undeniable. Nevertheless, it is possible to discover yet other sources, and the consequences for art of his interest in this mesh of metaphysics and pseudo-science are not fully revealed until it is related to other passages in the *Carnets*, such as, for example, the following entry:

> Tout est double et composé d'âme et de corps. L'univers est le corps de Dieu (mais ici le corps est dans l'âme). L'esprit a pour corps la matière. Il y a le corps du corps. Le rare a le dense pour corps et le dur est le corps du dense. Toujours et à l'infini l'épais et le mince se tiennent par le dedans et le dehors.
>
> (C i. 179)

At this point matters become even more complex, and the analogy that may be drawn between such passages and texts of the eighteenth century has to be slightly modified. This passage has more to do with a pseudo-Milesian view of the universe and creation than it has with either Bonnet or Plato. Here we have to take into account the inspiration provided by fake Ancient Greek philosophical texts. Their identity is revealed in a typically elliptic reference which comes a little earlier in the *Carnets*: 'Ils regardoient les ténèbres comme une toîle prête à recevoir les couleurs que lui donneroit la lumière, le silence comme un grand vide prêt à être rempli de sons, l'eau comme une pâte fluide prête à s'imbiber des saveurs (Vid. Ocellus pag. 40) (C i. 152)

The Milesian philosopher Ocellus Lucanus, who lived during the fifth century BC, is best known, ironically, for a work he did not actually write which first appeared under a Latin title, *De universi natura*, some time during the third or second century BC. This treatise is a clumsy attempt to fuse Aristotelian physics with stoic pantheism and was translated into French by the abbé Batteux in 1768, along with short works by Timaeus Locrus and a pseudo-Aristotle on the same subject. This book, which began life as a series of lectures to the Académie des Inscriptions, is still to be found in Joubert's library at Bussy, with the words 'acheté à Sens, juillet 1797' written on the flyleaf. If we turn to page 40 we find the following passage, which provides comprehensive proof of the influence of Ocellus on the entry quoted above while indicating that, behind the interest in Bonnet and the issue of genesis as it is discussed in the *Carnets*, lies an appreciation of Aristotle's understanding of the dynamic of germinal being and the creative power that operates between potentiality and actuality:

Dans la partie du Monde où la Génération et la Nature ont l'empire, il y a nécessairement trois choses. La première est l'être qui est le sujet des qualités sensibles et qui se trouve dans tout ce qui va à la génération. C'est une pâte qui reçoit toutes sortes de formes, qui se prête à tout, qui est aux autres produits ce que l'eau est aux saveurs, le silence au son, les ténèbres à la lumière, la matière à l'art. L'eau, qui par elle-même est sans goût et sans qualité prend le doux ou l'amer, le fade ou le piquant: l'air non frappé est prêt à rendre le son, la parole, le chant: les ténèbres sans couleur et sans forme, sont disposées à prendre le rouge, le jaune, le blanc; et dans les arts, ce qui est blanc peut être employé à la sculpture ou à la céroplastique indifféremment. D'où il faut conclure que tout est en puissance dans ce sujet avant qu'il y a eu génération, et qu'il a reçu ce qu'on appelle une nature. Il faut donc supposer d'abord ce sujet, pour que la génération ait lieu.[23]

Now it can be seen that, although Bonnet's theories contributed a stimulating contemporary background to Joubert's musings, it is in fact a pseudo-Milesian concept of Unity that lies behind his description of 'le Tout' and diagram of the Universe. As Ocellus wrote:

[23] Ocellus Lucanus, *De la nature de l'univers*, trans. l'abbé Batteux (Paris, 1768), 39–41. This work was known to and used by Joseph de Maistre (See Triomphe, 420). The works by Timaeus Locrus and a pseudo-Aristotle were included in the same volume by Batteux.

4. THE STATUS OF ART IN THE CARNETS

J'appelle Univers et Tout, le Monde pris dans sa totalité; car c'est pour cela qu'il a été nommé ainsi, parce que c'est un composé régulier de tout ce qui est ... Car rien n'est hors de lui ... tout est dans le Tout, tout est avec le Tout, ou comme partie, ou comme production.[24]

Even more importantly, however, these passages presented Joubert with yet another version of the idea that first emerged from the consideration of the position of the human soul in relation to Bonnet's nerve matrix: namely, that the genesis and movement of physical objects had to be related to some formless spiritual principle. In Plato this formless principle is space and Joubert's 'esprit élémentaire' is almost certainly a version of it. In March 1799 he wrote:

La terre est un point dans l'espace, et l'espace est point dans l'esprit. J'entends ici par esprit l'esprit élément, le cinquième élément du monde, l'espace de tout, lien de toutes choses, car toutes choses y sont, y vivent, s'y meuvent, y meurent, y naissent.—L'esprit ... dernière ceinture du monde.

(C i. 200)

In the passage by Ocellus, however, this spiritual principle is considered in Aristotelian terms as a material substratum. It appears to be this substratum that Batteux translates as 'l'être qui est le sujet des qualités sensibles et qui se trouve dans tout ce qui va à la génération'. There are references by Joubert to what might be interpreted as versions of an Aristotelian substratum, but he is far more comfortable when evoking the space necessary for soul to breathe and move freely: 'Il faut bien que l'âme respire,' he wrote; 'Ce vague est son air, son espace. C'est là qu'elle se meut à l'aise. Un seul trait (haustus) de cet élément suffit pour rafraichir en elle le principe de son bien-être qui est l'effet de ses tempérances (C i. 135).[25]

Given Joubert's preferences, he could not have been entirely happy with Ocellus' account of creation. The way Joubert focuses upon *le vide* and *la lumière* and their potential for transformation are indicative of this and remind us of the many passages quoted in Chapter 3 where space plays a definitive role in the creation of harmonious discourse. Furthermore, Joubert could not have failed to notice the single most significant feature of this passage. This consists in an Aristotelian attempt to identify the formless principle by reference to analogies

---

[24] Ibid. 23.
[25] For a discussion of the 'formless principle' in relation to Platonic space and the Aristotelian substratum, see F. Solmsen, *Aristotle's System of the Physical World* (Ithaca, NY, 1960), 123.

between nature and craft. Ocellus is forced from one analogy to another in his attempt to define the indeterminate and unknowable substratum, and, in his commentary on this passage, Batteux draws attention to the importance of this procedure by recalling the distinctions made by Timaeus Locrus between 'L'Idée', 'La Matière', and 'Les Êtres engendrés'. Timaeus declares that the second of these cannot be known directly 'mais seulement par analogie', and Batteux is quite incapable of letting this pass. Immediately he notes this use of the word *analogie* and writes:

L'analogie est la comparaison de deux rapports ou raisons; ainsi on connoît la matière par analogie quand on dit, la matière est quelque chose qui est aux formes primitives comme le marbre est à la statue, comme l'huile est aux parfums, comme le son est au chant.[26]

The only way we can identify or make contact with 'l'être' or 'l'esprit élémentaire' is by analogy, by likening it to the relationship that exists between the lump of raw marble and the art form into which the artist will change it. As Joubert wrote in February 1803: 'L'Ordre ou assortiment avec Dieu a l'analogie ou le rapport pour fondement' (C i. 367). Indeed, he himself, as we have seen, had used Bonnet's texts in analogical fashion to talk about the relationship between the physical world and spiritual reality but Joubert does not seem to have related this specific practice to the question implicit in the passage from Ocellus, which asks what the precise ontological status of art may be which attempts to identify an essentially unknowable spiritual principle. As Friedrich Solmsen has pointed out: 'For Plato and anyone sharing his convictions, to determine the nature of the formless must be a hard and unfair task. To identify the unknowable seems a self-contradictory proposition.'[27]

The paradox at the heart of Joubert's aesthetic is again coming into view and it is clarified by relating his own use of Bonnet to what he has to say *explicitly* about the process of analogy. We have already seen in Joubert's remarks on ideal poetry just how discreet the 'imitation du divin' must be, and it is significant that his statement of February 1803

---

[26] Académie des Inscriptions, *Mémoires*, xxxii (Paris, 1768), 13. I refer here to the version of these texts presented by Batteux to the Académie *before* their publication in book form. Joubert seems to have been familiar with both versions since he quotes at one point, among unpublished fragments, from a passage by Plutarch to be found in a section entitled 'Sentiment de Platon, dans son Timée' not included in the volume purchased in Sens.
[27] Solmsen, 122.

4. THE STATUS OF ART IN THE CARNETS

makes no claims for the success of analogy in an 'assortiment avec Dieu'. Elsewhere, indeed, he speaks of this trope in highly conventional terms which remind us strongly of the accepted rules of classical rhetoric as defined by Du Marsais and Rollin. After reading the following passage we may be forgiven for doubting the ability of analogy, of art in general, to convey anything much of the 'formless' and 'unknowable':

Mais les comparaisons les plus défectueuses sont celles où les objets extérieurs sont comparés à l'homme, et les corps à l'âme, au lieu de comparer les âmes au corps et l'homme aux choses du dehors. Par exemple, quand on compare une mer emuë à un cœur agité, la blancheur à l'innocence, le fracas de tonerre aux tempêtes de l'âme. L'homme se porte, se possède, il a un perpétuel sentiment de soi. Tout cela ne lui apprend rien et le resserre et le contracte au lieu de l'étendre [...] Notre illustre Chateaubriand commet quelquefois cette faute. Dans les comparaisons il faut passer du proche au loin, de l'intérieur à l'extérieur, de l'un à l'autre, et du connu à l'inconnu [...] Il faut en effet que toute comparaison et même toute figure, pour être noble et agréable, étende les vues de l'esprit, et non pas qu'elle les ressere ... De l'abstrait au concret; et du non vu au vu.

(C ii. 719)

The passage from abstract to concrete, indeed the entire analogical process as it is discussed above, occurs only when the artist's imagination is brought into play, and Joubert's descriptions of it, which will be discussed more fully in Chapters 5 and 6, are frequently in keeping with his analysis of the function and nature of comparison as well as with traditional classical hostility to the power of this faculty. The following remark—'J'appelle imagination la faculté de rendre sensible tout ce qui est intellectuel, d'incorporer ce qui est esprit, et en un mot de mettre au jour sans le dénaturer ce qui est de soi-même invisible' (C ii. 493)—is couched in language reminiscent of Marmontel or La Harpe writing in Le Lycée.[28]

This statement is typical of most of Joubert's remarks concerning the imagination, in so far as it carefully outlines both the scope and the intrinsic limitations of a faculty '[qui] revêt d'images' (C i. 282). His aside, 'sans le dénaturer', is important, since it implies that the imagination is capable of doing just that. Instead of making it easier for us to see 'ce qui est de soi-même invisible', the figures of the

---

[28] For Dumarsais on analogy and metaphor, see Œuvres (7 vols.; Paris, 1797); iv. 140; iii. 120, 129. La Harpe, Cours de littérature, ancienne et moderne (3 vols.; Paris, 1847). See the chapter on 'L'Harmonie du discours' in volume I. J.-E. Marmontel, Eléments de littérature (3 vols.; Paris, 1879), iii. 348.

imagination may sometimes obscure and themselves become the focus of attention:

Quand l'image masque l'objet, lorsque l'on fait de l'ombre un corps, quand le mot débauche l'esprit en le charmant, quand l'expression plaît tellement qu'on ne tend plus à passer outre pour pénétrer jusqu'au sens, quand la figure absorbe en soi notre attention toute entière, on est arrêté en chemin. La route est prise pour le gîte. Un mauvais guide nous conduit.

(C i. 213)

As La Harpe wrote: 'Les trois vices dominants de ce siècle' are 'l'enflure, les ornements recherchés et la fausse chaleur'.[29] When an imagination, like that of Joubert's friend Chateaubriand, is used simply to create a seductive style, it is, in fact, being false to its own intrinsic limits and betraying its basis in illusion. For the figures of the imagination are, as Joubert makes clear in an entry immediately preceding his remark about the image, of the same nature as the apparent opacity of the physical world. They are mere illusions, approximations, representations of the 'noyau de l'amande' or 'être invisible' camouflaged by the unpredictable but fascinating 'exfoliations' described in the works of Charles Bonnet. 'L'illusion', Joubert writes,

est dans le monde ce que la métaphore est dans nos discours. Nous ne voyons, nous ne sentons, nous ne croyons qu'à l'aide de quelque apparence qui montre une réalité. 'Il leur parlait en paraboles', et c'est ainsi que Dieu agit. Ne le disions-nous pas que c'étoit là le grand poète?

(C i. 213)

It is in the light of such a train of thought that the full implications of Joubert's recipe for an ideal poetry becomes clear. It is poetry that reflects an imagination which is true to itself only when it acts modestly as a 'magasin d'images', productive of illusions, of appearances 'qui montre une réalité': 'l'imitation du divin qui a fait toutes choses avec si peu et pour ainsi dire avec rien' (C i. 319). Any kind of art, or, as we saw in Chapter 2, any kind of scientific enquiry which distorts the illusory nature of the physical universe by lending it a solidity it does not possess is to be condemned. We recall, in this context, Joubert's objections to the microscope and telescope. On the one hand he considered that eyes were microscope enough: 'Que nos yeux sont une lorgnette, un microscope,—et que le toucher en est un

---

[29] La Harpe, i. 37.

autre. Que sans ces instrumens qui nous la grossissent, la matière échapperait à l'esprit tant elle est peu de chose devant lui' (C i. 193). In the *Génie du Christianisme* Chateaubriand concurred, comparing the type of metaphysics taught by Plato and Pythagoras, 'la science des Dieux et ... la géométrie divine', with the blinkered kind, '[qui] n'est qu'un microscope, qui nous découvre curieusement quelques petits objets qui n'auraient pu saisir la vue simple, mais qu'on peut ignorer ou connaître, sans qu'ils forment, ou qu'ils remplissent un vide dans l'existence'.[30] As for the telescope, it had tampered with the stars, whose light, as we have seen, was for Joubert of a purely spiritual nature: 'Les astres, plus beau à l'œil qu'au téléscope qui les dépouille de leurs illusions' (C i. 168).

Language which acted like the telescope was equally abhorrent and its rewards of little consequence. Thus, Joubert never tired of attacking the 'style qui étreint et ne prend rien. Qui trop étreint mal embrasse, dit un proverbe et: qui trop serre et ne tient rien' (C i. 371). Preferable by far are '[des] pensées [qui] s'entresuivent et se lient, comme les sons dans la musique, par leur seul rapport—harmonie—et non comme des perles enfilées' (C i. 320).[31] Or, as the contemporary poet Michel Deguy puts it in a version of the tenet to be found in countless manuals of rhetoric: 'Il s'agit de rapprochement. Non de fusion identificatoire; mais de rapprochement: il n'y aura de rapprochement que par le *comme*.'[32] It is clear that Joubert considered attempts at an identification between image and the spiritual reality it was supposed to make visible to be somewhat naïve. Even the analogies or *rapprochements* invented by the imagination could be interpreted as attempts to usurp the proper function of *esprit*, the faculty of intellect which alone, Joubert believed, was capable of intuitive contact with God and which should remain in control of the effusions of the imagination. It is significant, for example, that the 'natural metaphor' is the one '[qui] indique une vive intelligence en action, en mouvement, en jeu'. 'Elle avait l'air d'une idée' (C i. 233), he wrote. This may be compared with other remarks about the image, his belief 'que c'est une idée qui règle l'image' and that, although he always has 'une image à rendre', 'ce n'est jamais ma phraze que je polis mais mon idée' (C ii. 644).

Apparently, the 'imagination opératrice' is to be seen as a mediating faculty, 'quelque chose de moyen entre le sens et la pure intelligence' (C

---

[30] Chateaubriand, *Génie du Christianisme*, ed. M. Regard (Paris, 1978), 820.
[31] Joubert preferred 'perles défilées' (C i. 263).
[32] M. Deguy, *La Poésie n'est pas seule: Court traité de poétique* (Paris, 1987), 103.

i. 454). We recall Joubert's references to the need for 'atomes insécables ... *pour arrêter l'imagination*', and in the following quotation it is not surprising to find that, when employed in the task of 'imagining God', it can only go so far:

> Dans cette opération [...] le premier moyen est la figure humaine; le dernier terme est la lumière. Et dans la lumière la splendeur. Je ne crois pas que l'imagination puisse aller plus loin. Mais ici l'esprit continue ... l'étendue ... enfin l'infinité. Il faut recommencer. Cercle ravissant à décrire et qui recommence toujours. On le quitte, on s'y plonge, on en sort, on le reprend. N'en décrions aucun degré; n'exigeons pas que tout le monde l'achève; notre devoir, notre bonheur sont d'y tenir et non de le tracer.
>
> (C i. 442)

The final sentences of this remark are extremely important for an understanding of Joubert's suspicion of any finished art object that aspires to reflect, however faintly, the world of the spirit. Through constant intellectual effort we may attain to the presence of God, but the art produced by the imagination will only ever provide us with a barely adequate *esquisse* or tracing of the 'être invisible', and here Joubert voices his doubt as to whether any such project should be undertaken. If it is embarked upon, then we must 'mouler légèrement. L'air se moule légèrement. Ce qui retient si fortement la forme ne doit pas être assés spirituel' (C ii. 481). It is ultimately a journey we could spare ourselves 'si rien ne peut parvenir à l'âme et la toucher que par son idée; si tout ce qui est corps ne peut entrer dans notre mémoire même que par son idée ou par son ombre,—quel chemin épargné à l'art si ...' (C ii. 775).

The Status of the Image

Joubert once described himself as 'plus Platon que Platon lui-même' and his suspicion of art would appear to confirm his diagnosis, yet his conception of the image as 'une illusion [...] qui montre une réalité' was susceptible to positive interpretation when linked to his growing opposition to mimetic art forms.[33] Similarly, the playful sequence of 'ifs' that end the passage quoted above indicate that Joubert was probably aware that a vision of the world free from the vain pretensions of art was an unrealistic one and one that is undercut by his own unacknowledged enthusiasm for the creative process itself as distinct

---

[33] See *Correspondance*, Tessonneau, 52.

from the actual creation of finished specimens of style. 'Le monde est monde par la forme: par le fonds il n'est qu'un grain de matière' (C i. 152), he wrote. Yet, in the *Carnets*, Joubert loves evoking this 'grain de matière', this 'pellicule', 'écorce', 'goutte d'eau soufflée', this 'glu', just as much if not more than the 'esprit élémentaire' which lies behind it, or the art object, the 'brillants' into which it will be transformed.[34] What Joubert loves in the *chenille* is the latent butterfly. For him, as for Aristotle, the *point* is not simply a bit of mediocre friable matter but something pregnant of line: 'A celui qui tire la ligne du point. La ligne est dans le point comme la brassée du fil est dans un pelotton' (C i. 163). It is the action contained in the verb *tirer* that attracts him most, as well as the potential for action stored within the 'pelotton'. Just as Fabre d'Olivet called for the regeneration of poetry by seeking for its *essence* in the inspired works of Sophocles and Euripides and rejected the efforts of later centuries to formalize and tame it, so Joubert believed that the line which forms an element in a realized work of art is far less beautiful than the line which the imagination and intellect are only just beginning to conceive, a line entirely faithful to its own illusory nature.[35]

It is, indeed, important to pay careful attention to what Joubert has to say about the structuring power of line in the *Carnets*, for his remarks provide us with a fine example of how the approach to imagination and the role of the image outlined above feed into a dynamic view of human creativity. As Michel Delon has shown recently in his book *L'Idée d'énergie au tournant des lumières*, many writers during this period had recourse to 'les figures du mouvement centripète' in order to express the full intensity of the power they felt within themselves. Joubert's identification in the following quotation of those elements that constitute strength and durability is an example of this, illustrating, as Delon puts it, that 'la concentration constitue souvent une accumulation énergétique'.[36]

C'est avec ce qu'il y a au monde de plus menu, de plus mince, de moins spacieux, dans ce que fait la main de l'homme, c'est avec le point, avec la ligne, avec des lettres que s'opère dans le monde ce qu'il y a de plus grand, de plus fort, de plus durable, de plus irrésistible.

(C i. 185)

---

[34] C i. 181, 217, 147, 171. These images may be traced back to Bonnet, iii. 76, 110.
[35] Fabre d'Olivet, 'Discours'. Joubert's 'pelotton' is probably based on Bonnet's observations of the characteristic activity of a spermatozoon: iii. 113, 57.
[36] M. Delon, *L'Idée d'énergie au tournant des lumières* (Paris, 1988), 325.

Art is certainly the final goal envisioned here, but it is the process leading to it, the accretion of one phrase upon another, that seems to give Joubert most pleasure.

It is not entirely beyond the bounds of credibility either that this remark conceals a familiarity with what has come to be known as the 'extension' argument in Neoplatonic philosophy. This argument draws parallels between the basic concepts of geometry and differing stages in the soul's descent from Unity in the One to life in the material body. Thus, in Ficino, if Unity equals the One, then the point equals Mind; the line, soul, the plane, Heaven, and the solid, the subcelestial world. There is no absolute need to evoke this philosophical commonplace in order to understand Joubert's remark, but it is likely that he was familiar with it and, as we shall see in more detail shortly, sometimes made interesting use of geometrical models in ways that resemble his employment of biological analogies drawn from the work of Bonnet.[37]

Line, for Joubert, is creative of form, which in turn enables us to identify and create objects. The following pages will show, however, that Joubert is not so interested in the individual object as such but refers it constantly to 'Le Tout' out of which it is created. Thus, in 1797 he writes: 'On ne peut pas imaginer au *tout* aucune forme, car toute forme n'est que la différence visible et palpable de l'objet qui est revêtu d'elle' (C i. 131). The most beautiful form is that which, 'détachant le plus nettement une chose des autres, la laisse cependant le mieux en harmonie avec le tout' (C ii. 582–3). The beautiful art object is never self-sufficient but must relate not only to the spiritual source from which it springs but to the multitude of other objects which also owe their existence to the same creative origin:

Le beau, c'est l'intelligence rendue sensible [...] En un mot, une chose est parfaitement belle lorsqu'elle est telle que toutes les choses de la même espèce en auront quelque participation. Ce qui est vraiment beau est ce qui ressemble à son idée.

(C i. 214)

It would be difficult to find a more orthodox espousal of Neoplatonic aesthetics and it should be clear by now that Joubert's attitude towards

---

[37] The 'extension argument' is derived partly from Plato's *Laws* and became a philosophical commonplace read into *Timaeus* 32B and attributed ultimately to the Pythagoreans. See M. Allen, *The Platonism of Marsilio Ficino: A Study of his Phaedrus Commentary, its Sources and Genesis* (Berkeley, Calif., 1984), 105.

4. THE STATUS OF ART IN THE CARNETS

the imagination and the images and forms it creates is expressive of 'une tension vers l'infini'.[38] Indeed, it seems appropriate to refer again to Ficinian philosophy, to the Florentine's enthusiasm for the dynamic interrelationship existing between any one entity and all other things as a result of their mutual participation in the one good. As the critic Michael Allen puts it:

> Through its creative relationship with the one each thing is involved in a creative relationship with all other things, the one's creativeness ensuring that there is a like creativeness in the many. The whole of existence outside the one is therefore the result of a ceaseless flow of energy not merely downwards from the one but upwards from the many as well.[39]

This 'tension vers l'infini' may, however, be most accurately measured by insisting, paradoxically, on those elements that limit and define objects in the real world. Joubert's gaze moves immediately to the circumference of an object because it constitutes that line which identifies the nature of the relationship between an individual object and infinite space, a significant mark which defines the object as a form where space both begins and ends. In his commentary on the *Philebus*, Ficino points out that Plato calls God

> the limit of all things, then the measure of all things. Plato added that God was the universal measure, in order to show He is not the limit which is imprinted in things, but the limit which encloses all things from the outside and which separates all things into their proper natures by imprinting in them the inner limit.[40]

Joubert's emphasis on lines which limit and define is a product of a desire not simply to understand the 'proper natures' of individual objects but to concentrate on those points which link a particular physical entity to God and from which the intellectual leap into infinite space may be made. Something of this idea is expressed in a series of unpublished notes Joubert took in June 1813 while reading the *Thaetetus*: 'Quest-ce que scavoir?' he asks. 'C'est connoître les essences,' he replies.[41] Joubert goes on to consider how we come to know about and understand individual things, but his attention is focused again upon their limits, those *points* and *lignes* that not only

---

[38] Delon, *L'Idée d'energie*, 11.
[39] M. Allen, *Marsilio Ficino: The Philebus Commentary, a Critical Edition and Translation* (Berkeley, Calif., 1975), 46–7.
[40] Ibid. 386.
[41] MSS Bussy.

enable us to identify the *essence* of the individual object but themselves exist as shadows of *les essences*:

> Connoître une chose est encore sçavoir en quoi et par quoi elle diffère de toutes les autres. C'est distinguer et pouvoir assigner nettement ce qui constitue son individualité. Ce qui l'isole et la détache de tout le reste—c'est en concevoir la *rondeur*, c'est [...] ses limites ... c'est enfin avoir en vue et pouvoir en décrire tous les points, toutes les lignes, tous les profils, tous les contours.[42]

It is appropriate to recall here, as Patricia Ward points out,[43] that Joubert's reference to *rondeur* is a variation on the concept of unity in Aristotle's *Poetics*: 'Ce qui est arrondi en soi (dit Aristote) a bien plus de force et d'effet que ce qui est étendu' (*C* ii. 924).

Joubert's interpretation of the ambiguous status of line and contour, the way they can be used to create finite objects as well as to provide a glimpse of 'le Grand Tout', may be related to the growing complexity of his attitude to the image. Earlier we drew attention to the impoverished status of the *image* which masks the object it is meant to make visible. If we take into account *all* the *Carnet* entries on the nature of the image, however, as well as some important unpublished fragments, it becomes apparent that Joubert's Platonic suspicion of the imagination actually provided the stimulus necessary for him to undertake a re-examination of the nature of art, which led ultimately to a Neoplatonic faith in the power of image and metaphor. Thus, at various stages in his life, Joubert distinguished between the terms *copie* and *image*, aligning himself with critics like Quatremère de Quincy. In his book *De l'imitation* Quatremère attacks the early Romantics' emphasis upon *le pittoresque*. By this he understands 'la copie immédiate et presque graphique des objets de la matière'.[44] For a Platonist such as Quatremère de Quincy, slavish reproduction of material illusions was pointless; he preferred a different type of imitation which capitalized upon the inferior status of the image, suggesting ideal beauty by insisting, as Joubert does, on its inherent limitations.

We can watch Joubert moving towards this position while reading some of Plato's *Dialogues*. Thus, in an unpublished fragment dating from 1799 and not included by Beaunier in the *Carnets* he made the following notes:

---

[42] Ibid.
[43] *Critical Tradition*, 102.
[44] Quatremère de Quincy, *Essai sur la nature, le but et les moyens de l'imitation dans les beaux arts* (Paris, 1823), 82.

4. THE STATUS OF ART IN THE CARNETS 135

dans le Timée—idée, l'existence—le simulacre
le modèle, l'ouvrage, la copie ou l'ombre.[45]

The same year, however, while reading the *Phaedo*, he wrote 'Ce n'est pas là l'image mais une copie de la nature' (C i. 215), and this important distinction is insisted upon during his reading of the *Sophist*:

nb dans le sophiste
—l'image *est* comme une image peut être et non comme une réalité. Il y a donc l'être de l'image et l'être de la réalité. il y a l'être de l'apparence et l'être de la solidité.
ibid dans le sophiste
il y a dit-il le même et l'autre
L'être est le même et le non être est l'autre
comme le beau et le non beau,
le juste et l'injuste, le grand et le non-grand (différens et non contraires) car le non-grand peut être l'égal et non le petit.
tout est composé de *l'être* et du non-être, du même qui rend chaque chose semblable et collé à elle-même et de l'autre qui la rend différente et séparée de tout le reste. vid. Sophist 322.[46]

Here, Joubert implies that images should not be mistaken for mere copies, cannot in fact be confused in this way. Images belong to the world of appearance, of material illusion, and as such are totally *different* from the 'reality' they attempt to figure: 'l'image *est* comme une image peut être'. If we attend, therefore, to the true nature and status of images and do not pretend that we can use them to copy what cannot be copied, then we may realize the creative potential latent within them. Images begin to suggest where previously they had merely copied, usurped, and masked. For Quatremère de Quincy, as the critic Marguerite Iknayan puts it, the artist receives pleasure in 'recognizing the distance between the model and the image and from the act of comparing the two. The spectator receives pleasure which he would not get from the object precisely because it is an image, rather than the real thing'.[47] Or, as Joubert himself remarked: 'Nous l'avons dit, les poètes sont plus inspirés par les images que par la présence même des objets. Ainsi l'idée de la perfection est plus nécessaire aux hommes que les modèles' (C ii. 657). Here, again, Joubert finds inspiration in an

---

[45] Dated 7 Nov. 1799. MSS *Carnets*.
[46] MSS Bussy.
[47] M. Iknayan, *The Concave Mirror: From Imitation to Expression in French Esthetic Theory, 1800–1830* (Saratoga, 1983), 22.

intellectual ideal that stimulates creativity rather than in a static, finished model.

Far more promising, and indeed realistic, in Joubert's opinion, than the polished illusion of the finished art object, an illusion moreover which immodestly pretends to present us with an accurate copy of spiritual reality, is the illusory material of the physical world that goes into the creative process. During that process the potential for development seems endless and, in so far as this process constantly draws attention to the illusory material with which it works, more honest. We suggested earlier that, despite Joubert's definition of Bonnet's 'matter' as mere 'envelope corporelle', nevertheless it becomes caught up in the inevitable aspiration of all created things towards the divine, and it is unsurprising to find that Joubert's description of the birth of illusion itself is couched in language that owes much to Bonnet and to Ocellus:

L'illusion. Dieu la créa et la plaça entre les grains, les fruits, les chairs et le palais de la bouche et il en naquit les saveurs; entre les fleurs et l'odorat et il en naquit les parfums; entre l'ouïe et les sons et il en naquit l'harmonie, la mélodie etc., entre les yeux et les objets, et il en naquit les couleurs, la perspective et la beauté.

Elle est un peu de la nature qui s'amuse à nous donner quelque plaisir par quelque évaporation.

Elle diffère de l'erreur. Si je vois des couleurs sans voir aucun objet, comme dans les airs par exemple, je suis dans l'erreur. Dans le cas contraire je suis dans l'illusion et la vérité.

Toute illusion est produite par quelque émanation et est l'effet d'un nuage, d'une vapeur, de l'intervention d'un fluide. Si l'organe est vicié, si l'objet est mal disposé ou altéré dans ses parties constitutives, il n'y a point d'illusion. Une des deux parties manque alors de fournir l'enjeu, et le jeu d'illusion ne peut plus s'opérer.

Illusions. Elles ne peuvent donc être produites que par ces effluvions, ces écoulemens invisibles, ces subtiles émanations qui entretiennent des courans perpétuels entre les êtres différens. Ils ne peuvent donc donner et recevoir des sensations agréables, s'il ne se fait quelque part quelque déperdition de substance. Ainsi à la condition de changer et de dépérir est attaché le bien d'inspirer et de ressentir le plaisir.

(C i. 167)

What is most significant about this passage, apart from the insistence upon the inspirational nature of movement and change, is that, here, Joubert makes out a case for the dynamic, suggestive qualities of illusion. Just as he stresses the need to distinguish image from copy, so he emphasizes that illusion is not to be confused with error; 'une illusion *est*, comme une illusion peut être', we might say.

Bonnet's description of seminal liquid again seems to have been the inspiration here, providing him with the necessary imagery. The Swiss thinker's evocations of 'des globules mouvans', 'une évaporation plus ou moins abondante, plus ou moins accélérée de ce fluide',[48] all contribute to this long passage on illusion and are even more audible in the following entry, already quoted:

Les plus beaux sons, les plus beaux mots sont absolus et ont entre eux des intervalles naturels qu'il faut observer en les prononçant. Quand on les presse et qu'on les joint, on les rend semblables à ces globules diaphanes qui s'aplatissent sitôt qu'ils se touchent, perdent leur transparence en se collant les uns aux autres et ne forment plus qu'un corps pâteux quand ils sont ainsi réduits en masse.

(C i. 66)

Here we have a fine example of what happens when the *émanations* and *évaporations* of illusion are neglected. Bonnet's diaphanous 'globules mouvens' coalesce into an ugly, sticky mass of unregenerate matter through which no light may penetrate. Beautiful discourse gives way to cacophonous noise, reminiscent of Rabelais's 'coups de canon'. The illusions, the appearances, of the physical world take on an erroneous or spurious reality which obscures the spiritual dimension to which they may now give access.

Provided, therefore, that we recognize the true status of created matter in the divine scheme of things, then it is clear that Joubert believed much could be learnt about the nature of creativity and ideal beauty from its observation.

'ÂME' AND ANIMATION

We are now in a better position to understand how Joubert, the Platonist, was able to recognize that a valid creative relationship could operate between the material shadow and the spiritual ideal. Essentially, it is the relationship that exists between *âme* and *animation*, between divine reality and the animated flux of illusory matter.

Joubert's concern to define the precise nature and sphere of influence of these two forces is most graphically illustrated in annotations which

---

[48] Bonnet, iii. 77–8.

he made upon his copy of the influential commentary on Plato's *Dialogues* by the German scholar Tiedemann. On pages of Tiedemann's analysis of the *Politicus* Joubert underlined an attack, not only on the Manichean belief in the existence of two Gods, of two equal principles of good and evil, but on those who hold matter to be coeternal with, rather than created by, God.[49] Such men, and Tiedemann included Plato himself among them, attribute to God a certain power of moving and acting, 'movendi et agendi tribuit', but in their hands spirit becomes confused with, at worst, the directionless flux of matter and, at best, a mere 'attempt at' or 'effort towards' movement. Perhaps a little more neutral than Joseph de Maistre, who was shocked by Tiedemann's accusation, Joubert commented drily in the margin of the text: 'Ils confondaient l'Âme et l'Animation.'[50] The distinction is vital: soul, spirit, is of God the Eternal, the Unmoving, creator of a world of Being which is the world of stable and definite Form; *animation* is typical of the 'unstable flux of Becoming that is the sensible world'.[51]

As we now know, however, Joubert's remark need not be interpreted as a measure of his hostility towards *animation*. His interest in the creative flux of Bonnet's 'corps organisés', his descriptions of illusion, are persuasive enough, but it is when he comes to describe the nature of the soul itself that the intimate relationship between *âme* and *animation* is most clearly visible:

> L'âme est une faculté animante, déterminée à devenir et à subsister, une personnalité dès qu'une fois elle a contribué à quelque existence individuelle. L'âme est l'homme, c'est-à-dire ce qui, dans la personnalité humaine aime, pense et existe toujours dès qu'une fois cela a existé.
>
> (C i. 142)

Even more significantly, in 1813, while reading the *Theaetetus*, he noted: 'L'animation est une espèce d'âme' (C ii. 748).

The earlier quotation, with its emphasis upon *âme* as an active force in itself, may, of course, be related to the ideas of the *idéologues* who were debating the whole issue of *force* or *activité* at around the time that Joubert was making these entries in the *Carnets*. We have already referred briefly to a momentary similarity between Joubert and Cabanis, and all these men were, at some stage, interested in Bonnet, who

---

[49] Tiedemann, 157.
[50] See Triomphe, 422.
[51] R. T. Wallis, *Neoplatonism* (London, 1972), 57–8.

described the soul as an 'Etre Simple ... Cet Etre est une *Force*, une *Puissance*, une capacité d'agir ou de produire certains effets.'[52] One of the central desires of the *idéologues* was to prove that 'les principes réels des choses' must be located 'dans les forces'.[53] Joubert's description, however, seems to owe most to a Florentine Neoplatonic conception of the energized nature of the soul, and in this context it is worth quoting from a passage on Ficino by Gérando in his *Histoire comparée des systèmes de philosophie*. In his hands Ficino's spiritualism takes on just the kind of dynamic proportions that stimulated Joubert to write in the margin of Tiedemann's commentary on the *Convivium* 'Que le monde est plein de germes':

> il s'est livré avec une singulière persévérance à l'investigation de tous les faits qui servent à marquer la limite entre l'esprit et la matière, à mettre en évidence l'empire que l'âme exerce sur les organes du corps, à montrer l'énergie des forces qui appartiennent à ce foyer d'activité intérieure, et qui, en se répandant sur la nature entière, l'envahissent par une sorte de conquête intellectuelle.[54]

Another Neoplatonist, Ralph Cudworth, the seventeenth-century Cambridge philosopher, also of interest to Joubert, who made a trip to the Bibliothèque Mazarine in 1801 to consult his huge *Systema-intellectuale*, received similar treatment from Gérando.[55] Summarizing Cudworth's theories, Gérando noted that:

> L'âme ... n'est pas une simple *table rase*, destinée seulement à recevoir l'instruction qui lui viendrait du dehors, elle est surtout une force active et productrice; les connaissances ne commencent point à la sensation, mais s'y terminent au contraire.[56]

The relationship, as Joubert perceived it, between *âme* and *animation* is fully clarified when these passages and his own remarks are seen in

---

[52] Bonnet, vi. 22. We ought not to forget either, in this context, the abbé Batteux's comment on remarks by Timaeus Locrus: 'que les Anciens connoissoient sous le nom d'*Ame*, ce que les Modernes connoissent sous celui de *Force*' (Locrus, in Ocellus Lucanus, 57–8).

[53] J. M. baron de Gérando, *Histoire comparée des systèmes de philosophie, relativement aux principes des connaissances humaines*, pt. 2 (4 vols.; Paris, 1847), iii. 397–8.

[54] Ibid. i. 76.

[55] This visit by Joubert to the Mazarine was made in the context of a reading of Kant. It is intriguing to speculate whether Joubert found a parallel between the philosophy of the English Platonist and that of Kant. See C i. 287 and A. O. Lovejoy, 'Kant and the English Platonists', in *Essays Philosophical and Psychological in Honor of William James* (Columbia, NY, 1908). See Triomphe, 472, for Joseph de Maistre's knowledge of Cudworth. It is worth noting that Triomphe believes that 'Maistre a pu être orienté vers Cudworth par "le bel ouvrage de l'abbé Le Batteux sur le principe actif de l'univers"'.

[56] Gérando, *Histoire comparée*, ii. 353.

the context of a Ficinian emphasis on the soul as the source of all motion, or the soul as 'prime motion' or 'animation'.[57] As Ficino wrote in his commentary on the *Philebus*:

> The power to act and so to move will be present in bodies from the soul. So every act and movement of bodily objects is from the soul, which is an incorporeal essence joined to but not mixed with the body, connected to but not dispersed through it ... the whole soul is moved by itself: that is, it runs to and fro and brings to completion by means of time's intervals the works of nutrition, growth and reproduction, the products of reasoning and cogitation.[58]

Commenting on Ficino's similar treatment of soul in the preface to the *Phaedrus*, Michael Allen has noted that this emphasis upon the concept of motion stresses the 'soul's relationship to what is moved, its creative rather than contemplative relationship to the world'.[59] Joubert's reference to *animation* as 'une espèce d'âme' is not, therefore, to be interpreted as evidence of momentary confusion on his part, nor as a deliberate upgrading of the status of material flux, but simply as a recognition of the creative presence of soul in matter: that, without the *animation* intrinsic to *âme*, there would be no movement at all in the physical universe. Like Gérando, Joubert may indeed have been sensitive to the 'modern dialecticity' which contemporary critics are beginning to rediscover in Ficino's philosophy, his presentation of 'an ontological system with an emphasis on the organic union of all being and activity'.[60]

Repos

It is again to Ficino that we have to turn if we wish to understand Joubert's apparently paradoxical insistence throughout the *Carnets* on the need for *repos*:

> La force sans repos (dans Lavater). Des forces toujours en travail, une activité sans repos, du mouvement sans intervalles, des agitations sans calme, des passions sans mélancolie, des plaisirs sans tranquillité. C'est vivre sans jamais s'asseoir, vieillir debout, banir le sommeil de la vie et mourir sans avoir dormi.
>
> (C i. 178)

---

[57] Allen, *Phaedrus*, 69.
[58] Allen, *Philebus*, 100.
[59] Allen, *Phaedrus*, 79.
[60] Allen, *Philebus*, 47.

This passage need not be seen as a contradiction of Joubert's enthusiasm for *activité* and *mouvement* if *repos* is linked to the relationship that exists between *âme* and *animation*. Just as *animation* is not regarded by Joubert as the dialectical opposite of *âme* but as a physical reflection and translation of the prime motion of the soul, so *repos* must be regarded both as the final goal to which all the forces of animated nature tend *and* the still, spiritual centre where the soul abides in peace and from which these forces draw their energy. As Joubert wrote in a letter to Pauline de Beaumont: 'Vivre, c'est penser et sentir son âme.'[61] Here again, there is the desire for a moment of rest, of pause, first encountered in the 'Éloge de Cook', for the creation of an *espace* or 'ciel' where the human soul, glinting like a star, may breathe freely, where the perfectly organized human being may attune his soul to the music of the spheres. Like Ficino before him, Joubert predicates rest as the goal of motion and therefore of life. As Michael Allen argues in his study of the *Phaedrus* commentary, 'Soul's highest motion, its highest life is self-transcending and ultimately passes into the realm of Mind to become motionless and therefore in a way lifeless, in transvital rest.'[62]

Joubert's desire for *repos* therefore, need not be taken as an index of a contemplative philosopher's passivity, but as a recognition and identification of the final stage in the Phaedran ascent.

Joubert's version of a spiritually energized material universe continually 'turning back'—to use a Ficinian expression—to God was not easily come by. Initially, at least, his attempts to get to grips with the status of the physical cosmos led him to stress its ontological inferiority and to doubt the effectiveness of art that pretended to imitate or copy spiritual reality by relying on analogies drawn from the realm of illusory matter.

He uses Charles Bonnet to proclaim the reality of an immaterial spiritual principle lying behind the illusions of the physical cosmos, but in so doing is seduced by Bonnet's descriptions of living organisms and a universe of vital movement and creativity. Bonnet's insects remind him of Ficino's, which are constantly engaged in an artistic process of weaving and building that is part of the aspiration of all created things to return to their creator. It was precisely this vision of creativity that enabled Joubert to flout his own Platonic suspicion of the analogical

[61] Letter to Mme de Beaumont of 14 Sept. 1803.
[62] Allen, *Phaedrus*, 7.

process in general and plunder Bonnet's texts for metaphors with which to talk about the relationship between the physical world and spiritual reality.

The mere versifier, at three removes from Truth, whom Plato rightly condemned as unworthy of attention, was not of the same stature as the great Homer or the Neoplatonic poet directly inspired by God whose sensitivity to the Pythagorean music of the spheres was examined in Chapter 3. The art of this type of poet is an art of 'multiplication' not 'imitation', a multiplication and relating of one beautiful object to another in the knowledge that no single entity may successfully reflect Beauty itself. This is an art that deals in images as distinct from copies, that reflects the mobile, illusory nature of the matter out of which it is made, and that is conscious of and draws attention to its limited nature. It is an art that insists on the limits that define it, because to go beyond them is to risk an encounter with God of which only the human intellect is capable.

This emphasis on limits is to be regarded not as the declaration of an interest in the creation of imitative *objets d'art* but rather as the production of sketches whose lines and circles suggest what cannot be more accurately represented. Perfection did not lie, inevitably, for Joubert, in the future, as it did for men like Condorcet, but could be discovered in certain moments of the past. It was available to the poet in Homer; the sculptor found it 'dans les antiques, le philosophe dans Platon (s'il peut l'entendre), le moraliste dans Socrate et le Chrétien dans Jésus Christ. Notre condition est donc bornée à remplir les dimensions où peut atteindre notre ébauche' (C i. 315). And it is the 'ébauche', the *pointilliste* technique of the Cartesian mathematician, the Malebranchean geometer, or the Ficinian metaphysician that is the only method available to one who is eager to plot the existence of 'les purs esprits':

On ne peut les concevoir [...] sans quelque corps, sinon terrestre, au moins céleste ou, si on le veut, du moins mathématique, c'est-à-dire indiquant leurs bornes, leurs limites, leur privation d'infinité, d'immensité et leur donnant par conséquent quelque figure. Corps mathématique: j'entends par là un corps sans pesanteur, sans impénétrabilité, sans aucune des qualités qui caractérisent ou par lesquelles on définit les corps terrestres.

(C i. 446)

The physical world, its 'corps terrestres' formed by the matter of image, colour, sound, and light, becomes an *estampe*, a graph, a grid of points,

4. THE STATUS OF ART IN THE CARNETS 143

and lines which represent what cannot be represented in more human terms—a map which figures an *idea* we have conceived of the sensible universe from the images it presents to us:

> On entre dans [l'infini] en sortant de la matière comme, lorsqu'on parcourt ce monde en sortant de la terre, on entre dans la mer. Et représentez-vous nos cartes de géographie. Comme les pleins y sont découpés par les vuides qui laissent les mers et les lacs, de même le fini, si j'ose m'exprimer ainsi, est découpé par l'infini, le mouvement par le repos.
>
> (C i. 250)

Fini, infini, plein, vide, mouvement, repos—all terms which exist in creative tension with each other for the duration of the *Carnets* and which, far from being dialectical opposites, are expressive of the circularity of the ontological process already touched upon in Joubert's use of the word *rondeur*. Ideal art is expressive of that circularity and, by definition, is incapable of being brought to completion:

> Cercle ravissant à décrire et qui recommence toujours. On le quitte, on s'y plonge, on en sort, on le reprend. N'en décrions aucun degré; n'exigeons pas que tout le monde l'achève; notre devoir, notre bonheur sont d'y tenir et non de le tracer.
>
> (C i. 442)

It is a statement that might serve equally well as a description of the *Carnets* themselves, which continually postpone the moment of their 'resolution' into a completed book of *maximes* and point instead to their status as an embryonic romantic text which is, as Friedrich Schlegel argues, 'always becoming and never capable of completing itself'.[63]

---

[63] F. Schlegel, *Dialogue on Poetry and Literary Aphorisms*, trans. and ed. E. Behler and R. Stuc (Pennsylvania State University Press, 1968), 141.

5
Idea, Image, and Copy

In the previous chapters we discussed the difficulties Joubert encountered while trying to establish the status of art in the context of a Platonic approach to the illusory nature of the material world. This led to the discovery in Renaissance Neoplatonism of ideas that enabled him to adopt a relatively positive attitude towards human creativity. In the pages that follow we shall see how Joubert pursued these ideas, particularly those relating to the relationship between idea, image, and copy, into the realm of contemporary epistemology; how his reading of Bonnet and Ficino made it easier for him to take advantage of the sensualist philosophy of Condillac without becoming snared by materialism.

Joubert's reading of Bonnet and Ficino undoubtedly helps to modify any view of him as a strict Platonist, more concerned with contemplation of a divine realm of archetypes or *essences* than their reflection in the world of perishable matter. In a *pensée* of 1798, which compares the merits of a pear's flesh with its pips or seeds, it is interesting to observe the emergence of a slight preference in Joubert's careful choice of vocabulary:

Quelquefois, pour l'usage, c'est le trop qui est l'essentiel. C'est ainsi que la chair de la poire vaut mieux pour nous que ses pépins, quoique pour sa reproduction, qui est le grand but de la nature, le pépin soit le nécessaire, l'assés, et la chair soit le superflu, le trop.

(C i. 180)

Later, Joubert was to write: 'Rien n'est si subtil que les germes. Et rien cependant n'est si réel; et que dis-je? Ils sont la cause de toutes les réalités' (C ii. 833), but in the earlier entry we witness a paring down of the core rather than of the rind and fruit, a respect for the immediate pleasure and utility provided by the fully developed physical object before us, and, only then, acknowledgement of the less tangible importance of the seeds it reflects and by means of which it lives.

In 1803, however, the artistic analogue of this *pensée* again shows Joubert striving after the creation of harmony, an ordered balance between 'le trop' and 'l'assés':

> Pour qu'une expression soit belle, il faut qu'elle dise plus qu'il est nécessaire en disant pourtant avec précision ce qu'il faut. Il faut que le *trop* et *l'assés* s'y trouvent réunis et qu'il y ait en elle abbondance et oeconomie.
>
> (C i. 409)

This continual effort towards unity and reunification is apparent also in his reading of Bacon, in the same year, which develops his interest in La Bruyère's harmonious art of 'aggrégation' and its 'convenance entière, naturelle, unique': 'Dans Bacon: "Rapprocher les objets". Grand moyen de perfectibilité (si perfectibilité il y a). Moyen réel d'avancement dans leurs sciences ... Bacon dit que les élémens sont de grandes assemblées ou congrégations' (C i. 271).[1] Clearly, Joubert recognizes that the ordered harmony of parts is a crucial element of the type of progress which he confines, warily, in accordance with his suspicion of 'infinite perfectibility', to *'leurs* sciences'. Yet this desire for harmony does not necessarily stand in opposition to Joubert's interest in 'le trop'. As an analysis of a number of his other entries on Bacon shows, what interested him most in the Renaissance thinker was Bacon's attempt to establish correspondences between the superficially different branches of human knowledge, his desire to map the 'escoulemens' that linked mind and matter, 'le trop' and 'l'assés', the various movements to and fro which take place within the harmonious 'tout' decreed by divine wisdom. Locke and Condillac were learned men, of course, but, as Bacon said: 'Tous les hérésiarques [...] ont été des hommes sçavans.' Yes, added Joubert, 'mais aucun d'eux n'a été un homme d'esprit. Esprits secs ou fougueux, vrais "coupeurs de cumin", avides non de plaire et d'embélir, mais de dominer et de disséquer. "Airetikoi", diviseurs, séparateurs, dissécateurs, etc.' (C ii. 577). Opposing them were the poets who, under the divine inspiration of *phantaisie* or, as Joubert preferred, *imagination,* unlocked all the doors of compartmentalized knowledge. Poets were, or could be again, the standard-bearers of 'la philosophie primitive' or 'transcendante', and in

---

[1] Joubert refers to F. Bacon, *Neuf livres de la dignité et de l'acroissement des sciences,* trans. le sieur Golefer (Paris, 1632). For the reference to La Bruyère, see C i. 255.

this context we recall all the eighteenth-century discussions of poetry as the first, natural language of man, of poets as singing law-givers.

Yet, although Joubert may have been hostile to the analytical genius of Locke and Condillac in the context of Bacon's attempts '[à] unir la nature', he was fascinated by their obsession with 'la liaison des idées' and the communication between mind and matter. Ultimately, these philosophers were as important to Joubert as Bonnet and Ficino in his attempt to come to terms with the dynamic nature of the physical universe.

Locke, Condillac, and Innate Ideas

Just as Joubert came to regard Plato's doctrine of Ideas as a poetic fable and preferred to dwell on the spiritual impetus inherent in created matter, so his reading of Locke and Condillac forced him to question the logic of philosophers who believed in the existence of innate ideas imprinted by God on a passive human mind:

(Moi). 1. S'il y a ou s'il n'y a pas des idées que l'on peut appeller innées est une question qui tient essentiellement à la science, à la connoissance de l'âme; et non pas simplement une question d'école.
2. Si, lorsque la proposition en frappe l'oreille, l'idée d'une chose qui n'a jamais frappé les sens naît aussitôt dans notre esprit, y éclôt et s'y développe, on peut croire, on peut dire, on doit penser que c'est là une idée innée ou dont le germe étoit en nous, à peu près comme on suppose que le feu est dans les veines d'un caillou. Dieu existe, N. est juste, etc.
3. Ces idées, ou notions, ou sentimens innés ne sont point indestructibles en nous. Ils peuvent au contraire être très aisément défigurés, altérés, déplacés, etc. (Quoique éternel, tout cela est mobile et se chasse aisément) comme tout ce qui est germe.

(C i. 266–7)

Just as Joubert never denies the fundamental truths expressed by Plato's doctrine of Ideas, so, in this passage, he does not refute the reality of innate ideas. Nevertheless it is his description of their precise nature that is of most significance here.

Joubert's understanding of the animated nature of the human soul has been examined in some detail and it would appear from these remarks that he regarded innate ideas in much the same light: 'Quoique éternel, tout cela est mobile et se chasse aisément.' Just as his polemic on behalf of *âme* and *repos* concealed an appreciation of their dynamic nature so his 'idées, ou notions ou sentimens innés' exist in and contribute to a mind that is susceptible to change, growth, and, as we shall see, the influence of ideas coming from the senses.

Joubert's prefacing of this entry with a bracketed 'Moi' is important, for it underlines a deliberate attempt to distinguish his own thoughts on this matter from those of Locke and Leibniz, who seem to have formed the staple diet of the year 1800, as from those of Bonnet and Nollet, whose vocabulary can still be heard echoing in his mind. Between 1800 and 1804 Joubert undertook detailed critical readings of Berkeley, Locke, Bacon, Condillac, Leibniz, Kant, Bonald, and Malebranche, and it seems likely that this concentrated dose of philosophy was a response to the activities and publications of the Institut de France, whose members, influenced by Bonnet and Condillac, were debating feverishly questions relating to the operation of the mind. It is doubtful, however, whether Joubert was actually working on any specific Institut competition during these years. In September 1801, in the course of reading Kant, he noted that the Academy of Berlin had proposed the following subject for discussion:

'Démontrer d'une manière incontestable l'origine de nos connoissances, soit (ajoute le programme) en présentant des argumens non employés encore, soit en présentant des argumens déjà employés, mais en les présentant avec une clarté nouvelle et une force victorieuse de toute objection'. Cela est beaucoup trop plaisant. (Vid. Magaz. encyclop. N° 22, germinal.).

(C i. 301)

Whether this cutting dismissal refers simply to the optimistic desire for originality or to the actual subject itself is a moot point, but it is unlikely, in the light of this reaction, that Joubert would have been any less hostile to the competitions set by the Institut in Paris. What *is* significant about this remark, however, is that it points to his awareness of contemporary philosophical debate. Even if his programme of reading was not stimulated by any particular question, it may be seen as a deliberate testing of his own position against some of the ideas that were inspiring current discussion. There is a sense in which the notes on these great philosophers are a constantly renewed attempt by Joubert to write '(Moi)' at the beginning of an all-inclusive *pensée*, as he did in 1800; as he wrote, while reading Condillac later that year: 'Je me sers de leurs expressions et je les cite avec plaisir. J'aime à leur faire dire malgré eux ce que je pense. (Ce n'est jamais que notre propre pensée que nous appercevons, selon Condillac)' (C i. 279)

5. IDEA, IMAGE, AND COPY

Joubert began to read Locke in August 1800 and from the first it is apparent that the English philosopher's handling of the question of innate ideas left much to be desired:

> En combattant ce qu'ils [ses contradicteurs] entendoient par notions innées, il serre trop le sens du mot et a l'air d'agir et de se déterminer plus par raisonnement que par conviction. Il semble dans cette question avoir consulté les règles de la logique plus que son propre sentiment, son sens intime.
>
> (C i. 265)

Joubert was more prepared to hesitate between the terms *notion* or *appréhension innée*, both of which were more susceptible to the intuitive capacities of a *sens intime* than the rigid concept of *idées innées*. Although he *does* use this expression when noting what Locke has to say about it, Joubert continually steps back from a wholehearted adoption, ever ready with the refining nuance:

> Nous avons l'idée (ou apréhension) innée d'une certaine essence que nous ne pouvons voir (celle de l'esprit), nous n'avons de sens ou de sentiment inné que d'une certaine règle d'harmonie et d'ordre moral (celle du juste et de l'injuste). La manière dont cette essence ou nature existe et la croyance même de son existence, la manière dont ce principe ou règle doivent être apliqués et les règles particulières qui en dérivent sont des opérations de notre esprit susceptibles d'une infinité de variations et même de contradictions [...] C'est tout ce que je puis voir de plus clair sur ce sujet en ce moment.
>
> (C i. 266)

Rather than *idées innées*, Joubert would prefer, as we have seen, to talk about *germes*, and, as he began to read Leibniz, 'son mot monade. Monade veut dire unité' (C i. 267). This movement of *recul*, as it were, to a larger, more all-embracing concept of innateness which might in fact leave individual ideas more freedom to manœuvre is confirmed by a short remark of first September: 'Inné? Mais nos facultés sont innées' (C i. 268). By the time, therefore, that he came to read Leibniz's reply to Locke, the *Nouveaux essais sur l'entendement humain*, in April 1801, he was able, due to his own reflections on the question, to agree with the opinions of the German philosopher:

> Le raisonnement de Leibniz est fort bon. Nous avons de certaines idées qui nous sont innées, parce que nous avons un entendement qui nous est inné et qui ne peut pas plus subsister sans quelques représentations qu'un Miroir exposé au grand jour et à beaucoup d'objets ne peut subsister sans images.

5. IDEA, IMAGE, AND COPY

Nous portons en nous mêmes les idées (ou plutôt les germes des idées) que les sens ne pourroient nous donner et qui néanmoins nous sont indispensables.

Il n'est rien dans l'entendement qui ne soit entré par nos sens, excepté l'entendement même et par conséquent excepté les notions et les idées sans lesquelles l'entendement ne sçauroit subsister.

(C i. 288)

In a note to this page, Beaunier refers us to a reading Joubert gave to the correspondence of Leibniz and, in particular, a letter to 'Bierlingius, tom V, in-4° pag. 358. Ce qu'il dit de Locke. Vid. inf. 12 avril'. Following up this reference to the 1768 edition of Leibniz's complete works, it becomes clear that Joubert's remarks are a virtual translation of Leibniz's opinion of Locke and of the latter's confusion between 'necessary truths' and 'those perceived by demonstration'. As Leibniz put it: 'nihil est in intellectu, quod non fuerit in sensu, nisi ipse intellectus'.[2]

The greatest irony to emerge from Joubert's reading of Locke is the extent to which the English philosopher resembles Plato. It is significant, indeed, that he notices, first, the limitations common to both. On 9 August 1800 he notes that Locke merely disposes 'l'esprit à s'éclairer. Il l'y détermine et l'y induit plus qu'il ne l'y etc.', just as Plato 'ne nourrit pas l'esprit, mais [. . .] le dispose à se nourrir. Il ne fait rien voir, mais il éclaire' (C i. 266). In 1801, however, this had given way to an appreciation of the positive doctrine they held in common. Like Plato, Locke actually recognized 'des obligations antérieures à toutes les constitutions humaines', and Joubert immediately snares him with this confession, forcing Locke to admit to the theory of *notions innées* which his logic forced him to reject: 'La manière dont Locke a fait philosopher les hommes a détruit ces grandes maximes qu'il professoit. Il fut le dernier raisonneur qui eût en morale les grands principes que sa logique a décriés. Locke fut imprudent' (C i. 312).

Too rigid an adherence on Joubert's part to the concept of innate ideas would indicate that he believed man to be a largely passive creature, dependent upon God for all his important insights. As we have seen, however, Joubert struggles hard against this view and, in one of the passages quoted above, appeals, instead, to the knowledge afforded by a *sens intime*. This term occurs frequently in the *Carnets*

---

[2] G. G. Leibniz, *Opera omnia collecta* (6 vols.; Geneva, 1768), 358–9.

and contributes powerfully to Joubert's vision of a spiritually energized universe.

The French Jesuit, Buffier, was among the first to articulate clearly a philosophy of common sense based upon the intuitive information provided to each human being by their *sens intime*, and, as his *Traité des premières vérités* is to be found in Joubert's library at Bussy, it is quite likely that this work constituted a principal source. In March 1797, coming significantly after an entry on the soul's need for space and an expression of Ficinian visionary ecstasy beginning 'l'oubli des choses de la terre, l'intention aux choses du ciel', Joubert insists upon the reality of *sens intime*. It is, he declares, 'une faculté véritable ... C'est notre tact intérieur, distinct de tous nos autres sens. Il a comme eux des propriétés et une destination' (C i. 135). Two years later this 'sens intérieur' exists '[à] nous incliner à croire ce que nous ne pouvons connaître, affin que du moins nous ayons avec la vérité cette manière de posséder, ne pouvant en devenir maîtres autrement' (C i. 195). *Sens intime* is of little help in telling us about other people, but it is a sure guide to the truth about ourselves. As Maine de Biran wrote in his journal: 'Pour savoir ce qui est, il faudroit pouvoir lire dans toutes les âmes, être successivement chaque homme, et je n'ai pour moi que mon sens intime',[3] and Joubert was in complete agreement: 'Il est en nous pour nous parler de nous. Il nous entretient de notre âme, de son destin. Il se tait sur la destinée des autres êtres animés' (C i. 195). By far the most striking expression of this theory occurs in 1797, when Joubert evokes 'L'évidence intérieure intime' and then refers to it idio-syncratically as 'l'invidence' (C i. 149). It is significant that Joubert should think of *sens intime* at this particular moment for it comes after a series of passages inspired by Nollet's and Bonnet's interest in 'la liqueur séminale', allowing us to relate this primitive, instinctive sentiment to the entelechic tendency of the soul described by the *idéologues* as 'puissance active'. Maine de Biran speaks constantly of 'la tendance invincible de nos âmes', of Man '[qui] tende sans cesse vers quelque objet extérieur',[4] but perhaps the most eloquent expression of this movement is provided by the Dutch Platonist Hemsterhuis, in his essay *Sur les désirs*. 'Je crois qu'il est assez évident', he writes, 'que le désir de l'âme est une tendance vers l'union parfaite et intime avec l'essence de

---

[3] P. Maine de Biran, *Journal intime*, ed. La Valette Monbrun (2 vols.; Paris, 1927, 1931), i. 44.
[4] Ibid. i. 26.

l'objet désiré; et ensuite que l'âme tend proprement vers l'union parfaite et intime avec tout ce qui est hors d'elle.'[5]

Joubert's remarks about 'invidence' in 1797, however, are made also in the context of references to Leibniz. 'Les vérités de fait, qui sont l'objet d'une connaissance immédiate,' Gérando writes in a summary of some of the ideas of the *Nouveaux essais sur l'entendement humain*, which Joubert read around this time, 'sont exclusivement renfermées, suivant Leibniz, dans la conscience intime. Il n'y a proprement que l'expérience interne dont le témoignage soit direct.'[6]

The best summary, however, of the way in which *sens intime* and *puissance active, âme* and *objet extérieur*, are all related to one another in one dynamic matrix is provided by Ancillon in his *Essais philosophiques* of 1817. Joubert makes references to Ancillon in 1812, so it is just possible that this is a work he may have read at some stage. Ancillon writes:

Ce seroit une erreur de croire que ces faits primitifs naissent d'eux-mêmes dans notre âme, ou que nous les produisions par un simple acte de notre volonté. Il faut le concours de la force intelligente et des objets extérieurs pour les faire sortir de leur obscurité. Ils sont les résultats de la nature intime, et de la tendance primitive de l'âme, d'un côté; et de l'autre de l'action du monde extérieur, qui fait de cette tendance un véritable acte.[7]

Joubert's sensitivity to 'la tendance primitive de l'âme' is evident also in a number of remarks on the nature of vision. These may have been stimulated by a re-reading of the *Timaeus* in 1801, centring on the importance of the eye, which both receives and gives light: 'Que la vision se fait par le concours de deux lumières.—Add. 19 Mars: Et si les objets rayonnent vers nous, nous rayonnons vers les objets' (C i. 287), a remark which is taken up again in July and can be seen as an illustration of the theme central to these early years of the nineteenth century: what is the liaison between the human *entendement* and the physical universe, spirit and matter? How do we reproduce what is spiritually innate in the outside world of the senses? How do the senses, ratifying the existence of a world beyond ourselves, communicate with and indeed constitute that inner self? Are 'we' locked in? Can't 'we' get

---

[5] *Œuvres philosophiques de F. Hemsterhuis* (2 vols.; Paris, 1792; rev. edn. 1809), i. 71.
[6] Gérando, *Histoire comparée*, iii. 80.
[7] F. Ancillon, *Essais philosophiques ou nouveaux mélanges de littérature et de philosophie* (2 vols.; Paris, 1817), p. xii.

out? These questions and a hundred other unspoken variations underlie Joubert's considerations of vision:

15 juillet 1801. Vuë. il nous semble[8] d'abord que nous voyons avec nos yeux comme nous touchons avec nos mains, par l'imposition ou application de nos regards. Nous nous figurons aisément nos regards comme de longs rayons qui sortent de nos yeux à peu près de la manière dont nos sourcils sortent de nos paupières. Nos sourcils aident à nous donner cette imagination et aussi les apparences que nous avons l'occasion d'observer souvent dans les corps lumineux ou enflammés, tels que la chandelle, le soleil etc. d'où nous voyons, par de certaines dispositions de nos yeux en ces momens, sortir des rayons semblables à de longues baguettes d'or minces et divergentes. Nous nous figurerions donc aisément que nos regards vont toucher les corps et nous les font voir aussi. Mais à la réflexion cette idée ne suffit plus pour nous expliquer la merveille de la vision parce qu'elle laisse inexplicables des circonstances qu'un peu d'attention ne tarde pas à nous faire appercevoir.

Il y image; elle se peint ...

(C i. 293)

Not only does this passage touch on the theories of Plato and Berkeley, but Leibniz is also pulled into the vortex of Joubert's thought. This is made clearer by an entry of 20 December 1801, which is, in turn, clarified by the more substantial entry of 15 July and the questions that motivated it.

Leibniz. La lumière d'une chandelle vient-elle des objets qu'elle éclaire? Les idées innées sont nécessaires—comme les tendons et les muscles dont nous nous servons pour marcher (pag. 40) 'Ils ne pourront (dit Leibniz) raisonner sans caractères. Ils n'en ont pas besoin si les images leur en servent.' Or etc—Leibniz attribueroit donc la perception même à l'arbre, car il y a en lui une sorte d'entéléchie ou de force vive, de tendance.

(C i. 311)

There is the same desire to make metaphysical and aesthetic capital out of philosophies which regard ideas innate in us as 'inclinations or tendencies', agglomerations of forces that move the individual to act, rather than static entities locked within the mind;[9] the wish to see eyes as a source and not simply a receptacle of vision, discover objects illuminating candles, find strange trees darting glances at aspiring topiarists, stars which discreetly dispose to action: 'Les astres (dit Bacon) inclinent, mais ne déterminent pas' (C i. 271).

[8] The cautionary use of the verb *sembler* shows the influence of Berkeley.
[9] G. G. Leibniz, *New Essays on Human Understanding*, ed. P. Remnant and J. Bennett (Cambridge, 1981), 52.

IMAGE AND ANALOGY

The most interesting and important notes on the issue of innate ideas occur, however, when Joubert can be seen to move towards Condillac's position in the *Essai sur l'origine des connaissances humaines* and the *Traité des sensations*.[10] On 13 August 1800 he noted how Locke tended to confuse ideas with sensations, 'comme lorsqu'il dit que la douleur est une idée, et l'idée de la douleur. Il n'est pas vrai que la sensation ne se reçoit que par l'idée' (C i. 275).

In early 1802, Joubert returned to Locke and again took him to task for this error. From his vocabulary, however, it is particularly clear that he has just been reading Condillac, and it is this fact that should be kept in mind for the moment, since the implications of these musings reflect back upon and confirm the direction of his thoughts on the French philosopher:

Locke dit que nous ne connoissons que nos idées. Qu'est-ce que cela fait, pourvu que nos idées ressemblent à ce qu'elles nous représentent? Nous ne voyons ainsi que les images peintes dans la rétine de notre œil mais si l'image ressemble à l'objet, qu'est-ce que cela fait? [...]

'L'esprit (dit Locke) ne connoit pas immédiatement les choses, mais seulement par les idées qu'il en a.' Qu'est-ce que cela fait? Autant vaudroit dire qu'un soldat ne tue pas immédiatement son ennemi, mais seulement par l'intervention de l'action par laquelle il frappe [...] Il y a deux existences que l'homme enfermé dans lui-même pourroit connoître, la sienne et celle de Dieu: je pense, je suis, donc Dieu est. Mais la sensation seule peut lui apprendre celle des corps ... Il a produit la matière nécessairement et par son existence; et le monde volontairement et par sa bonté.

(C i. 312–13)

Here, there is a distinct sense of frustration on Joubert's part. He is heartily sick of the whole question of *idées innées*, of the claustrophobia of thinkers who refuse to see beyond the contents of their own minds, the sole guarantors of reality; again there is a movement outwards, an almost pragmatic concern for the physical objects of the outside world, for images which represent or translate the spiritual and mental realities that lie behind them.

---

[10] E. B., Condillac, *Essai sur l'origine des connoissances humaines* (2 vols.; Amsterdam, 1788). Joubert owned this edition and read the *Traité des systèmes* and *Traité des sensations*, which make up vols. ii and iii respectively of Condillac's *Œuvres complètes* (23 vols.; Paris, 1798).

It is precisely this concern that emerges from yet another passage on innate ideas written 18 May 1800:

Distinguons donc deux espèces d'idées dont les unes se font par image et peinture: telles sont celles qui entrent en nous par les yeux et les sens ouverts. (On les conçoit mieux, en effet, en les imaginant ainsi). Les autres se font par empreinte, par gravure et imprimerie. Elles n'entrent point par les sens, mais elles passent au travers, comme les caractères d'une planche passent au travers d'un papier pour s'aller tracer sur un autre.

En considérant les idées sous cette dernière forme surtout (celle d'empreinte) on conçoit qu'elles sont quelque chose d'aussi réel que les figures d'une estampe. Et les figures d'un tableau n'ont-elles pas aussi quelque réalité indépendante de la toile? Ne les communique et ne les multiplie-t-on pas par le calc? Eh que dis-je? ne les sépare-t-on pas réellement de la toile par des mordans? Ne transporte-t-on pas tous les jours des tableaux tout entiers et en personne, pour ainsi dire, d'une toile sur une toile, d'un bois sur un bois? Une idée a donc la réalité qu'a toute figuration.

La notion du juste et de l'injuste, du difforme et du beau viendront de l'empreinte de Dieu qui est mise en nous et qui nous rend en quelque sorte participans de ses pensées et (si je puis ainsi m'exprimer) de ses dégoûts et de son goût.

(C i. 249)

In Chapter 4 we saw that, in order to define the nature of the spiritual substratum, Ocellus and his translator, Batteux, were forced to draw analogies from the realm of created matter and human art. An identical process is at work in the passage quoted above, in which artistic analogy is again used to articulate the nature of immaterial phenomena, to illustrate the difference between innate ideas and those coming from the senses. Typically, one of the most important remarks Joubert makes, here, is in parentheses. The distinction between the two types of ideas may be grasped more easily, he asserts, by comparing them to the difference between an engraving and a painting: '(On les conçoit mieux, en effet, en les imaginant ainsi).'

By the end of the passage, indeed, the importance of Joubert's recourse to analogy is plain for all to see. Introduced initially to facilitate our understanding of the nature of two types of idea, Joubert is gradually seduced by the appropriateness of his comparison, and immaterial ideas are seen to be dependent upon the analogical process itself for a sense of their very reality: 'Une idée a donc la réalité qu'a toute figuration.' Initially the analogy enables us to see, to focus upon the idea; ultimately, due to the fact that human beings function, of necessity, in the realm of material reality, we are able to 'see' the idea solely *in terms of* the analogy that makes it visible.

Essentially this constitutes a recognition of the visual metaphor underlying most empiricist epistemology which was so energetically attacked by the Scottish philosophers of common sense. Men like Thomas Reid, James Beattie, and Dugald Stewart agreed with Locke and Condillac that, as there is no natural language of the mind, so we have no alternative but to apply physical descriptions to mental processes, to describe by means of analogy. As Paul Hamilton writes however: 'Reid and his compatriots declared that these analogies should not be allowed to impose on us and set the conceptual boundaries of discussions of mental phenomena. This was seen as a misuse of analogy which led the philosopher into error. Reid wrote that "we contemplate the operation of our minds, only as they appear through the deceitful medium of such analogical notions and expressions"'.[11]

As we recall from the previous chapter, Joubert was quite aware of the 'deceitful' character of this process. He was not reluctant to criticize those who used figures of speech in such a way that they obscured the spiritual truths they were supposed to reveal, but we saw, also, that this misuse of language stemmed precisely from an inability to recognize its 'deceitful' or, as Joubert preferred to call it, its 'illusory' nature. Those who do, those who recognize that 'une image *est* comme une image peut être',[12] those who keep its proximate, deceitful character in mind, will not be led astray but will see truth more clearly. Far from appealing, as the Scottish philosophers did, to the authority of 'ordinary' language in preference to the analogical language of philosophers, Joubert recognizes that the philosopher and metaphysician are locked into language that is inherently figurative. As we shall see shortly, in the context of his reaction to Condillac's thoughts on this matter, Joubert was happy to make a virtue out of this necessity.

Something of his enthusiasm for the communicative medium which enables us to visualize the immaterial idea is, as we have suggested, visible in the *pensée* of 18 May. It is worth examining even more closely the distinction Joubert makes here between engraving and painting, for it may be related to his understanding of the validity of the image examined in Chapter 4. There, it became evident that, from a Platonic point of view, art could only offer an *esquisse* or *tracing* of the

[11] Quoted by P. Hamilton, *Coleridge's Poetics* (Oxford, 1983), 37.
[12] MSS Bussy.

spiritual reality it aspired to reflect, and, in the passage of 18 May 1800, ideas imprinted on the mind by God are compared to 'les figures d'une estampe' (C i. 249). These 'figures' have a reality independent of the 'fonds', be it paper, wood, or mind, on to which they are subsequently traced. They offer us a 'sketch' of a 'higher reality'. Except, as we have noted, Joubert does not quite put it like that and prefers to reverse the terms of the equation. The status of the 'higher reality' is guaranteed by, is dependent upon, the reality of the 'sketch'.

So far so good; Joubert links the art of the engraver, the artist who works primarily with the lines and contours associated with the power of the intellect, to the creator of innate ideas. But he does not stop there: 'Et les figures d'un tableau n'ont elles pas aussi quelque réalité indépendante de la toile?' Joubert then proceeds to make a case for the painter, for the artist who works with images and colours which originate in impressions drawn from the human senses: 'Une idée a donc la réalité qu'a *toute* figuration' (C i. 249). Giving this statement its proper emphasis, we are reminded again of Joubert's rehabilitation of the image. We understand that the painter's art is not necessarily inferior to that of the engraver, simply that it is different because it works with different materials in the sphere of material reality.

Joubert's recourse to aesthetic analogy in order to clarify the workings of the human mind, and the increase in prestige for the artistic process which this strategy entailed, did not occur in an intellectual vacuum. His writings on this issue were stimulated, as we have said, by readings of both Locke and Condillac, and it is important to note that Condillac's constant recourse to aesthetic examples in order to illustrate the development of mental faculties is one of the distinguishing features of his thought. This is a process which both Jacques Derrida and Marian Hobson have studied, and it seems likely that Joubert was sensitive to it.[13] The long *pensée* of 18 May comes close to being a paradigm of Condillac's method, Joubert simply preferring to compare his examples of mental phenomena to engravings and paintings, whereas Condillac has recourse to the illusions of the theatre. Condillac's use of aesthetic examples is, indeed, a symptom of the deeper implications of his philosophy as a whole, where 'concern had shifted from the objects of knowledge to the nature of knowledge and finally,

---

[13] J. Derrida, *L'Archéologie du frivole: Lire Condillac* (Paris, 1973). M. Hobson, *The Object of Art: The Theory of Illusion in 18th Century France* (Cambridge, 1982).

to the mechanics of thought and perception'.[14] Marian Hobson's account of the aesthetic models underlying his description of the evolution of the faculties helps to show that,

> while apparently conducting a sensualist version of faculty psychology in the *Essai sur l'origine des connaissances humaines* . . . [he] is in fact developing a far more powerful account of the mind . . . From an intention which is merely associationist . . . there derives a much deeper notion of subjectivity.[15]

Indeed, Condillac's tendency to discuss the nature of the human mind and its immaterial content in terms of analogy and metaphor help to reinforce his explicit emphasis upon the role of language in the actual creation of, as distinct from the mere reproduction of, knowledge. As Condillac wrote:

> Le pouvoir de réveiller nos perceptions, leurs noms, ou leurs circonstances, vient uniquement de la liaison que l'attention a mise entre ces choses, et les besoins auxquels elles se rapportent. Détruisez cette liaison vous détruisez l'imagination et la mémoire.[16]

This liaison, Condillac argues, 'est produite par l'usage des signes, et que, par conséquent, les progrès de l'esprit humain dépendent entièrement de l'adresse avec laquelle nous nous servons du langage'.[17] In Joubert's entry for 18 May the way he expressed himself made it seem that the contours of a mental idea were clearly visible only when they were envisaged in terms of an analogy produced by the imagination. Condillac's statement regarding the dependency of the human mind— and functions such as memory and imagination—on language for its perceptions is at the origin of Joubert's *pensée*. Certainly there can be little doubt that it lies behind the following *Carnet* entry of 14 November 1800:

> Ainsi donc la mémoire est le miroir où nous voyons notre histoire; mais ce miroir n'a de taim (n'est entamé) et nous ne pouvons y rien voir que lorsqu'il est doublé par ces signes dont la ténacité jointe à la matérialité ne permet plus que tout passe à travers de etc. et s'en échappe.

(C i. 280)

Yet again there is concern for that which gives material form to what would otherwise be invisible and unknowable, locked within the

---

[14] I. F. Knight, *The Geometric Spirit: The Abbé de Condillac and the French Enlightenment* (New Haven, Conn., 1968), 178.
[15] Hobson, 242–3.
[16] Condillac, *Essai*, i. 51.
[17] Ibid. i. 126.

confines of the human mind. A memory becomes a memory only when we speak it, otherwise it passes through our mind and fades away. Similarly the perception of relationships between ideas in the mind is dependent on and constitutive of the imagination, which, in turn, relies upon language to articulate the correspondences or *liaisons* it establishes. On 17 November Joubert wrote: 'Peut-être (et probablement) il seroit vrai de dire que nous ne concevons que ce que nous pouvons nous figurer' (C i. 80);[18] on 19 November: 'et la métaphore ne lui [a la métaphysique] est pas moins nécessaire que l'abstraction' (C i. 281). The argument is virtually identical to that which emerges from Batteux's commentary on Ocellus and Timaeus Locrus. The true nature of the universe may only be visualized by means of the material signs of language. Analogy and metaphor are among the *figures* which enable us to articulate the world. As he wrote on 20 November: 'Vérité. L'entoura de figures et de couleurs affin qu'elle soit regardée.' The movement outwards, the obsession with *medium* so clearly illustrated in the *pensée* of 18 May, the effort to make connections between spiritual and material realms, these are the impressions that emerge most strongly from Joubert's reading of Locke and Condillac: 'Ce n'est pas assez d'avoir recours à la matière pour se faire une idée de l'esprit, ou à l'esprit pour se faire une idée de la matière', wrote the latter in his *Traité des systèmes*.[19] 'Oui,' contradicted Joubert, '(quoi qu'en dise Condillac) nous avons besoin de recourir à la matière pour nous faire une idée de l'esprit, et besoin de recourir à l'esprit pour nous faire une idée de la matière' (C i. 281).

The Imagination

Condillac's statement about the progress of the human mind inevitably arouses curiosity about the nature of the linguistic skill on which it is said to depend. In what does this *adresse* consist? Condillac himself believed that it lay in the steady development from primitive figurative sources of abstract philosophical language. This language, in so far as it helps to 'réveiller nos perceptions', is creative of Man's reason.

As we saw, however, in the context of a brief comparison with the Scottish philosophers of common sense, and as his remarks about the equal importance of metaphor make clear, Joubert was more than ready

---

[18] See Chastel, 75, for the importance of *figure* to Ficino.
[19] Condillac, *Œuvres complètes*, ii. *Traité des systèmes* (Paris, 1798), 193.

to rely upon the 'deceitful' medium of figurative language. He saw quite clearly that Condillac's understanding of the term *adresse* fed directly into Condorcet's theories about human perfectibility and his attack upon Condillac's use of the term *liaison* may be read as a variation on his frequently expressed antipathy to materialistic notions of 'progress':

C'est de l'impossibilité de raisonner que naquirent les arts, l'apologue, etc. (Voyez Condillac, d'après Warburton, traité des hyéroglyphes). Et c'est encore de l'inaptitude à raisonner ou de l'ennui de raisonner sans cesse que naissent dans les âmes vives la poésie, l'éloquence, la métaphore. Voilà certes un grand avantage.

(C i. 280)

An understanding of the human mind and its potential for development did not necessarily lie at the end of a sequence of rigorously argued propositions; knowledge was not necessarily the product of attention to an endless series of liaisons which the human mind established between one perception and another. On the contrary, Joubert's appeal is to the image-making faculty, the imagination of poets: 'Voulés-vous connoître le mécanisme de la pensée et ses effets? lisez les poètes. Voulez-vous connoître la morale, la politique? lisez les poètes. Ce qui vous plaît chés eux, approfondissés-le: c'est le vrai' (C i. 43). Poets, the standard-bearers of Bacon's 'philosophie primitive' or 'transcendante', are men who instinctively reach for analogy, image, and metaphor in order to articulate immaterial truths and express mental ideas, because they know that figurative language is the only kind that will provide them with a perspective upon these invisible worlds. It is, in fact, the only 'natural' language available to Man since it admits to and expresses most vividly the essentially material or 'corporeal' nature of *la parole* which, as the critic Jean-Louis Chrétien says, is 'l'incorporation de la pensée, insaisissable et évanescente hors de ce corps même'.[20]

The true metaphysician, Joubert writes, 'est un opticien qui [...] rend les êtres qui sont invisibles, ou en leur donnant une forme ou en plaçant sur nos yeux d'invisibles lunettes' (C i. 295) and his proper style is one which consists in giving 'un corps transparent à ce qui n'a pas de corps' (C i. 289). 'L'art d'écrire en métaphysique', he remarks, 'consiste à rendre sensible et palpable ce qui est abstrait' (C i. 135). It is not

---

[20] Chrétien, 471.

surprising, therefore, to find that the faculty of imagination which makes this process possible is described in almost identical terms: 'L'imagination', Joubert says, 'est éminemment la faculté de revêtir de corps et de figure ce qui n'en a pas' (C i. 282). When he declares that 'C'est par l'imagination qu'on est métaphysicien' (C i. 278), this faculty would seem to have been endowed with the freedom to move beyond the subordinate role which we examined in Chapter 4, in accordance with the status of its product, the image.

The degree of truth contained in such a statement, however, is best determined by defining even more closely the nature of Joubert's objections to the abstract language of thinkers such as Condillac and Kant.

Joubert began to read Kant in March 1801 and was as hostile to his use of language as he had been to Condillac's:

Nota.—Kant paroit s'être fait à lui-même un langage pénible. Et comme il lui a été pénible à construire, il est pénible à entendre. Ce qui a fait souvent sans doute qu'il a pris son opération pour sa matière. Il a cru se construire des idées en ne se construisant que des mots. Mais il y a dans ses phrases et ses appréhensions quelque chose de tellement oppaque (et brun) qu'il ne lui étoit guère possible de ne pas croire qu'il y avoit là quelque solidité [...] Nos transparences et nos légèretés nous trompent moins.

(C i. 297)

What Joubert implies here—particularly in the phrase 'il a pris son opération pour sa matière'—is that abstract language, by virtue of its inherent opacity, nearly always mistakes its own rhetorical manner for the subject it is supposed to clarify. In a sense abstract language is language that pretends it is not language at all, not a corporeal, expressive medium, but part and parcel of what it is examining. Abstract language, in Joubert's eyes, is guilty of pretending to bypass the essentially analogical character of language itself and of attempting to fuse with the subject it is supposed to be examining, thus providing the reader with direct access to mental ideas, a process we saw Joubert reject in Chapter 4. Inevitably such ignorance of the natural characteristics of language merely leads to obscurity, the reader having to spend most of his time deciphering a supposedly expressive medium.

These objections are similar to those which Joubert directed against the 'image qui obscure', but, as we have seen, there is another type of image, which draws attention to its figurative nature and to the limitations of such a nature, providing us with a perspective on the immaterial truths or mental ideas we wish to consider. As Joubert points out, 'Nos transparences et nos légèretés nous trompent moins' (C i. 297). 'L'imagination', he wrote elsewhere, 'est du moins forcée à se tenir plus près de la réalité et ses erreurs ont cet avantage de plus et ce danger de moins qu'elles sont plus visibles' (C i. 442). The images produced by the imagination should help us to see more clearly:

> En métaphysique, bien imaginer, c'est bien voir. Et même en physique, si on n'imagine pas on ne voit qu'à demi. Et qui ne fait rien imaginer ne montre rien clairement et ne fait rien connaître. L'essence et l'être de la matière elle-même sont tout spirituels.
>
> (C ii. 586)

Yet we have to be very careful indeed when drawing attention to the way Joubert champions the imagination and the figurative language it produces, for the dangers of exaggerating its spiritual efficacy are very real. The dividing-line between the 'image qui obscure' and the 'image qui est comme une image peut être' is a very thin one, and Joubert never entirely loses sight of a Platonic perspective on its material nature. 'Nos transparences et nos légèretés nous trompent *moins*' (C i. 297); the final, nuancing word still speaks of Joubert's enthusiasm for the image but simultaneously implies that it does not provide us with direct or immediate access to truth; we remain at a certain necessary distance from it.

Indeed, it is the issue of perspective that is all-important. Jean-Louis Chrétien, in an otherwise excellent article on Joubert, states that a metaphysical style which uses the figurative language natural to it would be, for Joubert, 'une science où il suffirait de voir pour savoir'. He goes on to argue that this style 'nous placerait—sans chercher à nous convaincre ni à nous persuader—au juste point de vue, d'où l'objet apparaîtrait dans l'évidence'.[21] By and large, Chrétien's remark is justified, but he would have caught the precise nuance of Joubert's aesthetic if he had insisted more emphatically on the phrase 'au juste point de vue'. As Chrétien makes clear earlier in his article, the power of visual metaphor to give us access to metaphysical truth may only be *fully* realized in heaven or in a future spiritual life '[où] il n'y a qu'inspection et tout ce qu'on regarde est vérité' (C i. 221). While we remain on earth, the good metaphysical style 'est une vision qui supplée à l'obscurité où nous sommes ici-bas', but the distance

[21] Ibid. 470.

between *voir* and *savoir* remains considerable.[22] It is a distance created by our natural, human dependence on the phenomenal, material nature of *la parole*, whose very figures draw attention to that which makes it different from the immaterial ideas it is trying to express. Yet, without an acknowledgement of this quintessential difference, of the distance it opens up between *signe* and *signifié*—an acknowledgement that abstract language fails to make according to Joubert—no measure of perspective on truth is possible. As Pascal wrote, 'trop de proximité empêche la vue',[23] or, as Joubert put it, 'la masse offusque' (*C* i. 147).

Figurative language does not attempt to fuse or engage too closely with the object of its attention but sheds light on, renders more transparent, the difficult, obscure truths that lie locked within our minds. Out of a recognition of the inherent limitations of *la parole* springs an appreciation of its suggestive as opposed to mimetic power, of the need for a creative 'distance' or *espace* in which the individual word will have freedom to manœuvre. Indeed, this may be related to what was said in Chapter 4, regarding Joubert's apparent preference for the artistic process itself as opposed to concern with the finished art object, a recognition of the value of *l'indéterminé* in art, of *le vague*: 'On pourrait déterminer avec précision beaucoup d'occasions où il faut employer le vague' (*C* i. 402), wrote Joubert, who gave his supreme approbation to ancient Greek authors '[qui] disaient toujours la vérité, même solide, avec des paroles flottantes' (*C* ii. 520).

Despite Joubert's dislike of Kant there are moments when this understanding of the nature of language and its relation to *le beau* and *le vrai* remind us of what the German philosopher has to say in the *Critique of Judgement* about the way the imagination produces 'symbols' when it has to deal with experience of the sublime. Kant believed that, when confronted with the sublime, we are forced to use the expressions we employ in understanding the world but that we use them to signify a feeling for another order of things altogether, that we make aesthetic and epistemological capital out of the very inadequacy of the language at our disposal. The poet or metaphysicians' 'analogical use of language produces symbols by which we try to grasp in imagination thoughts and feelings which escape the conditions and determining knowledge of objects'.[24]

---

[22] Ibid. 471.
[23] Pascal, *Pensées*, 157.
[24] Hamilton, 53.

For a word to function as a symbol it must have space to suggest, to breathe, to resemble only in so far as a dream resembles reality. 'Il faut qu'un spectacle soit beau', Joubert writes, 'qu'on y croie imaginer et rêver ce qu'on y entend, ce qu'on y voit, que tout nous y semble un beau songe' (C i. 370). As Jean-Louis Chrétien comments, 'Rendre totale la précision de l'œuvre, c'est la paralyser et paralyser l'âme qui la contemple.'[25] It is much better to *désigner vaguement*, to *faire bruire*, to leave something to the imagination of the reader: 'Peut-être est-il vrai que l'esprit du lecteur aime à achever et qu'il ne faut lui donner que ce qu'il faut pour achever facilement et être rappellé de lui-même à l'ouvrage, etc. Je finis trop' (C i. 47). The type of art envisioned here is of the kind that suggests, that does not impose its meaning tyrannically on the reader, an art '[qui] ne soit que la trace d'un mouvement de la pensée, dont la spatialité et la mobilité propres lui importent plus que le produit'.[26]

In the light of this emphasis upon the suggestive power of the imagination, Chrétien is undoubtedly correct to describe it as 'le commencement de la vision béatifique', and his insistence that Joubert regarded it, not as a 'vision dégradée', but as a 'vision inchoative, le véritable commencement de cette vision plénière', fits in well with the important role of the poet in the Ficinian ascent and Joubert's high regard for his inspired character.[27]

Chrétien deduces from this, however, that in Joubert's ontological scheme the imagination is to be regarded as superior to '[le] seul entendement', yet in Chapter 4 we quoted a number of entries which state quite clearly that the reverse is true. In Chapter 6, therefore, we shall look again at the status of the imagination in the *Carnets* to try to discover if a resolution of these apparent contradictions is possible and examine how Joubert's aesthetic affects his judgement of individual works of art.

[25] Chrétien, 491.
[26] Ibid. 472.
[27] Ibid. 471.

6
Imagination and the Form of the Carnets

BONALD

The status of the imagination in the *Carnets* is probably best examined in the context of Joubert's reading of works by the vicomte de Bonald and Malebranche's *De la recherche de la vérité*.

Joubert first read Bonald during the early 1800s and the *Carnets* record the substantial measure of disagreement that existed between these two political allies.[1] One of the main points of contention arose over the related questions of literature, language and the role of the imagination. Bonald held that literature was the expression of 'society', but Joubert believed that 'il y a des livres tellement beaux que la littérature n'y est que l'expression de ceux qui les ont faits' (C ii. 522). This was written in November 1805, but it merely serves to confirm remarks made reading the *Théorie du pouvoir* in 1802:

> La société exporte par et pour les individus et non les individus pour et seulement en vue de la société. Les poètes ont cent fois plus de bon sens que les philosophes, et ceux-là en cherchant le beau rencontrent plus de vérités que ceux-ci en cherchant le vrai.
>
> (C i. 327)

Here again, we meet Joubert's growing confidence in the creative powers of the individual, of the poet, discovered in the context of reading Bacon and Ficino as well as the implication that spiritual truth is more easily apprehended by the artist than by the philosopher.

When it came to Bonald's theory of language, its origin and development, there was equal disagreement. This theory was first

---

[1] Like Bonald, Joubert worked for a number of years as an 'inspecteur général' for the Université Impériale.

outlined between 1800 and 1802 in the *Essai analytique, Du divorce*, and the *Législation primitive*, and received its most extensive exposition in the *Recherches philosophiques sur les premiers objets des connaissances morales* of 1818. Basically, Bonald held that, without the spoken word, thought was impossible. Consequently, Man could not have invented language, for, in order to do so, he would have had to have conceived the idea of inventing it. He could not have had this idea without formulating it in words in his mind; therefore, language was of divine origin and logically beyond the inventive capacities of Man. Bonald also believed that language was responsible for the creation among men of civilized society. If he had adhered to Condillac's or Gérando's belief that language was man-made, then it would have followed that society was an equally temporal, mundane affair in which anybody might try his hand at law-making or constitutional improvisation, a point of view with which he had little sympathy. He believed in the existence of a 'langue primitive', given by God to Man, and that the fossil of this language could one day be discovered through the science of etymology. He did not believe that a word created an idea but, rather, that it revealed the innate idea to itself and to the world; in this he came close to the theory of knowledge outlined by Plato in the *Cratylus*. There is surprisingly little overt criticism by Joubert of Bonald's theories of language in the reading of the 1800s and, for a guide to his attitude, it is better to turn to the remarks he made while reading Condillac and Bacon.

While reading Condillac in November 1801 Joubert had agreed that the 'faculté d'inventer les langues est une industrie naturelle à notre intelligence' (C i. 306) and, although he seemed prepared at one point to admit the existence of a divinely inspired Adamic language, he described this strategy merely as a 'convenient hypothesis', thereby joining Court de Gébelin, Hugh Blair, and Condillac himself in their concern for the specifically human attributes of language.[2]

A vivid illustration of Joubert's dissatisfaction with Bonald's handling of these issues can be found by consulting his own copy of the *Recherches philosophiques* at Bussy.[3] We recall the apocryphal account of the vandal Joubert, tearing pages from the books in his library, but the fate of this particular work makes Chateaubriand's story sound a little less fantastic. Opening volume i of this edition we find that

[2] See C i. 417.
[3] L. de Bonald, *Recherches philosophiques sur les premiers objets des connaissances morales* (2 vols.; Paris, 1818; 2nd edn., 1826). Joubert owned a copy of the 1818 edn.

pages 188–230 have been crossed out with a thick, red crayon and on page 230, in the top left-hand corner, the figures '(42p ...?)' can be seen. These pages constitute Bonald's critique of Condillac's theory on the origin of language; rather than bothering to refute his arguments, Joubert simply indicates their inadequacy with a stroke of the pen.

Joubert also found fault with Bonald over his attitude to the imagination. For Bonald, the development of the imagination was an initial but inferior stage in the growth of the human mind, most visible in children and the mentally deformed. As Henri Moulinié interprets:

L'enfant ... n'a que la faculté d'imaginer. Il a des images, comme en témoignent ses gestes, il n'a pas d'idées, faute de mots pour les exprimer. Il *imagine*, il ne peut idéer ... chez lui, comme chez les peuples primitifs, l'imagination précède l'entendement. C'est donc au seul exercice de l'entendement que Bonald limite la nécessité de la parole pour penser.[4]

As we have seen, however, Joubert was prepared to give far greater scope to the imagination, and it is fascinating to find him outlining his thoughts on this matter in the margins of his copy of Bonald's *Recherches philosophiques* of 1818. If we turn to volume ii of this work, we find that the margins of several pages devoted to a definition of the imagination have been covered in Joubert's handwriting. This is particularly interesting, not only because the remarks correspond precisely with entries in the *Carnets* for 21 April 1818, but because they seem to prove conclusively that Joubert's conception of the imagination had remained virtually unchanged in the decades since 1800.[5] Numbering his notes 1–7, Joubert summarized a lifetime's thought in the margins of a book written by a man 'qui écrit les yeux fermés'.[6]

I. dites = l'imaginative plutôt que l'imagination = ou Art d'imager. la première en effet est une faculté grossière et presque matérielle qui est surtout dominante dans ceux qui ont peu d'esprit et un esprit peu actif—faculté molle qui reçoit et ne produit rien. L'autre est active ... elle met en mouvement ... formes ou couleurs tout ce qui peut-être pensé.
II. Plait à celle là et tout ce qui soit aisément maitrisé.

---

[4] H. Moulinié, *De Bonald* (Paris, 1916), 230.
[5] See *C* ii. 872.
[6] Bonald, *Recherches philosophiques* (1818 edn.), ii. 192–3. Cf. Saint-Martin's attitude to Milton 'livré à son "imaginative"' in *Le Ministère de l'homme-esprit* (Paris, 1802), 383; quoted by A. Becq, *Genèse de l'esthétique française moderne: De la raison classique à l'imagination créatrice, 1680–1814* (2 vols.; Pisa, 1984), 865. It should be noted that Joubert shared this hostility to Milton, who was culpable, in his eyes, of employing 'l'imaginative' in 'le poème épique'.

3. Ainsi par exemple ... sont de l'écume ou des ... de la /terre [—] entre aisément dans l'imagination qui est délicate, qui aime les choses déliées et qui se détourne de là avec dégout, avec mépris, avec horreur et nous observerons ici que l'irreligion, le matérialisme qui exercent puissamment et augmentent même ...
4. l'imaginative répond à la = phantasia = des grecs et l'imagination à l'ingénium .= des Latins = ingenium cui sit.
5. Les enfans et même quelquefois les imbéciles ont beaucoup d'*Imaginative*— les grands poètes ont beaucoup d'*Imagination*.
6. en laissant dominer son *imaginative* on fait des ouvrages *fantasques*, grotesques, lugubres, bouffons, des ruines de Volney, des Candides, en se livrant à une heureuse imagination on fait *Télémaque*.
7. l'imaginative est propre à se représenter l'enfer et l'imagination a concevoir le paradis—on peut employer avec succès l'imaginative dans le *drame* mais non dans le poème épique.

Other pages of the *Recherches philosophiques* are equally revealing. At one point Bonald indulges in an attack upon materialists like La Mettrie and Cabanis '[qui] se *figure* un limon qui bouillone aux rayons d'un soleil ardent; des corpuscules qui s'agitent'. Here 'l'imagination trouve la pâture qu'elle demande': 'L'imagination se *figure* aisément tout cela, et l'on peut assurer que nos adversaires n'y voient pas autre chose, et qu'ils ne font que revêtir de grands mots de forts petites images.'[7]

For someone like Joubert, whose study of thinkers such as Bonnet, Nollet, and Ocellus had contributed profoundly to his personal aesthetics, such an attack must have been viewed with mixed feelings and, possibly, some amusement. Whatever the case, he contented himself by writing: '($N^A b\dagger = \dagger$se figurer$\dagger = \dagger$)' in the margin, repeating exactly the same formula a few pages later, taking from this expression precisely the meaning Bonald meant him to take, but viewing it, probably, from a positive angle that would have horrified the vicomte. As with Condillac and Locke, Joubert used his source to make it speak against itself for his own purposes.

The Testimony of Malebranche

In 1804 Joubert undertook a critical reading of Malebranche's *De la recherche de la vérité* and found that, like Bonald, 'Toutes ses explications sont d'un matérialiste, quoique tous ses sentimens et toute

---

[7] Bonald, *Recherches philosophiques* (1818 edn.), ii. 179.

sa doctrine fussent entièrement opposées au matérialisme' (C i. 437). When Leibniz had given a similarly critical reading to this work, he had noted on the flyleaf of *his* copy that 'l'auteur est fertile en conceptions et malheureux en preuves',[8] and Joubert's criticism of Malebranche as a 'visionnaire de raisonnement' of his 'abstractions qui le trompèrent' is in the same mould (C i. 436).

His opening attack, indeed, recalls his appreciation of Leibniz's belief that it is the understanding or mind, the 'entendement' itself, that is innate in Man: 'Mais à quoi bon chercher une essence à l'esprit. Il est lui-même essence. Il n'est qu'essence ...' (C i. 437), while a series of quotations from Malebranche, jotted down during a slightly later reading of the same work, and not reproduced by Beaunier, includes paragraphs dealing with philosophical positions rejected by both men: 'La IVe opinion est que l'esprit n'a besoin que de soi même pour appercevoir les objets; et qu'il peut en se considérant et ses propres perfections découvrir toutes les choses qui sont au dehors.'[9] Joubert then noted, possibly with some satisfaction, Malebranche's comment on the following page: 'il me semble que c'est être bien hardi que de vouloir soutenir cette pensée'.[10] As we saw earlier, however, Joubert did not appreciate the way Malebranche made ideas 'des êtres réels': 'Platon à qui on l'a tant reproché n'avait pas à beaucoup près été si hardi. Ce qu'il ne donnoit que comme une manière d'expliquer, celui-ci l'affirme comme une vérité, indubitable' (C i. 438).

We saw, in the context of Joubert's reading of Bonald, how beauty in the hands of poets was just as profound a source of truth as *le vrai* was for philosophers and this partly explains his disgust at the fact that:

Le mot de *beau* pris substantivement ne se trouve pas une seule fois dans Malebranche. Il paroît qu'il n'en avoit jamais eu l'idée et que, en effet, le beau étant le bien de l'imagination et cette faculté lui paraissant essentiellement nuisible, son bien devoit lui paroître un véritable mal.

(C i. 441)

Joubert pinpointed the reasons for Malebranche's suspicion of the imagination with some precision in his copy.[11] There he would have read that the scholastics believed:

---

[8] A. Robinet, *Malebranche et Leibniz, relations personelles* (Paris, 1955), 152.
[9] N. Malebranche, *Œuvres complètes*, ed. G. Rodis-Lewis (20 vols.; Paris, 1962), i. 433. Joubert used the 1674 edn. (Paris, André Pralard). MSS Bussy.
[10] *Œuvres complètes*, i. 434. MSS Bussy.
[11] *De la recherche de la verité* (Paris, 1764), bk. 6, ch. iii, p. 30.

6. IMAGINATION AND THE FORM OF THE CARNETS

qu'il y a dans les corps quelques entitez distinguées de la matière; n'ayant point d'idée distincte de ces entitez, on peut facilement s'imaginer qu'elles sont les véritables ou les principales causes des effets que l'on voit arriver.

Here, Joubert wrote, we have the cause which determined him to attack the imagination: 'La philosophie de l'école lui en paroissoit pleine.' But this was not only an inadequate reason, as far as he was concerned, but poor erudition: 'Au contraire', he continued, 'cette école avoit admis une foule d'êtres inimaginables' (C i. 443).

Under this onslaught on the faculty of the imagination Joubert was prepared to admit, however, that there were many people 'qui imaginent mal', but, rather than use this word of them at all, we see him solving this problem by relating it to his distinction between *phantaisie* and *imagination*: 'Ceux là n'imaginent pas par l'imagination, mais par combinaison. Ils imaginent sans imagination' (C i. 444), he wrote. He was also ever ready to catch Malebranche out in the very exercise of the faculty he claimed to despise, focusing with relish on the latter's relation of the Fall: 'Voila les douleurs et les plaisirs (deux modes) devenus par nécessité des êtres poétiques et actifs, sous la plume de cet homme qui a tant décrié sans distinction toutes les sortes d'imagination!' (C i. 446-7). Perhaps it was time, now, to distinguish where Malebranche himself had failed to do so: 'Il paroit qu'au fonds il n'étoit ennemi que de l'imagination qui admet trop les êtres logiques et de celle qui dans la pratique traite les phantômes comme de solides réalités. etc.' (C i. 447). His objections to Malebranche's view of this faculty culminate in the following remarks:

> Il ne prend jamais l'imagination que comme une faculté corporelle et la mémoire des images etc. La profondeur et la netteté des vertiges de l'imagination dépend de la force des esprits animaux et de la constitution des fibres du cerveau.
>
> (C i. 447)

What! Joubert exclaims, 'jamais de l'âme et de l'âme seule? Est-il bon, en métaphysique, de tout expliquer ainsi par la matière seule, par les fluides et les solides?' (C i. 447).[12]

Attitudes such as these must have seemed a complete negation of all the theoretical ground he had covered since the early 1780s, and Joubert's revenge was typically scathing. Beside Fénelon's candle and the pure light of Plato, Malebranche was 'cette allumette!' (C i. 441).

---

[12] Cf. *Œuvres complètes*, i. 192.

Yet Joubert's defence of the imagination is not, as we have suggested, entirely unambiguous. J. M. Cocking has rightly insisted on the partiality involved in setting aside Joubert's religious and moral ideas, stating that he was

> primarily a Christian Platonist with a Jesuit background and though he proscribed moral didacticism in art ... still expected his artists and their creations to be morally wholesome. He maintained, moreover, for most of his life quite clearly, the dependence of the imaginative upon the intellectual; in our intuitions of God, he said, 'l'esprit' continues when imagination stops short.[13]

Cocking's last remark is an obvious reference to the entry quoted in Chapter 4 in which the imagination is compared unfavourably to the power of 'l'esprit' to 'imagine' God. This is an idea that can be found as early as 1799, when Joubert writes that 'Par delà ce qu'on voit, l'esprit s'y élance toujours' (C i. 220). The imagination is an undeniably powerful and sometimes creative faculty but, as it is dependent on the organ of sight, it has its limitations and must remain, ultimately, tributary to the purely intellectual capabilities of the *esprit*. This, it may be noted, is a limitation his 'imagination' shares with that of Diderot.[14] As Joubert was later to insist: 'Dans le ciel personne ne sera poète, car nous ne pourrons rien imaginer au delà de ce que nous verrons ... Cultivons donc l'intelligence, cette éternelle faculté qui sera toujours exercée et qui suffira au bonheur' (C ii. 657). In May 1796 Joubert noted that 'L'imagination est l'œil de l'âme' (C i. 124), and this gives P. A. Ward sufficient grounds for linking him to Coleridge and other English romantics, but, if we glance further down the page in Beaunier's edition, we notice that he adds: 'La raison. L'imagination est sa dame d'atours' (C i. 124), proving that it is dangerous not to recognize the disjunctive nature of Joubert's equations, since this may lead to unbalanced, partial judgements.[15] Just as, in Latin, we have to search a little for the verb which will give the sentence its correct meaning, so the sequence of Joubert's thought is not always immediately obvious: 'Il y a des vérités qu'on a besoin de colorer pour les rendre

---

[13] J. C. Cocking, 'Joseph Joubert and the Critical Tradition', *French Studies*, 37 (1983), 220–1 (a review of P. A. Ward's *Critical Tradition*).

[14] D. Diderot, *Œuvres complètes* (Paris, 1875), ii. *Rêve d'Alembert*, 178: 'L'imagination, c'est la mémoire des formes et des couleurs.'

[15] Cf. C ii. 511: 'Tant que la raison la retient par quelques fils, l'imagination peut s'élever impunément.' See also Becq, *Genèse de l'esthétique*, 874, who quotes a review in the *Archives littéraires de l'Europe* of a work by Th. Barnes, who describes the imagination as 'la servante de la maison, toujours aux ordres de l'esprit'.

visibles. Tout ce qui tient à l'imagination surtout ne peut avoir d'existence extérieure que par les formes et les couleurs' (C ii. 578). Just as we might emphasize the positive orientation of the imagination towards the creation of a formal, coloured artefact, it is equally necessary to confront a statement like this with the existence of God, who cannot be coloured and made visible as in a child's reading book. A part of spiritual reality, or, rather, *the* ultimate goal of spiritual reality, remains stubbornly beyond the figurative capabilities of mankind. In a sense, Joubert may be said to be sensitive both to 'la perspective aristotélicienne [qui] permet ... de concevoir cet aspect actif ... de l'imagination' as well as to that of Plato, for whom 'l'idée existe réellement et préalablement en tant qu'intelligible; aussi est-ce la raison qui est seule concernée et qui la contemple'.[16]

Indeed, in the context of reading Malebranche, and despite his criticism of the metaphysician's hostility towards the imagination, we can find a straightforward approval of the need to ratify the evidence of the senses and imagination by referring it to the intellect:

Voici cependant un correctif qu'il faut admettre; 'Les idées des sens et de l'imagination ne sont distinctes (peut-être il vaudroit mieux dire: ne sont nettes) que par la conformité qu'elles ont avec les idées de la pure intellection.' Cela est fort bien observé, et fort bien dit et fort exact.—Ajoutez ce qu'il ajoute. 'C'est ... l'idée qui règle l'image.'

(C i. 438)

If we turn back now to Joubert's reading of Bonald, it becomes clear why he could often find sympathy with criticism of 'des hommes à imaginations'.[17] Imagination is not the totally unambiguous aid to spirituality it might at first have seemed, and, although Joubert might have written freely of the need 'à rendre sensible tout ce qui est intellectuel' (C ii. 493), he was equally capable of underlining, in his copy of Bonald's *Recherches philosophiques*, the following statement:

Mais c'est une vérité importante de l'analyse de l'esprit humain ... que ces deux facultés d'idéer ou concevoir, et d'*imaginer*, sont distinctes l'une de l'autre, à tel point que nous ne saurions imaginer ce que nous concevons, ni concevoir ce que nous imaginons; ou, en d'autres termes, que nous ne pourrions nous former des images de nos idées, ni des idées de nos images.[18]

[16] Becq, *Genèse de l'esthétique*, 429.
[17] Cf. C i. 303: 'Prendre garde aux éblouissemens de l'imagination. Y renoncer, s'y soustraire, s'en défier.'
[18] Bonald, *Recherches philosophiques* (1818 edn.), ii. 78–9.

Nor, for that matter, given Joubert's own remarks, is it merely coincidental that, a little further on in the same volume, we can find apparent agreement with Bonald's belief that we know God only by means of our reason: 'Mais aujourd'hui ce n'est pas là ce qu'on appelle connoître, on ne croit plus à ses propres idées, on veut des images.'[19] Most striking of all, however, is what happens when we look at Joubert's famous distinction between *l'imagination* and *l'imaginative* in the light of this train of argument. Critics eager to pin the badge of originality on Joubert's lapel concentrate blindly upon the differences between active and passive imagination, ignoring an essential element of his equation. Joubert describes *l'imagination* as a 'faculté intellectuelle' and as 'l'imaginative de l'esprit' (C ii. 563). Here even the much vaunted imagination becomes a passive function of the intellect, mere phantasy in the presence of *esprit*.

We recall, then, the kinds of works produced by the creative imagination listed by Joubert in the margins of his copy of Bonald and note that it is responsible for *Télémaque*. No mention is made of Chateaubriand, and, in this connection, it is worth remembering that Joubert's idol among the French poets was La Fontaine. Similarly, if we look at his copy of Rivarol's *Discours préliminaire*, we discover that the following remark has been heavily underlined: 'Enfin, lorsqu'on parle du côté idéal des choses, on n'entend pas le côté qui fait image, mais au contraire celui qu'on ne sauroit peindre, le côté intellectuel.'[20] This being so, before undertaking any kind of construction, be it edifice, poem, play, or journal, we must ask ourselves:

Si le plan doit s'établir par les tons et par les images, ou par les pensées et les sentences propres au sujet et qui en sont en lui les points fixes. L'esprit (en ce cas) tient-il plus de la nature de l'oreille et de l'œil que de celle de tout le corps, de l'homme entier? Enfin faut-il commencer par les tours (*turres*) ou par le sol et les pavés? Grande question!

(C i. 434)

We are reminded here of Joubert's liking for Leibniz's 'atomes insécables', their creation of limits beyond which the imagination cannot reach, limits upon which he might build something solid and enduring; his recognition of the power of eye and ear, but also his attention to the

---

[19] Ibid. 85.
[20] A. Rivarol, *Discours préliminaire du nouveau dictionnaire de la langue française* (Paris, 1797), 26. Joubert's copy may be found at Bussy.

6. IMAGINATION AND THE FORM OF THE CARNETS

entire physiology of Man. By the time he came to read Malebranche a little later in the year, his *image* and *tour*, his image *of* the tower, had become subservient to, had transformed themselves into, idea and geometrical shape, the idea *of* a geometrical shape:

> Et l'image d'un quarré, par exemple, que l'imagination trace dans le cerveau n'est juste et bien faite que par la conformité qu'elle a avec l'idée d'un quarré que nous concevons par pure intellection. Il falloit ajouter que la figure même du quarré n'est juste que par là, ou par cette conformité. Cela est vrai et très fécond en conséquences théoriques, pratiques, métaphysiques et poétiques.
>
> (C i. 438)

Here, we are confronted once more with the competing claims of *gravure* and *peinture*. In Chapter 5 Joubert was observed promoting the figurative capacities of *tableau* along with those of the engraving, but this entry, where the '*image* d'un quarré' depends upon the '*idée* d'un quarré' for a sense of its own accuracy calls that interpretation into question. Indeed it suggests that we need to look again at Joubert's understanding of the elements that constitute a painting and, in particular, at the role of colour.

Shortly before his entry of 18 May 1800, in which he compared different types of ideas to paintings and engravings, Joubert noted that 'dans les arts, non seulement la peinture, mais aussi le simple dessin, n'existe que par les couleurs, ainsi que l'écriture. Rien ne peut être séparé et distinct à nos yeux que par deux ou plusieurs couleurs' (C i. 247). In Joubert's hands colour performs exactly the same function as the lines and contours that gave shape to the universe in Chapter 4. Colour for Joubert is not primarily any particular colour, red, blue, white, or black, but, like line, that which *distinguishes* one thing from another. Thus he is able to conceive of both painting *and* engraving in terms of the 'colours' out of which they are made. It is possible, writes Joubert in 1802 'que les couleurs ne soient pas les mêmes pour tous les yeux, mais les *rapports* d'une couleur à une autre, leur *opposition* ou leur *harmonie* se font uniformément sentir à tout le monde' (C i. 350). Frequently, giving colour and form to an object are seen as virtually synonymous activities: 'Rendre coloré, *ou* figuré ce qui est diaphane ...' (C ii. 591), he writes, and, to the extent that it may be possible to consider *couleur* as the particular *quality* of an object, then one might be justified in substituting one word for the other in the following entry, without betraying Joubert's idea: 'Quelquefois la qualité peut tenir lieu de forme pour distinguer une matière de toute autre. Par exemple, un morceau d'or ou de diamant incrustés dans un mur s'en détachent par leur éclat' (C ii. 583).

Colour, for Joubert, includes black and white, light and shadow. 'Le simple dessin', he remarks, 'n'existe que par les couleurs' and in this context *couleur* comes close to identification with *ombre*. The abbé Nollet had written that 'l'ombre n'est donc autre chose à proprement parler, qu'une lumière éteinte, par l'interposition d'un corps opaque',[21] and this opaque body well defines the necessary 'matter' of the following *pensée*: 'Si la lumière entre dans les couleurs—qui néanmoins ne deviennent visibles que lorsqu'elles sont fixées, arrêtées, agglomérées, par une matière propre à produire cet effet' (C i. 248). Such an interpretation of the word 'colour' throws a rather different light on the apparent promotion of *tableau* in the *pensée* of 18 May. It was, perhaps, due to this understanding that Joubert was able to pass so quickly and easily from *tableau* to *estampe* and back again and, through this subtle reciprocal process, actually weaken the traditional barriers between ideas that were believed to originate in the senses and those that were thought to be innate, imprinted on the mind by God. Joubert uses two *different* terms, *tableau* and *estampe*, to typify them, but it is what they have *in common* that is of vital importance and is insisted upon by the author: the key word here is *aussi*. Behind *tableau* lurks the conventional notion of a coloured painting; behind the more representational, less imitative outlines of *estampe* is the idea of *couleur* as *ombre*.

It is important to recognize, therefore, that what Joubert has to say about the creative imagination complements rather than contradicts his enthusiasm for *esprit*. What he is most concerned with is defining their relevant spheres of activity. Imagination is of this material world, producing images which enable us to get some kind of perspective on immaterial reality. *L'esprit*, on the other hand, provides us with an intellectual diagram. Yet its figures, lines, and numbers work symbolically just as the images of the imagination do, both engraving and painting providing us, in their different ways, with a sketch or *esquisse* of a reality that lies beyond the senses.

It is perhaps easier for us to reconcile Joubert's attitude to the imagination with his understanding of the human intellect if we

---

[21] Nollet, v. 79. Cf. C i. 294: 'Pourquoi se fait-il une ombre? Parce que la lumière est interceptée', and C ii. 481: 'Partout où entre un corps, un objet, la lumière est diminuée . . .'

6. IMAGINATION AND THE FORM OF THE CARNETS

recognize that during the eighteenth century a dynamic conception of *raison* and *esprit*, evolved in earlier centuries, still pertained and that, to Joubert, the gap between the *entendement* and the *imagination* was not as wide as we may suppose.

Annie Becq, for example, has proved that a dynamic interpretation of these words was quite common during the seventeenth and eighteenth centuries. In this respect she capitalized on Jeanne Haight's study of these concepts, which was inspired, in turn, by remarks of Jules Brody about Boileau. For Boileau, *raison* is 'a kind of intellectual "sense"', an 'eye of the mind', which includes 'an intuitive and feeling aspect enabling man to make contact with eternal truth'.[22] It is more than likely that Joubert was alive to the spontaneous capacities of *raison* and *esprit*, to this sense of creativity implicit in the seventeenth century's understanding of these words.

What we may have in the *Carnets*, therefore, is a growing appreciation of the independent powers of imagination, which, nevertheless, sometimes continues to operate *within* the context of traditional seventeenth- and eighteenth-century notions of 'la raison créatrice'. This at least is an attempt at synthesis of which Joubert would probably have approved. The *Carnets* are a sometimes bewildering kaleidoscope of these competing visions of the world, and to dismiss their author as either reactionary Platonist, half-hearted sensualist, or confused Cartesian is to ignore an extremely intelligent testimony to the richness of the complex experience that constitutes the closing years of the eighteenth century and the opening years of the nineteenth in art and philosophy.

The Form of the Carnets

J. M. Cocking rightly links Joubert's Cartesian pride in the intellect to a desire for moral wholesomeness in the arts, and an examination of this leads us again to an appreciation of the fragmentary style of the *Carnets*. The early 'Éloge de Pigalle' forms a marvellous paradigm of the competing aesthetics touched on in preceding pages, but, before we look at this in any detail and note the general importance of Joubert's

---

[22] See Becq, *Genèse de l'esthétique*, 647–51, and J. Haight, *The Concept of Reason in French Classical Literature* (Toronto, 1982), 137. She quotes J. Brody, *Boileau and Longinus* (Geneva, 1958), 84–7.

interest in painting and sculpture as a key to the understanding of his own art, it is appropriate to consider his attitude to the theatre.

Joubert did not like the theatre much. He approved of Corneille and found him spiritually uplifting, but Racine, 'le Virgile des ignorans' (C ii. 560), although recognized as a fine poet, was dismissed probably because the pictures of tortured love presented by the great seventeenth-century playwright unleashed unwonted passion in the soul of the spectator. Racine was morally unhygienic. Rather than trace this prejudice laboriously over page after page of the *Carnets*, however, I should like, instead, to focus on one example which forms a stimulating parallel to remarks Joubert makes about some of the other arts, sculpture in particular. Beaunier has been unable to date this passage and consigns it to the final pages of his edition (C ii. 933-4).

Far from being the description of great theatre, it recounts, initially with some enthusiasm, what can only be described as an equestrian spectacle, a mixture of circus and vaudeville acts which took place in the 'amphithéâtre anglois, rue et fauxbourg du Temple'. Its star was a certain 'sieur Astley, fils', an athlete of some talent, 'qui dansera le *Sérieux*, et fera l'exercice du drapeau: le tout au grand galop'. On the whole, Joubert liked what he saw and for interesting reasons: 'J'aime ces spectacles qui me représentent une nature fantastique, soit qu'ils embélissent la nature réelle comme les décorations d'un opéra, soit qu'ils en offrent les ridicules comme la danse des chiens' (C ii. 933). What is noteworthy about this is that no attempt is made to imitate reality: fantasy prevails. Here the old warning to actors never to act with children or animals is happily ignored. If the actor were to be upstaged by them, we feel Joubert would approve. Why this should be so becomes evident when we turn the page and read his reservations with regard to the performance of one particular species:

Les tableaux que présente le singe sont beaucoup moins intéressans. Cet animal a trop de traits communs avec l'homme pour que l'imitation qu'il fait de nous ait cette pureté d'illusion qui dans toutes les imitations est la cause principale du plaisir qu'elles produisent. Trop de réalité se mêle à ces sortes de représentations. D'ailleurs cet animal en copiant l'homme le rend plutôt difforme et vil que risible. En nous copiant les petits chiens ne rendent sensibles que l'extravagance de nos modes et de nos manières, au lieu que le singe dont les traits expriment fortement un naturel vicieux à la manière des hommes, n'est propre qu'à nous attrister par cette image de notre dépravation. Les premiers dans leurs exercices sont encore intérressants par l'expression de leur docilité timide qui perce à chaque minute; l'autre ne nous montre qu'un impudent qui se satisfait lui-même en se livrant au pire de tous les génies qui est celui de l'imitation.

(C ii. 934)

This outright condemnation of mimesis probably means the passage was composed around the same time as the remarks directed against it in his notes on 'La Bienveillance universelle'.[23]

Joubert objects to the antics of these monkeys because there are too many points of resemblance with human beings. There is scope only for servile copying of the type which Joubert came to reject. It is significant that the word *image* does not occur in this passage, owing to a lack of 'distance' between man and monkey and the resulting absence of perspective from which images might operate. There is also a very seventeenth-century concern for the indignity inflicted upon Man by such unwholesome caricature. It is instructive to compare this attitude to that of the Platonist Villoteau, writing in the preface to his *Recherches sur l'analogie de la musique avec les arts*. In a note he writes:

Je prie le lecteur d'approfondir la maxime de Platon, que les mœurs des pièces de théâtre doivent être plus parfaites que celles du parterre; maxime qui ne peut être contestée par ceux qui font du théâtre une école de mœurs. Je crois qu'il y découvrira la pleine réfutation de ce beau système inventé par Aristote, que le théâtre purge les passions par les passions mêmes. Aristote a pris le théâtre tel qu'il étoit de son temps, et l'a voulu justifier; ce qu'il a fait avec plus de subtilité que de vérité. Platon a considéré le théâtre tel qu'il doit être, et n'y a trouvé nul trait de ressemblance avec ce qu'il est.[24]

There is a request here for the type of theatre, if theatre there must be, typified by that of Corneille, a theatre of heroes and heroines suffering nobly for the edification of the audience; the imitation of ordinary men and women is outlawed, not simply because it runs the danger of stimulating the passions, or providing onlookers with bad examples they might inadvertently or deliberately try to copy in their own lives, but because it calls into question the moral integrity of the actor himself, of the actor as human being. It is the fear that the impersonation of a bad or inferior character will have a harmful effect upon the impersonator. Evidence that this attitude, common to both Joubert and Villoteau, is rooted in seventeenth-century aesthetics can be found by looking at Joubert's copy of Boileau's *Art poétique*. There, we find

[23] See C i. 43–56.
[24] Villoteau, *Recherches*, i, p. xl.

'Chant III', l. 352, underlined in red wax crayon; the passage leading up to it involves a description of ancient Greek comedy:

> La Comedie apprit à rire sans aigreur, 350
> Sans fiel et sans venin sut instruire et reprendre
> Et plus innocemment dans les vers de Ménandre. 352

This line, which particularly attracted Joubert's attention, has an important commentary attached in a footnote that is worth quoting in full:

> La Comédie a eu trois âges, ou trois états differens chez les Grecs. Dans l'ancienne Comédie on se donnoit la liberté, non seulement de représenter des avantures véritables et connues, mais de nommer publiquement les gens. Socrate lui-même s'est entendu nommer; et s'est vû jouer sur le Théâtre d'Athènes. Cette licence fut reprimée par l'autorité des Magistrats; et les Comédiens n'osant plus désigner les gens par leur nom firent paroître des masques ressemblans aux personnes qu'ils jouoient, ou les designerent de quelque autre manière semblable. Ce fut la Comédie moiënne. Ce nouvel abus presque aussi grand que le premier, fut encore défendu: on ne marqua plus les noms ni les visages; et la Comédie se réduit aux règles de la bienséance. C'est la Comédie nouvelle, dont Ménandre fut l'Auteur, du temps d'Alexandre le Grand.[25]

The tragedies of Corneille, the comedies of Menander, might pass muster, but, on the whole, Joubert was of the opinion that 'les spectacles physiques n'apellent point les idées morales'.[26]

The same opinion underlies Joubert's general dislike of the novel. In 1806 he sent an 'invective contre les romans' to Mme de la Briche, believing that the frivolities of Mme Cottin and the more serious work of Mme de Staël represented a gross distortion of reality: 'Dans les nouveaux romans ... la vie humaine est une toile rouge et noire,' he wrote with unconscious foresight; 'Parlons raison. Quand la fiction n'est pas plus belle que le monde, elle n'a pas le droit d'exister' (E 210).

This is an idea that recurs in many of Joubert's statements about sculpture and painting. Particularly interesting is his 'Éloge de Pigalle' of 1786, which shows the same concern for seventeenth-century standards of good taste, as well as a desire to reflect an Ideal Beauty or Morality, that is evident in his remarks about the theatre and the novel. Also present, however briefly, is a third element which, as we saw, only

---

[25] Œuvres de M. Boileau-Despréaux, avec des éclaircissements historiques (new rev. edn., 2 vols.; Paris, 1745), i. 289. Joubert's copy is at Bussy.

[26] MSS Carnets, unpublished fragment, dated 7 Nov. 1799.

6. IMAGINATION AND THE FORM OF THE CARNETS

came into its own in the context of his reading of Condillac. We find a plea on behalf of the autonomy of the art object, for an understanding of the idea that 'une image est comme une image peut être'; a statue by Pigalle:

honore à jamais et le pays et le talent qui la créa. Ce n'est pas là simplement une image, mais un objet réel. Ce n'est pas simplement un ouvrage, mais un être qui prend dans l'univers une place, au rang des êtres véritables, et s'y maintient comme un sujet éternel d'observation et d'étude.

(*E* 42)

This independence, however, is compromised by Pigalle's lack of *pudeur*; on seeing many of his statues we experience the same kind of discomfort produced in us by the excesses of the vaudeville theatre. Indeed the vocabulary Joubert uses here is applicable to *both* art forms. We experience 'le mécontentement que vous cause la peinture de la difformité toutes les fois qu'elle n'est pour nous qu'un *étonnant spectacle*. Avec une idée de plus, Pigalle aurait toujours aisément mérité tous les *suffrages*' (*E* 43). Here, there is yet another request for a suggestive image at the expense of a simple copy, an 'idée de plus' that will reflect a certain idealism. His statue of Voltaire contains the 'trop de réalité' harmful to theatre audiences: 'la décrépitude y est peinte avec excès' (*E* 43). Joubert would make a few slight alterations and render the hero more Cornelian: 'en nous montrant son corps usé par ses travaux et par l'étude encore plus que par le temps', seeming to say to us 'Soyez justes et ne me refusez pas ma louange, car vous voyez de quel prix j'achetai la gloire' (*E* 44).

In contrast with the great sculptors of antiquity, who, when obliged to represent ugliness, made sure that 'la difformité même offrait encore à la pensée une invisible image de la beauté absente', Pigalle's old man 'n'offre pas des traits où fut la jeunesse, mais des traits où l'on dirait que la jeunesse ne fut pas' (*E* 44). In Joubert's opinion the sculptor, Lebrun, had been much more effective than Pigalle in achieving this ideal goal. In a fragment entitled by Beaunier 'Le Tombeau de la Mère de Lebrun' (*C* i. 77), Joubert notes how it is possible to tell from the statue 'qu'elle avoit été jeune et belle, avant d'être agée et morte'. While visiting the Église Sainte-Geneviève, he noticed how a crucifix 'en y offrant aux yeux un corps fait pour être livré à la sépulture devrait cependant y faire entrevoir le principe et le germe d'une résurrection surnaturelle et prochaine' (*E* 61), a formula which Lebrun had been equally successful in following:

On voit de plus à la confiance avec laquelle elle ressuscite pour le jugement qu'elle vécut toujours vertueuse. La vie qu'elle vient de reprendre est dans sa chair; l'impression de la tombe qu'elle quitte est à la surface de sa peau légèrement terreuse et pâle.

(C i. 77)[27]

In nearly all these passages Joubert is describing a form of art which should be familiar to those who recall his interest in Bonnet and the creative activity of living organisms. These statues are art forms whose influence extends beyond the contours that define them as *objets d'art*. Rather than drawing attention to themselves as perfectly achieved copies of the aged human beings they represent, they provide us with images capable of suggesting these people at different stages of their lives. The dead hand of mimesis is challenged by a form of art that strives to free the imagination, to permit a glimpse of the spiritual 'principe et germe' first discovered concealed beneath the 'exfoliations' of Bonnet's animated matter. As Joubert wrote: 'toute figure n'est que la trace subsistante d'un mouvement déjà cessé' (C i. 289).

The effect of Lebrun's statue, however, is spoiled a little, according to Joubert, due to the rather futile imitation, by the church's architect or interior decorator, of an angel summoning all by trumpet to the Day of Judgement. As Joubert comments: 'Il auroit mieux vallu représenter simplement dans la voûte une trompette entre des nuages. L'imagination auroit achevé le tableau. Cet accessoire même étoit inutile: l'artiste avoit sçu l'exprimer dans la figure principale' (C i. 77). As in the theatre, we have yet another example of wasteful exaggeration. Joubert took up this same example much later in February 1802, concluding that 'il ne s'agit pas tant de peindre quoi que ce soit que d'en donner l'idée' (C i. 320). It is interesting to note that this *pensée*, with its criticism of the ridiculous effects produced by heavy-handed mimesis, its criticism of the intrusively *narrative* effects of poor church sculpture, comes immediately before this entry: 'Il faut que les pensées s'entresuivent et se lient, comme les sons dans la musique, par leur seul rapport—harmonie—et non comme les chaînons d'une chaîne, comme des perles

---

[27] Joubert might, judging from this *pensée*, have accepted Quatremère de Quincy's opinion that the ideal 'in its acceptation of generalization and search for a type, is not limited to beauty: there is also a 'laideur idéale', even an 'horrible idéal'. See Iknayan, 24–5. Joubert would have agreed with Lessing, however, as the trend of these remarks shows, that the expression of extreme pain ought to be softened and veiled in the visual arts, as Laocöon's scream is softened to a sigh (Lessing, *Du Laocöon*, trans. Ch. Vanderbourg (Paris, 1802; Joubert owned this edition).

enfilées' (C i. 320), a sequence of thought which thus bears eloquent witness to the close relationship in Joubert's mind between his own method of looking at art objects, his own expectations of them, and the fragmentary style of the *Carnets* themselves.

A similar movement occurs if we return to Pigalle's sculpture, whose 'luxe d'accessoires' (*E* 47) can be seen as a superior version of these annoying church decorations, and forms an instructive parallel to the chaotic excesses of the theatre—rather like the judgement of manic caricatures performed by eighteenth-century monkeys:

On se plaignoit du temps de Cicéron que les acteurs et les musiciens s'éloignoient de l'antique gravité pour se précipiter dans une hâte et une vivacité folles. Les spectateurs exigeoient encore ceppendant tant de sagesse et de sobriété dans l'expression, qu'ils blâmèrent Pylade de donner à son geste trop de liberté un jour qu'il jouoit Hercule furieux. Il ôta son masque et leur cria: 'Foux que vous êtes! je représente un plus grand fou que vous'.

(C i. 65)

Here we have another example of the 'forces sans repos' Joubert condemned while reading Lavater, activity for activity's sake, forgetful of the 'antique gravité' that animated the soul of the great actor. It is a passage that recalls the similar story quoted by Joubert while reading Du Bos, concerning the respective merits of the actors who played Agamemnon as an 'homme grand' and a 'grand homme'. As A. W. Schlegel wrote of the theatre of the Greeks, 'ils auraient moins regretté la perte d'une nuance de vivacité dans la représentation, que celle d'une nuance de beauté'.[28]

Pigalle's 'œil savant' discovered 'mille traits' in his subjects 'et dans chaque partie une infinité de parties', but the unifying line of *contour*, so dear to the ancients, always eluded him. The key to success in these arts, their way to perfection, was not the furious unrelenting activity of the theatre, this piling of *geste* upon *geste*, the effusions of the heart or the epicurean multiplication of *trait* preferred by modern sculptors, but the awareness of space which the art object would come to fill. Joubert would, indeed, have been happy to subscribe to the opinion expressed by Quatremère de Quincy that:

une répétition trop nombreuse de petites impressions ne produirait jamais l'idée de grandeur. Il faut que notre esprit soit tenu de faire un effort pour embrasser

---

[28] Quoted by Becq, *Genèse de l'esthétique*, 823.

l'idée de l'étendue, et le trop de petites divisions, loin d'augmenter, diminue en nous cette puissance.[29]

The ancients had left their statues room to breathe, stepped back from them with a certain *pudeur* thus allowing them time to *evoke* an ideal beauty that could not be physically captured:

> Cette nature, qui n'est parmi nous émue que par intervalles et qui est réduite, pour s'exprimer aux brusques mouvements qui sont permis à l'homme seul ou aux expressions partielles et presque imperceptibles du sourire et des larmes qui suffisent à l'homme assis et retiré dans sa maison, exercée perpétuellement chez les anciens, obligée à se montrer en présence d'un nombre infini de spectateurs, était accoutumée à se déployer avec décence et dignité dans les moindres mouvements ainsi que dans la contenance du corps tout entier, et lui donnait une physionomie qui, par l'habitude, y demeurait inhérente et devenait ineffaçable, selon des lois que la physique pourroit aisément expliquer. On ne doit pas s'étonner de la supériorité des anciens. Ils voyaient l'objet de leur art aussi parfait que pouvait le souhaiter l'imagination même. Ils le voyaient toujours en haleine, toujours ému. Ils le voyaient à sa place et comme ils devaient le peindre: je veux dire environné de l'univers.
>
> (E 51)

Given the way Joubert's appreciation of particular art objects reflects the aesthetic examined in earlier chapters of this study it is not surprising to find that much of the critical vocabulary he devotes to painting or sculpture may be applied quite readily to the type of discourse practised in the *Carnets* themselves.

Thus the paradigmatic movement of *pensées* '[qui] se succédassent dans un livre comme les astres dans le ciel, avec ordre, avec harmonie, mais à l'aise et à intervalles' (C i. 263) presides over the way Joubert contemplates a painting by David:

> Il faut pour qu'un grouppe se forme et soit réel à l'œil qu'il y ait une liaison entre le mouvement de chaque figure et de celle qui suit; il faut que les attitudes des personnages s'enchaînent l'une à l'autre; il faut qu'il y ait [...] une graduation bien ménagée et des nuances qui se fondent; il faut que l'esprit, aussi bien que l'œil, les embrasse d'un seul regard, il faut qu'elles forment une (ou plusieurs) unités [...] bien distinctes et dont le souvenir soit facile. Dans le *Bélisaire*, la femme, l'enfant et le vieillard grouppent parfaitement; le soldat ne groupe point, ni avec les premiers personnages, ni avec ceux qui sont peints dans le lointain, ni avec le lieu, ni pour ainsi parler avec lui-même.

---

[29] Quoted ibid. 550–1.

6. IMAGINATION AND THE FORM OF THE CARNETS

Pour qu'une figure grouppe avec elle-même, il faut qu'elle ait une vérité d'expression comme de conformation qui la replie sur son propre individu et lui donne un mérite absolu et indépendant. C'est ce que cette figure n'a aucunement; son attitude et son expression sont fausses et mentent à la nature encore plus qu'au sujet.

(C i. 58)

The evocation of a 'figure [qui] grouppe avec elle-même' makes us think of Joubert's desire for '[des] mots [qui] quadrent avec les pensées' (C i. 148), but the whole question of what he understands by *aggrouppement* in painting and its equation with linguistic discourse is not made explicit until June 1800, some fourteen years after his note on David: 'L'art de groupper ses paroles et ses pensées. Alors il faut que la pensée, que la phrase et la période s'encadrent de leur propre forme, subsistent de leur propre masse, se portent de leur propre poids' (C i. 255).

What is more, he turns yet again to a writer of the seventeenth century for an illustration of this formal cohesion:

Labruyère (disait Boileau) s'étoit épargné la peine des transitions. Il s'en étoit donné une autre, c'est ce[lle] des aggroupemens. Pour la transition, un seul rapport suffit. Mais pour l'aggrégation il en faut mille, car il en faut une convenance entière, naturelle, unique.

(C i. 255)

This partly explains Joubert's need 'à polir son idée' before risking its expression in words. It is not sufficient to strew them here, there, and everywhere, in a scattered attempt at the truth. They must be weighed and then placed with such grace as may be necessary to show that all these thoughts spring *naturally* from the same distinctive perspective. The light shed by the *Carnets* on the subjects they discuss should be like the light cast by a stained-glass window:

Un million de petits vitraux unis par les ligamens du plomb qui les enlacent ne forment qu'un seul tout; leurs innombrables parties se réunissent à l'œil en un ensemble commun, et dans leurs compartimens divisés donnent un jour diminué qui est convenable aux temples.

(C i. 78)

More continuous discourse, on the other hand, might offer the same effect as 'Ces vers quarrés [qui] n'offrent rien que de mesquin dans leur proportion moyenne et dans leur multiplicité. Il est trop facile de les compter et le jour qu'ils produisent est trop crud' (C i. 78). When we look at a good stained-glass window, its effect depends, perhaps to a greater degree than many other art forms, on the participation of the spectator's eye. The tiny particles of glass come together to form a whole under the pressure of the cohesive sweep of the human gaze: 'leurs innombrables parties se réunissent à l'œil' (C i. 78).

The idea of 'nuances qui se fondent', in the 1786 entry, is taken up again in the observation on the technique of Lantara, and mediates usefully between Joubert's appreciation of painting and that of music: 'Lantara ne se servoit jamais que d'un seul pinceau [...] C'est que, retenant toujours quelque teinte de la couleur qu'on venoit d'essuyer, il en laissoit apercevoir le mélange sur la toile et donnoit ainsi plus d'harmonie à tous les tons' (C i. 62). Here, the presence in the final line of characteristics stipulated in the August 1800 *pensée* is evident, but it also relates to Joubert's desire for the perceptible existence in each art object of an echo that reflects its constitutive elements, thus, presumably, strengthening its ability 'à groupper avec elle-même':

> Tout son dans la musique doit avoir un écho; toute figure doit avoir un ciel dans la peinture; et nous qui chantons avec des pensées et peignons avec des paroles, toute phrase et chaque mot devrait aussi dans nos écrits avoir son horizon et son écho.
>
> (C i. 63)

We might think like peripatetics and assume that the thoughts we find in the *Carnets*, being intrinsically autonomous, are incapable of forming a whole, but this would be foolish:

> Dans le chant, chaque note, quoique individu, se lie à une autre et fait continuité par une espèce de retentissement qui sert en quelque sorte d'articulation intermédiaire. De même, chaque point se joint à un autre point, par une espèce de gonflement qui sert de moyen de contact et d'identification entre les deux.
>
> (C i. 196)

The 'retentissement', 'écho', 'ciel', and 'mélange' of colour and tones form, almost, an image in negative, a diaphanous reflection of elements in the composition which swell like tiny molecules or the precarious balloons of the Montgolfier brothers to ensure a more graceful form of communication and expression than that provided by continuous analytical discourse. Significantly, it is when musicians split up into separate groups, are heard at a distance, recognized by their echo which impresses the listener with the distinctive power of perfume, that they are at their most evocative:

> Ces musiciens qui marchent par petites troupes parcourent aussi la ville pendant le jour. En été, vous croiriés être quelquefois dans cette ville de Bagdad dont parlent les Mille et une nuits, où les rues étoient arrosées d'eaux de senteur et où les maisons retentissoient de chansons d'allégresse. Les bouquets qui sont entassés dans les quarrefours et qui embaument l'air, les musiciens ambulans qui concertent de distance une multitude d'honnêtes gens aux fenêtres; tout cela réuni a quelquefois un charme inexprimable et dont il est difficile de conçevoir une idée.
>
> (C i. 73)

It is interesting to compare this aesthetic distance and echo with a passage heavily underlined by Joubert in his copy of the translation of Hogarth's *Analyse de la beauté*. During a discussion of shadow in painting, he drew attention in his usual manner to the following paragraph:

> Il y a une si grande analogie entre les ombres et les sons qu'il est facile d'expliquer les qualités des unes par celles des autres; car ainsi que les sons, à mesure qu'ils deviennent plus foibles ou plus forts, donnent à l'oreille une idée de leur éloignement; de même les ombres nous font juger de la distance des objets par leur degré de force ou d'adoucissement. Quant à leur analogie relativement à la beauté, on peut remarquer que comme les ombres dégradantes plaisent à l'œil, de même les sons flattent l'oreille quand ils s'enflent insensiblement ou qu'ils s'affaiblissent de même.[30]

This reference to the distancing powers of shadow, in turn, reads like a theoretical formulation of concrete observations made by Joubert as a young man; for this is precisely what we take out of his evocation of the rain 'qui allonge tous les objets [...] Cette espèce de teinte brune que l'humidité donne aux murailles, aux arbres ... ajoute encore à l'impression que font ces objets' (C i. 51–2).

In our discussion of Bonnet we suggested in passing that the *pensée* evoking 'les plus beaux sons, les plus beaux mots' was, perhaps, stimulated by 'ces globules diaphanes qui s'aplatissent sitôt qu'ils se touchent', and the remark following on from this one, noting the diastole and systole of music, might profitably be compared to the

---

[30] G. Hogarth, *Analyse de la beauté*, trans. Hendrik Jansen (2 vols.; Paris, 1805), i. 178. Joubert's copy is at Bussy.

similar oscillation involved in architecture, an equation, indeed, that Joubert makes quite explicit: 'Comme, dans la musique, le plaisir naît du mélange des sons et des silences, des repos et du bruit, de même il naît dans l'architecture, du mélange bien disposé des vuides et des pleins, des intervalles et des masses' (C i. 83).

Poetry, as we have seen, was for Joubert 'architecture de mots' (C ii. 498), and the careful weaving of space and matter characteristic of the art of the architect is present too in that of the poet, who does, however, favour the essential moments of rest in any structure over and above those of movement:

Que les paroles, les ouvrages, la poésie où il y a plus de repos (mais un repos qui nous émeut) sont plus belles ou plus beaux que ceux ou celles où il y a plus de mouvement. Que le mouvement donné par l'immobile est le plus parfait et le plus délicieux.

(C ii. 751)

Joubert is playing skilfully on words here. He makes no plea for a static, monolithic type of poetry, but declares that even the moment of rest, of pause before speech, must move us, must be emotive, the perceived *rapprochement* in that especially privileged space, where we have time to take in what has happened and what is about to happen, of 'mot et motion'.[31] Unfortunately most poets are unaware of the need for this stimulating vacuum: 'Les peintres disent qu'il y a des tableaux où il n'y a pas d'air. Nous avons aussi des poèmes à personnages où il n'y a pas de lieu, d'espace' (C ii. 606), a remark which reminds us of Joubert's condemnation of the frenetic activity of the theatre. This space acts almost as a kind of preservative;[32] when we recall beautiful lines of poetry, 'c'est toujours dans l'air qu'on le lit', quite detached from their context: 'On ne les imagine point sur la feuille où ils sont collés' (C ii. 491), and it is this which allows them to move like music and perfume: 'Les beaux vers sont ceux qui s'exhalent comme des sons ou des parfums' (C ii. 604). He contrasts this languid movement with the impulsion given by poets 'qui dardent les vers. Ceux de Voltaire sont lancés. Sa vivacité seule les produit; ils jaillissent et ne coulent pas' (C ii. 604), a diagnosis which evokes an early *pensée*, written around the expression 'mettre son esprit en bouteilles':

---

[31] Cf. Becq, *Genèse de l'esthétique*, 563, on Winckelmann and 'la noble simplicité', and on Fréron and 'le thème du repos'.

[32] Cf. C i. 180: 'Des stances—ou divisions—ou pause—ou compartimens. Que tout ouvrage d'esprit s'il est bien fait, est ainsi distribué.'

Cela se dit de ces esprits qui, pour faire éclater leur feu, ont besoin d'être contenus et comme captivés par un sujet fixe, un temps court. Alors ils éclatent et donnent des jets semblables à ces vins qui ne pétillent et ne montrent leur jeu que lorsque, enfermés dans un petit espace et contenus entre les murs d'une bouteille, leur fermentation se concentre et prend une vivacité que plus de liberté anéantiroit.

(C i. 116)

The problem about linking these two passages, however, is that it involves, possibly, the distorting powers of hindsight. Although, in the light of the later entry, Joubert seems to be describing a Voltaire-like mind, he could equally be seen to be engaged in self-description, if the earlier passage is read on its own. Many of Joubert's less considered *Carnet* entries do strike us with the force of a 'jet', all the stronger for their concision and elliptic qualities. It is clear, even from the tone of the early passage, that he does not really set much store by this kind of mind, but this should not prevent it from being read as self-criticism, underwriting his self-doubt as a writer, his frequent lapses of confidence in the power of the imagination: 'Peu d'esprits sont spacieux', he admitted; 'peu même ont une place vuide et offrent quelque point vacant. Presque tous ont des capacités étroites et occupées par quelque sçavoir qui les bouche' (C ii. 603).

We are presented with an ambiguous picture of the *Carnets*: as a disjunctive encyclopaedia of pickled, bottled *bons mots*, all jostling feverishly for attention; as a string of pearls, or stars, each one glinting and enlightening its neighbour from the preservative freedom of its own space. This space ensures 'Que le mot n'étreigne pas trop la pensée. Qu'il soit pour elle un corps qui ne la serre pas[. . .] (corps de baleine)' (C ii. 804).

Once again we find that it is the literature of the ancients that provides the best examples of this kind of *pudeur*. Among their writings we cannot find a single instance 'd'un discours suspendu par un autre que par celui-là même qui parle'. They are full of 'réticences' as opposed to 'interruptions': 'Circonstance remarquable chez eux, où entre un discours et un autre il s'écouloit quelque intervalle' (C i. 71). Tranquil, calm as the savages of Tahiti, they waited their turn 'et auroient . . . cru offenser le dieu de la parole, s'ils n'avoient pas permis à un discours d'arriver à sa fin et de parvenir à sa perfection'.

It is precisely the type of discourse that Joubert wishes for in the important entry of 1 August 1800, its evocation of 'pensées [qui] se succédassent dans un livre comme les astres dans le ciel' (C i. 263). We can see now that what it suggests, essentially, is a wedding of space to movement in language which, when translated into rhetorical terminology, denotes the desire for a fusion of *energeias* with *enargeias*.[33] Joubert's *pensées* are to be modelled upon the movement of stars whose patterns clearly display the Pythagorean harmonies of the cosmos. From the earth they appear to be beautiful but static points of light. The idealist knows, however, that a spiritual energy shines from these stars and is the home to which the human soul must tend. Joubert's *pensées* are therefore imbued with what the critic Michel Delon has called 'une énergie de l'âme qui est symptôme d'infini', to which writers as different as Quatremère de Quincy and Mme de Staël subscribed, but if they are to be clearly expressed, 'l'antique énargie' is not to be neglected.[34]

That, at least, was the ideal, and it is interesting that this is one of a number of *pensées* which are singled out for special treatment in Joubert's *Carnets*. Here, the evidence of the original manuscripts is of great significance. We have referred quite justly to the energetic bustle of the *Carnets*, yet there are pages where only one or two *pensées* are to be found, written with great care and placed on the page so that the surrounding margins are as significant a part of the 'meaning' of the *pensée* as the actual words themselves. Here we find Joubert 'composing' the single page in a way that he did not compose a book of maxims. He composes the fragment mentioned above with regard to its diagrammatic potential, its ability to picture forth a spiritual landscape; not only do we read about thoughts which move according to the pattern of stars in the night sky but we see black ink marks moving evenly across the white spaces of the page, providing us, almost, with a negative image, in the photographic sense, of the relationship between microcosm and macrocosm.

Such evidence obviously calls to mind the work of Mallarmé, yet what should be noted first is the contrast such individual pages make with the rest of the *Carnets* and what they can tell us about the tension at the heart of Joubert's own activity as a writer. The presence of these carefully composed pages next to others which are so cluttered as to be virtually indecipherable illustrates once more the various dichotomies we have been examining. On the one hand we have pages which

---

[33] Delon, *L'Idée d'énergie*, 37.
[34] Ibid. 118.

attempt to convey something of the Platonic space in which Joubert believed all things and beings existed. They are pages which pay homage by means of a brief, modest *esquisse* to the spiritual energy that animates the universe. They do not aspire, however, to the independent status of art. They do not constitute a book of maxims concealed within the unending pages of the *Carnets* but are jostled by the disorganized results of a mind whose feverish, creative activity is as symptomatic of its author's nature as his own clearly articulated desire for *repos*.

It is an interesting fact that Joubert's house in Villeneuve-sur-Yonne is full of *gravures anglaises*, which he seems to have collected with considerable enthusiasm, most of which represent caricatures of famous English politicians and satirize contemporary political events. What did he see in them? One of them represents a line of people strung out across the canvas, each representing a different attitude, a different thought within the tiny compass of the engraving's frame; it is the world in miniature. It is also a grotesque tug-of-war between opposed parties, and caricatures of men and women enslaved by their passions, a crowded scene where every available space is filled by satiric comment hardly leaving the spectator room to breathe before he is hustled on to the next one. They provide us with an ideal image of the tension that cuts across the *Carnets* themselves.

It may be that Joubert would have liked to turn the tug-of-war into the kind of dance created by the type of lines described by Hogarth in the closing pages of his book, *L'Analyse de la beauté*:

Les lignes que forment plusieurs personnes dans une contredanse ou danse figurée font un agréable effet, sur-tout lorsqu'on peut embrasser d'un seul coup-d'œil toute la figure, ainsi que cela a lieu des loges hautes d'une salle de spectacle. La beauté de cet espèce de danse mystique, comme l'appellent les poètes, dépend de ce que les danseurs se meuvent dans une variété de différentes lignes, parmi les quelles la ligne serpentine doit tenir la première place, disposées d'après les règles de la complication etc.[35]

In this context it is worth recalling Saint-Martin's appreciation of the dance, the *élans* of its movements leading Man towards the freedom of an ideal sphere of action.[36] It is an ideal movement Joubert would like to follow, but reality keeps breaking in: 'Les danses des peuples barbares', like the writings of Voltaire, or the 'esprits mises en bouteilles

[35] Hogarth, i. 246–7.
[36] See Iknayan, 92.

ne sont composées que de sauts et de gambades brusques et désordonnés, en tournant en rond, ou en courant en avant et en arrière, avec des mouvemens convulsifs et des attitudes forcées'.[37]

Villoteau reminds us that Dionysius Halicarnassus, in his *Traité de l'arrangement des mots*, describes the style of the Ancient Greeks as 'musical et coupé en petites phrases'.[38] Joubert recognizes it as typical of 'esprits étendus qui, voyant au loin et beaucoup, veulent peu dire', but only *after* he has been completely honest with himself and noticed that: 'Dans la plaisanterie on ne dit qu'une partie de ce qu'on pense; on n'envisage dans son sujet que de certains côtés. De là, le style bref et coupé est naturel à cette affection' (C i. 396). The fundamental antinomy of the *Carnets* is noted without comment in the stoic reticence of *pensée*, and it is from this that the richness of Joubert's journal flows. Each time he looks out at painting or sculpture, building or play, listens to music or watches a dance, he can be caught staring mercilessly into the divided soul of his own art.

[37] Hogarth, i. 246–7.
[38] Villoteau, *Recherches*, i. 203.

Final Profile

'On n'envisage dans son sujet que de certains côtés'. This line of reasoning, the acknowledgement of partiality, of human limitation inherent in it, might well have been adopted by Sophie Joubert as she came to draw the portrait of her uncle. For Hogarth's 'ligne serpentine' returns us to the enigmatic contours of Joubert's profile which have so puzzled generations of critics. Joubert refuses to confront our inquisitive gaze directly but stares to right or to left, a 'Gioconda' smile upon his lips.

It is possible that a deliberate aesthetic decision lies behind this strategy, and this is intriguingly confirmed by Joubert's underlining of passages in his copy of Lavater's *Essai sur la physiognomie*. Sophie's portrait, it should be noted, is a drawing, not a painting, and we find in it the *ombres* and *lignes* he preferred to *couleur*. 'Quoi de plus imparfait que le portrait de la figure humaine dessinée d'après l'ombre!' exclaimed Lavater. 'Et cependant de quelle vérité n'est pas ce portrait! Cette source si peu abondante n'est que plus pure'. A little later in the same chapter Joubert indicated his interest in the remark that 'La silhouette n'offre qu'une seule ligne de la figure qu'elle représente', 'quoi de plus simple que le seul contour extérieur du profil?—Dix fois il l'entreprendra et à peine une fois saisira-t-il cette ligne.' This difficult art of concentration, of pure delineation, is applied most appropriately to the human head: 'Elle est le siège principal de l'esprit, le centre de nos facultés intellectuelles.'[1] We note that Sophie limits herself to a head and shoulders and recall Joubert's early remark, made in the context of reading the *Timaeus*: 'La tête de l'homme est tout l'homme. C'est là que nos principaux sens ont leur place invariable dans l'empire de la raison' (C i. 35–6). Behind Lavater's studies of physiognomy are those of Ficino and there is no doubt that Joubert was aware of the

---

[1] J. G. Lavater, *Essai sur la physiognomie, destinée à faire connoitre l'homme et à le faire aimer* (3 vols.; La Haye, 1783–6), ii. 157, 327, iii. 234. Joubert's copy may be consulted at M. du Chayla's home in Villeneuve.

traditional Neoplatonic analogies between microcosm and macrocosm, of the way in which 'le visage humain renvoie aux formes célestes; la sphère ramène à l'âme'.[2] As much is indicated by Joubert's underlining of passages at the start of Lavater's work, with their evocation of 'la face humaine, cette divinité présente, mais cachée; elle s'y peint comme dans un miroir magique', his exhortation, 'Étudiez-le! dessinez ses contours, copiez-le comme le soleil se peint dans une goutte d'eau.'[3]

Lightly sketched in its oval frame, Joubert's portrait trembles on the edge of non-existence, as if reflected precariously in a drop of dew, a 'goutte d'eau' which the sun might cease to illuminate at any moment. But we understand, with the aid of Lavater, why a profile was the only form of art that would glimpse accurately the 'author' of the *Carnets*:

> S'agit-il d'un visage dont l'organisation est, ou extrêmement forte, ou extrêmement délicate, le caractère peut-être apprécié bien plus facilement par le profil que par la face. Sans compter que le profil se prête moins à la dissimulation, il offre des lignes plus vigoureusement prononcées, plus précises, plus simples, plus pures, et par conséquent la signification en est aisée à saisir; au lieu que très-souvent les lignes de la face en plein sont assez difficiles à démêler et à déchiffrer. Un beau profil suppose toujours l'analogie d'un caractère distingué, mais on trouve mille profils, qui, sans être beaux, peuvent admettre la supériorité du caractère.[4]

Here again we find enthusiasm for a representational *esquisse* or profile which provides a suggestive perspective upon that which is essential to man while implying that the limitations of such an art are an accurate measure of its genuineness and authority.

Sophie's portrait of Joubert is a miniature and it is worth noting that the *pensée* where Joubert describes himself as 'Tourmenté par la maudite ambition de mettre toujours tout un livre dans une page, toute une page dans une phrase et cette phrase dans un mot', so often used to define a lyrical art of heuristics, supposedly a typical product of the creative imagination, comes immediately after this entry:

> C'est toujours ce qui termine ou limite une chose qui en fait le caractère, la précision, la netteté, la perfection. C'est là ce qui l'isole, ce qui l'enserre, ce qui la sépare du reste, ce qui l'enferme à soi et ce qui la ramène à soi. C'est par cela qu'elle subsiste, qu'elle est distincte, qu'elle est absolument complète.
>
> (C ii. 818)

---

[2] Chastel, 94.
[3] Lavater, i. 6–7.
[4] Ibid. iii. 235.

It cannot be denied that this casts a rather different light on the famous *pensée* that follows, and testifies again to the dangers of quoting Joubert's entries out of context as detachable maxims. Now the 'Chinese box' approach to his subject-matter, or the form of linguistic *emboîtement* to which he subjects it, can be seen as yet another illustration of the sense of limit intrinsic to every human undertaking. We can hear, in fact, a chastened echo of Joubert's 1804 diagnosis of his failure to complete 'La Bienveillance universelle': 'Le fonds manqua. Il aurait fallu déterminer "quelles en devaient être les bornes" ' (C i. 443). At the same time he noted the principal idea behind another study which never came to fruition: 'En 1783. L'ouvrage où j'avais été engagé par Diderot aurait dû se réduire à ce point-ci: des perspectives pour l'esprit, et s'il peut se contenter sans elles'; against this was opposed the question of infinite perfectibility: 'si la même étendue qui le rend capable de concevoir une grande idée ne lui rend pas inévitable le désir d'une gloire sans bornes' (C i. 433).

It was Joubert's considered opinion that the mind needed some kind of 'perspective' from which to operate, a guiding line which would distinguish what was possible and necessary from the *flou* of infinite subject-matter. Present in his 1815 approval of 'ce qui la sépare du reste' is an echo of his appreciation of the 'forme qui le détache de tout le reste', discovered in the philosophy of Plato and Plutarch. Had Joubert discovered that 'forme' earlier, his journalistic articles might have been finished. More likely, he would have reduced them, out of an acute sense of *pudeur*, to the more modest, limited proportions of the notes towards his *Éloge de Cook* or of the *Carnets* themselves.

The miniature portrait was a typical product of civilized 'salon' society, and it should not be forgotten, in this context, that Joubert was a regular attender of Mme de Beaumont's salon in the early 1800s. Salon society frequently gave rise, also, to a highly sophisticated form of epistolary art, as friends and acquaintances not able to attend in person corresponded with each other for their mutual entertainment and instruction. Those who refuse to see past Joubert's inability to finish journalistic articles, and the temptation of the tired reader to characterize the *Carnets* as a *fourre-tout*, forget the powerful testimony of his correspondence, which, mutilated though it may have been by the same company of nineteenth-century editors, still contains some of the most perfect examples in French literature of complete, coherently argued letters. What is more, the recent discovery of a letter in the

Archives de Guitaud shows Joubert playing very skilfully with the whole concept of the fragment, proposing even that a letter, or at least the postscript to a letter, may indeed be considered as a form of fragment.[5]

A number of Joubert's letters, and this new discovery in particular, typical of a custom that goes back to the seventeenth century and continues into the nineteenth, are designed to be communicated in salon society to a fairly large group of people. It is interesting to relate this to the influence on le *moraliste classique* of this milieu and the *nouvelle rhétorique* of maxim and fragment which he evolved to express its concerns.[6] If one considers the logical connection that asks to be made here, the *Carnets* may be regarded as the continuation, in the study, of 'les subtilités du distinguo', taken out of the *modus scholasticus* of traditional rhetoric practised at school, and sieved through a tangential *ars dicendi* of salon debate and repartee.

Successive biographers tell us that Joubert was a delightful and persuasive conversationalist and it is not unduly frivolous in this context to describe him as a man who could not stop talking. Joubert never published a collection of *maximes* and *pensées* because, in a sense, his writing was truly conversation forced underground, the stream of consciousness of a voice, lowered because he had to replace friends and acquaintances from time to time with books and his own company. To publish would have been to betray the oral sources of his inspiration. Joubert's need for *la plaisanterie* constitutes a recognition of the essentially creative nature of the intellectual banter which characterized salon society and of the stimulatingly provisional nature of its discoveries. As we recall, 'dans la plaisanterie on ne dit qu'une partie de ce qu'on pense; on n'envisage dans son sujet que de certains côtés. De là le style bref et coupé est naturel à cette affection' (C i. 396).

In this light, the *Carnets* and their author are both representative of their period and milieu and of something more personal. Joubert refuses to be pinned down and conveniently defined by portraits of him as 'moraliste', 'Rousseauiste' turned imperialist, or conversationalist turned closet writer. Such labels are inadequate and do not do justice to the obsessive aesthetic interest which the act of writing had for him. It is this dimension that is the distinguishing feature of his thought and underlies every sphere of debate in which he engaged. Even an

---

[5] See D. P. Kinloch, 'The Art of the Missing Postscript: Some Unpublished Manuscripts of Joseph Joubert', *Nottingham French Studies*, 24/2 (1985), 12–27.

[6] Van Delft, 236, 247.

examination of Joubert's ideological or political stances is forced, ultimately, into a consideration of their expression, simply because the very process of putting pen to paper was fraught with a tension frequently more compelling than the ideas he was trying to voice:

> Mais en effet quel est mon art? quel est le nom qui distingue cet art des autres? quelle fin se propose-t-il? que produit-il? que fait-il naître et exister? que prétends-je et que veux-je faire en l'exerçant? Est-ce d'écrire en général et de m'assurer d'être lu? Seule ambition de tant de gens! est-ce là tout ce que je veux? ne suis-je qu'un polymathiste? ou ai-je une classe d'idées qui soit facile à assigner et dont on puisse déterminer la nature et le caractère, le mérite et l'utilité?
> C'est ce qu'il faut examiner, longuement et jusqu'à ce que je le sache.
>
> (C i. 216)

Successive generations of critics have tried to answer these questions for him, failing to recognize the intrinsic importance of their repetition, the way in which Joubert draws attention to their existence for him *as* questions, or rather, the insistent variations on one particular question, enshrining in miniature the real indecision that characterizes his use of *pensée* or fragment throughout his life. Such indecision is tributary to the approval and suspicion of imagination itself as it alternates from one end of the *Carnets* to the other and to the ambiguous relationship of imagination to 'la raison créatrice'.

This is apparent from the 'Éloge de Cook' on, where the incessant repetition of, and variation upon, certain phrases and paragraphs testifies not simply to the way in which the ideological indecision that characterizes it is *paralleled* by aesthetic hesitation, but to the *overriding* corrosive interest provided by the stutter of art itself. There is a sense in which Cook's mission may be seen, and perhaps was so by Joubert himself, as a physical reiteration of his insistent, indefatigable questioning: 'Quel est mon art?', as explorer and writer probe time and time again for a passage through the glistening coral that protects the 'patrie céleste' of Otahiti.

Perhaps even more striking is the way this aesthetic dimension helps to resolve the contradictions, or at least to appreciate a certain level of compatibility, between competing ideological attitudes. Thus, the increasing scepticism of many remarks about politics is refracted through occasional nostalgia for an *art* of politics, common ground being provided by the supple magic of illusion. Similarly, Joubert's echoes of Maistre's statement that 'la faiblesse et la fragilité d'une constitution sont précisément en raison directe de la multiplicité des articles constitutionnels écrits',[7] achieves poetic resonance if this 'constitution' may refer also to that of the *Carnets* themselves.

La multitude des paroles qui remplit nos livres annonce notre ignorance et les obscurités dont tous nos sçavoirs sont remplis. Si nous étions parfaitement éclairés, il n'y auroit dans nos livres de morale que des maximes, dans nos livres de physique et de spiritualité que des axiomes et des faits. Tout le reste n'est qu'un remplissage et n'y montre que nos recherches, nos efforts et nos embarras.

(C i. 126)

This quotation returns us again to the actual manuscripts of the *Carnets*, to the feverish creativity of nearly illegible pages where Joubert seems to put a premium upon the constant process of research itself, on creation as act rather than result. These pages outnumber their quieter neighbours where one or two carefully inscribed *pensées* float in a sea of white paper and seem designed to be read diagramatically, the emphasis firmly upon the spatial significance of the composed page, of its role as emblem or hieroglyph 'où tout serait dit à la fois', as Blanchot puts it.[8] They represent genuine intellectual achievements, discoveries of unknowns that emerge from the process of continuous endeavour. As such they please and surprise Joubert, who accepts and retains them among his *Carnets*. These are pages whose patterns are based upon the familiar emblem of stars in the night sky, the stars that guided Captain Cook and at which Joubert gazed on a sleepless night in August 1800, providing us with an image of motion as transvital rest, an image of âme or prime motion in the dignified *animation* of *pensées détachées*.

The juxtaposition of these different types of writing in Joubert's *Carnets* may have been creative of the tension that finally prevented him from publishing, yet both testify to the important status of human creativity, to the need for man to strive, however unsuccessfully, to provide an image of the spiritual reality that animates the universe. This need to create invades every area of human endeavour in which Joubert interested himself and it is no coincidence that the sudden depth given to political and metaphysical concerns by questions of aesthetics occurs at moments when Joubert lapses, or relaxes creatively, into the strategy of fable. At crucial moments Joubert tells himself stories, fabling the paradise of Tahiti, family unit, and the birth of

[7] Maistre, *Essai*, para. ix, p. 26.
[8] Blanchot, 'Joubert et l'espace', 76.

illusion, so essential to art, always consistently hostile, as his brand of Platonism shows, to those who would systematize and demythologize the limited utopias provided by the images of an Ideal Reality. The relatively commonplace rejection of mimesis becomes, in Joubert's hands, an urgent and nuanced interrogation of the nature and role of art itself. We witness Joubert, attracted by the underlying aesthetic models provided by the pseudo-science of Charles Bonnet and the metaphysics of Ficino, stepping forward to proclaim the validity of art in the face of that Reality, by insisting on the status of *image* as distinct from *copie* in ways which testify to a conception of poetic language that prefigures the aesthetics of symbolism by more than half a century.

Joubert's continual stress upon the need for a space, a distance that must exist between an image and the thing it seeks to make visible, is a startlingly precocious recognition of the power that defines art, 'ce pouvoir de représenter par l'absence et de manifester par l'éloignement qui est au centre de l'art', as Blanchot puts it.[9] It is in this that Joubert recognizably anticipates Mallarmé and it is this that would have enabled him to exercise a wide and stimulating influence upon the poets and aesthetic thinkers that came after him had he been gifted, as he most certainly deserved, with more intelligent and courageous editors. As it is, we are only now beginning to come to terms with his legacy.

A natural result of this aesthetic is the distance Joubert puts between himself and the realm of Platonic 'essences'. When we start to examine his debt to Plato, there is a tendency to end up discussing everyone Joubert read but Plato. In fact, his knowledge of the Greek philosopher, profound though it certainly was, is constantly refracted through his interest in other writers, and it is more accurate to regard the philosophy of the *Dialogues* as a source to which he deferred when in need of arbitration, rather than as a set of doctrines to which he referred constantly. This is supported by the emphasis firmly put on the dynamic movement from mind to matter at the expense of an obsessive concern for innate ideas. A similar process emerges as a consideration of metaphysical and epistemological issues modulates naturally for Joubert into a discussion of painting, while we are confronted with the existence of an idea dependent on a comparison drawn from aesthetics for a sense of its own reality.

---

[9] Ibid. 84.

Ultimately, however, all attempts to make conclusive statements about the nature of the aesthetic concerns in which Joubert interests himself, or for that matter about the level of consciousness behind the tendency of *Carnet* entries to reflect upon themselves, are compromised by the complexities involved in producing an 'edition' of Joubert. Joubert did not publish his *Carnets* in any form and this simple fact cannot be repeated frequently enough. The portrait, or rather *portraits*, of him that we possess today depend upon what each editor of his private journal has decided to put in or leave out. On such decisions depend our view of Joubert as a writer acutely conscious of the moral and artistic limitations inherent in humanity, as well as occasional glimpses of the lyric power expressed by the alternating centrifugal and centripetal rhythms of heuristic discourse. One day his 'maudite ambition' will remind us of Mallarmé's 'livre idéal', but on another it may strike us as a rather more mundane process of summary and *résumé* of books by other men, their 'substantifique moëlle' profitably compressed into the mnemonic wisdom of a single phrase or word. This same process, on the other hand, can be dignified by interpreting it as indicative of Joubert's profound awareness of 'intertextuality' as the necessary condition of writing, and the creative reader is called upon to step into the breach, make connections, trace sources, and delineate the relationship of author to his own texts and those through which he works.

All these competing and complementary elements may be found in Beaunier's edition of the *Carnets*, but each must be subjected to the vision of a man, overwhelmingly aware of the infinite number of choices and alternatives open to him in every sphere of activity and reflection in which he is engaged, but unwilling to decide on a definitive statement or version. The closest we may come to him is by drawing a parallel again with the figure of James Cook, and of the achievements and limitations of his voyage, as he is satiated but momentarily by each fresh discovery and forced to return only with a map, a sketch of what he has seen. Similarly Joubert, from the confines of his armchair, seeks constantly, in everything he writes, after the vision of an art, a structuring line or *contour*, that memory, imagination, and intellect might figure to reproduce a mnemonic of the 'partie céleste' which it can only faintly reflect. Such a map, such an art, presents us inevitably with a brief, barely adequate profile of Reality. Joubert understood this. He does not look at us directly from his portrait, because he knows we cannot confront him either in this way, that none of us would be able to hold the other's gaze for long in the 'miroir magique' of this world. We look at him as he looked at his friends, as we hope he might look at the shadows of posterity—with characteristic realism and generosity: 'Quand mes amis sont borgnes, je les regarde de profil' (*C* ii. 553).

Appendix: Joubert's Reading of Plato

For the convenience of the reader of Beaunier's edition of the *Carnets*, I reproduce below a list of Joubert's references to specific Platonic dialogues and, where possible or useful, to specific passages within them. References to these passages are given by means of the marginal sigla derived from the pagination and page subdivisions of the 1578 edition of Plato by Henri Estienne, which is conventionally used for references to the text of Plato. Occasionally Joubert does not mention a specific dialogue explicitly, even when his remarks obviously draw their inspiration from it, and I have indicated such references with an asterisk.

Beaunier edition		*Dialogue*	*Estienne edition*
Page	Reference		Page
35–6	Summary of 'la physiologie platonicienne'	TIMAEUS*	
44	'Le beau est un;'	REPUBLIC* or	6.507b
		LYSIS*	216d
57	'Je définirai la matière "la pâte dont sont faits les corps."'	TIMAEUS*	
90	'Socrate disoit des morts . . .	CRATYLUS	
	Tous les héros étoient Batude . . .	CRATYLUS	398c
91	'Alors dit Axiochus . . .'	AXIOCHUS (a dialogue attributed to Plato in the 1588 edition)	
92	'On sonnoit le point du jour . . .'	LAWS	
	'La faculté de se mouvoir . . .'	CRATYLUS*	401d

APPENDIX

Beaunier Edition		Dialogue	Estienne edition
Page	Reference		Page
	'Platon appelle roi ...'	CRATYLUS*	393b
	'La musique, les arts n'expriment que des simulachres ...'	CRATYLUS*	423d
93	'L'eau cherche a tout coaguler ...'	TIMAEUS*	
	'Parménide ... L'un est un ...'	PARMENIDES	
94	'... Solon ...'	TIMAEUS	22b
	'L'intellect est à l'âme ...'	TIMAEUS	30b
	'La chose la plus propre à lier ...'	TIMAEUS	31c
	'La beauté nait ...'	TIMAEUS	33c (?)
	'... il n'avoit pas besoin d'oreilles ...'	TIMAEUS	33c
95	'Il y a ... de la lumière dans les yeux ...'	TIMAEUS	45b
	'La thèorie des couleurs ...'	TIMAEUS	67c,d
176	'Que ce viscère ...'	TIMAEUS*	
180–1	'L'amour ... fils de la pauvreté ...'	SYMPOSIUM	203b,c,d,
213	'On pourroit soutenir ...'	ALCIBIADES A (attributed by Ficino)	
214–15	'Le Phoedon ...'	PHAEDO	76d
215	'Platon. Amour, fils de Porus ...'	SYMPOSIUM*	203b,c,d
216	'Dans le Phèdre ...'	PHAEDRUS	
220	Unpublished notes from several dialogues	SOPHIST	259b
		LYSIS	216d
		LETTER VII	342b
244	'Ce que Socrate dit ...'	PHAEDO	76d,e
			100c
286	'il y a dans toute espèce de couleur une sorte de flamboiement ...'	TIMAEUS	67c,d
	'... deux espèces de causes ...'	TIMAEUS	28
477–8	'Poésie. Ce qui la fait ...'	ION*	
491	'Dieu, seul miroir ...'	ALCIBIADES A	
493	'La valeur ... la science des choses terribles ...'	LACHES	199b

Beaunier edition		Dialogue	Estienne edition
Page	Reference		Page
493–4	Summary of several dialogues	APOLOGY ALCIBIADES A ALCIBIADES B EUTHYPHRO CRITO PHAEDO	
513	'Dans Plato, au Théétète …'	THAETETUS	
531–3	'Les douleurs de l'enfantement …' etc.	THAETETUS	150c,d,e
573	'Vid. la caverne de Platon'	REPUBLIC*	7.514
600	'Il n'est et n'a jamais …'	TIMAEUS	
658	'Socrate dans le Banquet …'	SYMPOSIUM	219a
718	'La poésie n'est pas un art, mais un enthousiasme'	ION*	
721	'Lettre première …'	LETTERS (to Dion)	
747	Unpublished notes and extracts	THAETETUS (summary) LETTERS (to Dion)	
747–8	'Il fait de l'âme'	THAETETUS	
753–7	'Il n'y a … de toujours vrai …'	PHILEBUS	59c
839	'Dire des choses agréables à Dieu.'	PHAEDRUS	273e

Select Bibliography

Primary Sources

(i) Editions of the Pensées, Carnets, and Correspondance

Recueil des pensées de M. Joubert (Paris, Le Normant, 1838).
Pensées, essais et maximes de Joseph Joubert, suivis de lettres à ses amis, ed., with an introduction by, P. de Raynal (2 vols.; Paris, C. Gosselin, 1842).
Pensées, essais, maximes et correspondance de J. Joubert, ed., with an introduction by, P. de Raynal (2 vols.; 2nd rev. edn., Paris, Le Normant, 1850).
Pensées, essais, maximes et correspondance de Joseph Joubert, ed., with an introduction by, P. de Raynal (rev. edn., 2 vols.; Paris, Didier, 1861).
Pensées, essais et maximes de Joseph Joubert précédées de sa correspondance, ed., with an introduction by, P. de Raynal and articles by Sainte-Beuve, Sylvestre de Sacy, Saint-Marc Girardin, Gérusez, and Poitou (2 vols.; Paris, Didier et Cie, 1862). (The editions of 1866, 1869, and 1874 from Didier, and those of 1888, 1895, 1909, 1911, and 1920 from Perrin, reproduce the edition of 1862. The 1866 edition also contains a 'table analytique' of the *pensées* by Wallon.)
Correspondance de Joseph Joubert, ed., with an introduction by, P. de Raynal (9th edn., Paris, Perrin, 1895).
Pensées de Joseph Joubert, repr. of 1st edn., with an historical preface by Arnaud Joubert (Joseph's brother), and ed., with an introduction by, V. Giraud (Paris, Blond et Cie, 1909).
Textes choisis de Joseph Joubert, ed. V. Giraud (Paris, Plon-Nourrit et Cie, 1914).
Lettres de Joseph Joubert à Mme de Vintimille, ed. A. Beaunier (Paris, Devambes, 1921).
Pensées de Joubert, ed. L. Cerf (Paris, Firmin-Didot, 1929).
Pensées de Joseph Joubert, repr. of 1st edn., with historical prefaces by Arnaud Joubert and Chateaubriand, ed., with an introduction by, V. Giraud (Paris, la Société des Médecins Bibliophiles, 1930).

Pensées, maximes, essais de Joubert, with correspondence, ed., with an introduction by, H. Peyre de Bétonzet (Paris, Hatier, 1932).
Pensées et correspondance de Joseph Joubert, ed., with an introduction by, P. Valentin (Paris, Gautier, 1938).
Les Carnets de Joseph Joubert: Textes recueillis sur les manuscrits autographes, ed. A. Beaunier (2 vols.; Paris, Gallimard, 1938).
Les Pensées de Joubert, ed. Mgr Grente (Paris, Maison de la Bonne Presse, 1941).
Correspondance de Louis de Fontanes et de Joseph Joubert, ed. R. Tessonneau (Paris, Plon, 1943).
Pensées de Joubert, ed. M. Vox (Lille, Danel, 1945).
Pensées de Joubert (Paris, Payot, s.a.).
Les Pensées de Joubert, ed. Cardinal Grente (Paris, Maison de la Bonne Presse, 1953).
Pensées et lettres de Joubert, ed. R. Dumay (Paris, Grasset, 1954).
Maximes et pensées de Joubert (Paris, Silvaire, 1961).
Pensées de Joubert, ed. G. Poulet (Paris, Bibliothèque 10/18, 1966).
Essais, 1779–1821, with previously unpublished material ed., with an introduction by, R. Tessonneau (Paris, Nizet, 1983).
Lettres de Joseph Joubert à Pauline de Beaumont et Louise Angélique de Vintimille, ed. R. Judrin (Quimper, Calligrammes, 1984).
Pensées, jugements et notations, ed. R. Tessonneau (Paris, Corti, 1989).

(ii) Texts by Joubert published in academic journals

Sainte-Beuve (ed.), 'Pensées, maximes, jugements et correspondance de Joubert', *Revue des deux mondes*, 29 (Jan.–Mar. 1842), 936–68.
Pailhès, G. (ed.), 'Lettres inédites de Joubert à Mlle de Fontanes', *Le Correspondant*, 190 (1898), 453–80, 751–770.
Paumes, B. (ed.), 'Trois lettres de Joubert à Claude Grancher', *Revue hebdomadaire* (19 July 1913).
'Le Journal intime', *Nouvelle Revue française* (1 Jan. 1937), 66–79.
Riberette, P. (ed.), 'A propos de Joubert. Une lettre inédite à Suard', *Bulletin de la Société Chateaubriand*, 18 (1975), 40–2.
Kinloch, D. P., 'The Art of the Missing Postscript: Some Unpublished Manuscripts of Joseph Joubert', *Nottingham French Studies*, 24: 2 (1985), 12–28.
For other letters and fragments by Joubert consult *Studien* and Tessonneau, *Éducateur*.

(iii) Translations of Joubert's Pensées

Some of the Thoughts of Joseph Joubert, trans. G. H. Calvert, preceded by a notice of Joubert by the translator (Cambridge, Mass., W. V. Spencer, 1867).

Pensées of Joubert, selected and trans., with the original French appended, by H. Attwell (London, MacMillan, 1877).
Lyttelton, Katherine, (ed.), *Joubert: A Selection from his Thoughts*, with a preface by Mrs Humphrey Ward (London, Duckworth, 1898).
Pensées and Letters of Joseph Joubert, ed. and trans. H. P. Collins (London, Routledge, 1928).
'Joubert, "Gedanken und Maximen"', *Die Französischen Moralisten*, trans. and ed. F. Schalk (Wiesbaden, Dieterich'sche Verlagsbuchhandlung, 1952).
Joubert, *Riflessioni dai Diari*, trans. and selected by G. Saba (Rome, G. Casini, 1957).

(iv) Other primary sources

Asterisked works may be found in Joubert's libraries in Villeneuve, Paris, and Bussy-le-Repos, and have been annotated by him.
ACADÉMIE DES INSCRIPTIONS ET BELLES LETTRES, *Mémoires de littérature* (Paris, 1663–1793), especially xxxii (1768), xxxvii (1769).
ANCILLON, F., *Essais philosophiques ou nouveaux mélanges de littérature et de philosophie* (2 vols.; Paris, Paschoud, 1817).
——*Essais de philosophie, de politique et de littérature* (4 vols.; Paris, Gide, 1832).
ANDRÉ, LE PÈRE Y., *Œuvres, contenant un traité de l'homme selon des différentes merveilles qui le composent* (4 vols.; Paris, Ganeau, 1766).
*——*Essai sur le beau* (rev. edn., Paris, Ganeau, 1770).
Année littéraire, ed. M. Fréron (Paris [Amsterdam], 1757–90), 1773, 1774, 1785, 1786.
ANSSE DE VILLOISON, J.-B. G. d', *Remarques ... sur quelques inscriptions grecques de marbres antiques et de pierres gravées, principalement sur celles qui sont en forme de dialogue* (s.l.a.n.) (BN 8† Zz 3965).
——*De triplici theologia mysteriisque veterum commentatio*, in G. de Clermont-Lodève, baron de Sainte-Croix, *Recherches historiques et antiques sur les mystères du paganisme*, 2nd edn., ed. S. de Saci (2 vols.; Paris, de Bure, 1817), ii. 3–111.
BACON, F., *Neuf livres de la dignité et de l'accroissement des sciences*, trans. le sieur Golefer (Paris, Dugast, 1632).
*——*La Politique du chevalier Bacon, chancelier d'Angleterre* (Londres, Jacques Tonsson, 1742).
BALLANCHE, P. S., *Œuvres complètes* (4 vols.; Paris, Didot aîné, 1830), iv.
BATTEUX, Ch., *Principes de littérature* (5 vols.; Paris, Desaint et Saillant, 1764).
*——*Les Quatre Poétiques d'Aristote, d'Horace, de Vida, de Despréaux* (2 vols.; Paris, Saillant et Nyon, 1771).
——*Traité de l'arrangement des mots, traduit du grec de Denys d'Halicarnasse* (Paris, Nyon l'aîné et fils, 1788).

Bibliothèque française, ouvrage périodique ed. C. Pougens, 4 (Paris, Honnert, Aug. 1800).

*BOILEAU-DESPRÉAUX, N., *Œuvres* (2 vols.; Paris, David l'aîné et Durand, 1745).

*BONALD, L.-G.-A. de., *Théorie du pouvoir politique et religieux dans la société civile* (3 vols.; s.l., s.n., 1796).

*——*Morceaux divers* (s.l., s.n., 1796).

*——*Essai analytique sur les lois naturelles de l'origine sociale ou du Pouvoir du ministre et du sujet dans la société* (Paris, s.n., 1800).

*——*Du divorce considéré au XIXe siècle relativement à l'état domestique et à l'état public de la société* (Paris, Le Clère, 1801).

——*Législation primitive considerée dans les derniers temps par les seules lumières de la raison* (2 vols.; Paris, Le Clère, 1802).

——*Recherches philosophiques sur les premiers objets des connaissances morales* (2 vols.; Paris, Adrien Le Clère, 1818; rev. edn., 1826).

BONNET, Ch., *Œuvres d'histoire naturelle et de philosophie* (7 vols.; Neuchâtel, Fauche, 1779).

BOSSUET, J.-B., *Œuvres*, ed. l'abbé Velat and Y. Champailler (Paris, Gallimard: Pléiade, 1961).

BOUGAINVILLE, L. A. de, *Voyage autour du Monde par la frégate la Boudeuse et la flûte l'Etoile* (Paris, Saillant et Nyon, 1771; repr. Maspéro, 1980).

BOYÉ, *l'Expression musicale mise au rang des chimères* (Paris, Esprit, 1779).

*BUFFIER, C., *Traité des premières vérites et de la source de nos jugements, où l'on examine le sentiment des philosophes de ce temps sur les premières notions des choses* (Paris, Veuve Mongé, 1724).

BUFFON, G.-L., *Histoire naturelle générale et particulière* (15 vols.; Paris, Imprimerie royale, 1749).

BURKE, E., *Œuvres posthumes . . . sur la Révolution française* (London, s.n., 1799).

*——*Reflections on the Revolution in France*, ed. C. C. O'Brien (Harmondsworth, Penguin, 1969).

CABANIS, P. J. C., *Rapports du physique et du moral de l'homme*, ed. L. Peisse (Paris, J.-B. Bailliere, 1844). (The first edition was published by Crapelet in 1802.)

Catalogue des livres de feu M. Ansse de Villoison (Paris, Debure, 1806).

Catalogue des livres de la bibliothèque de feu Antoine Bernard Caillard (Paris, Debure, 1807).

Catalogue des livres de feu M. le baron de Sainte-Croix (Paris, Debure, 1809).

CHABANON, M. P. G. de, *Sur le sort de la poésie en ce siècle philosophique* (Paris, Sébastien Jorry, 1764).

——*Observations sur la musique et principalement sur la métaphysique de l'art* (Paris, Pissot, 1779).

——*De la musique considérée en elle-même et dans ses rapports avec la parole, les langues, la poésie et le théâtre* (Paris, Pissot, 1785).
CHATEAUBRIAND, R. de, *Mémoires d'outre-tombe*, ed. M. Levaillant and G. Moulinier (2 vols.; Paris, Gallimard: Pléiade, 1958).
——*Génie du Christianisme* (Paris, Garnier, 1930).
——*Essai sur les révolutions, Génie du Christianisme*, ed. M. Regard (Paris, Gallimard: Pléiade, 1978).
CHATEAUBRIAND, C. B. DE LA VIGNE, Vtesse de, *Madame de Chateaubriand, Mémoires et Lettres*, ed. J. le Gras (Paris, Henri Jonquières, 1929).
CHÊNEDOLLÉ, Ch.-J. Lioult de, *Le Génie de l'homme* (Paris, Nicolle, 1807).
——*Études poétiques* (2nd edn., Paris, Gosselin, 1822).
——*Extraits du Journal ... (1803–833) d'après des manuscrits inédits*, ed. Mme P. de Samie (Paris, Plon, 1922).
CHÉNIER, A., *Œuvres complètes*, ed. P. Dimoff (3 vols.; Paris, Delagrave, 1911).
*CHRISTINE DE SUÈDE, *Ouvrage de loisir ou Maximes et sentences de Christine, Reine de Suède* (s.l.a.n.).
COLARDEAU, C.-P., 'Ode sur la Poésie comparée à la Philosophie', *Œuvres* (Paris, Ballard, 1799), ii.
COMBES-DOUNOUS, J. J., *Introduction à la philosophie de Platon, traduite du texte grec d'Alcinoüs* (Paris, Didot, an VIII).
——*Essai historique sur Platon* (2 vols.; Paris, Gautier et Bretin, 1809).
*CONDILLAC, E. B. de, *Essai sur l'origine des connoissances humaines* (2 vols.; Amsterdam, Nyon et Barrois, 1788).
——*Œuvres complètes* (23 vols.; Paris, Houel, 1798). ii. *Traité des systèmes*; iii. *Traité des sensations*.
CONDORCET, J. A. N. de, 'Esquisse d'un tableau historique des progrès de l'esprit humain', *Œuvres*, ed. A. Condorcet O'Connor and M. F. Arago (12 vols.; Paris, Firmin Didot, 1847), vi.
COOK, J., *Voyage au pôle austral et autour du monde, écrit par Jacques Cook, commandant de la Résolution, dans lequel on a inséré la relation du capitaine Furneaux et celle de MM. Forster* (5 vols.; Paris, Hôtel de Thou, 1778).
COURT DE GÉBELIN, A., *Le Monde primitif analysé et comparé avec le monde moderne* (9 vols.; Paris, Durand, 1787). (The 1st edn. was published by the author himself between 1773 and 1784.)
*CROUSAZ, J. P. de, *Traité du beau où l'on montre en quoi consiste ce que l'on nomme ainsi par des exemples tirés de la plupart des arts et des sciences* (Amsterdam, François Lhonoré, 1715).
CUDWORTH, R., 'The Digression concerning the Plastick Life of Nature, or an Artificial, Orderly and Methodical Nature', in *The True Intellectual System of the Universe* (London, Richard Royston, 1678).

*Dacier, A., *Les Œuvres de Platon* (2 vols.; Paris, s.n. 1701).
*—— *La Vie de Pythagore, ses symboles, ses vers dorés* (2 vols.; Paris, Rigault, 1706).
Dacier, le bon Joseph, *Notice sur M. de Villoison* (Paris, Imprimerie impériale, 1806).
Destutt de Tracy, A.-L.-C., *Projets d'élémens d'idéologie à l'usage des écoles centrales de la République française* (Paris, P. Didot l'aîné, an IX).
Dictionnaire de l'Académie française (rev. edn., Nismes, Pierre Beaume, 1786).
Diderot, D., *Œuvres complètes*, ed. J. Assézat (20 vols.; Paris, Garnier, 1875).
Documents sur la révolution française. Département de l'Yonne, 'Procès-verbaux de l'administration départementale de l'Yonne, de 1790 à 1800', i. (BL 9225 C. 27).
Du Bos, l'abbé J. B., *Réflexions critiques sur la poésie et sur la peinture* (rev. edn., 3 vols.; Dresden, Georg Conrad Walther, 1760).
Du Marsais, C. C., *Œuvres* (7 vols.; Paris, Imprimerie de Pougin, 1797).
Dupuis, Ch., *Origine de tous les cultes* (4 vols.; Paris, Agasse, 1795).
Emeric-David, T.-B., *Jupiter: Recherches sur ce Dieu, sur son culte, et sur les monuments qui le représentent, ouvrage précédé d'un essai sur l'esprit de la religion grecque* (2 vols.; Paris, Imprimerie royale, 1833).
Encyclopédie, ou dictionnaire raisonné des sciences, des arts et des métiers, par une Société de gens de lettres, mis en ordre et publié par M. Diderot (Paris, Briasson, David, Lebreton, Durand, 1751–65; facsimile repr., Pergamon Press, 1969; Readex Compact Edition, 5 vols.)
Fabre d'Olivet, A., *Les Vers dorés (de Pythagore) expliqués et traduits pour la première fois en vers eumolpiques français, précédés d'un discours sur l'essence et la forme de la poésie chez les principaux peuples de la terre* (Paris, Treuttel et Würtz, 1813).
—— *La Musique expliquée comme science et comme art et considérée dans ses rapports analogiques avec les mystères religieux, la mythologie ancienne et l'histoire de la Terre, ouvrage posthume* (Paris, édition de l'Initiation, BN: V 26798, 1896).
Féraud, L'abbé, *Dictionnaire critique de la langue française* (Marseilles, J. Mossy, 1787).
Ficino, M., *Discours de l'honnête amour sur le Banquet de Platon*, trans. from the Tuscan by G. le Fèvre de la Boderie (Paris, Jean Macé, 1578).
Fleury, Abbé C., *Traité du choix et de la méthode des études* (includes the *Discours sur Platon*) (Paris, Aubouin, Emery et Clousier, 1686).
Fontanes, L. de, *Œuvres* (2 vols.; Paris, Hachette, 1839).
Frisell, F., *Vue générale de la constitution de l'Angleterre depuis son origine jusqu'à nos jours avec quelques remarques sur l'ancienne et la nouvelle constitution de la France* (Paris, Le Normant, 1837).
Gautier, Th., *Préface de Mademoiselle de Maupin*, ed. G. Matoré (Paris, Droz, 1946).

GÉRANDO, J. M. baron de, *De la génération des connoissances humaines* (Berlin, Decker, 1802).

——'Plato', in Michaud (ed.), *Biographie universelle*, xxxi (Paris, Desplaces, 1843), 495–505.

——*Histoire comparée des systèmes de philosophie, relativement aux principes des connaissances humaines*, pt. 2 (4 vols.; Paris, Ladrange, 1847).

*GROTIUS, *Le Droit de la guerre et de la paix par M. Grotius, divisé en trois livres, où il explique le droit de nature, le droit des gens, et les principaux points du droit public ou qui concerne le gouvernement public d'un État, traduit de Latin en françois, par M. de Coutrin* (2 vols.; Amsterdam, Abraham Wolfgang, 1788).

GROU, le père, *Dialogues de Platon* (2 vols.; Amsterdam, 1770).

GUINGENÉ, P. L., *Histoire littéraire d'Italie* (14 vols.; Paris, Michaud, 1811–35).

*HARRIS, J., *Hermès, ou recherches philosophiques sur la grammaire universelle*, trans. F. Thurot (Paris, Imprimerie de la République, an IV).

HEMSTERHUIS, F., *Œuvres philosophiques* (2 vols; Paris, 1792; rev. edn., Paris, Haussmann, 1809).

*HIS, C., *Théorie du monde politique ou de la science du gouvernement considérée comme science exacte* (Paris, Scoel et Cie, 1806).

HOGARTH, G., *Analyse de la beauté*, trans. Hendrik Jansen (2 vols.; Paris, Levrault, Schaell, 1805).

*HUME, D., *Histoire de la maison de Stuart sur le trône d'Angleterre* (2 vols; London, s.n., 1760).

*——*Histoire de la maison de Plantagenet sur le trône d'Angleterre depuis l'invasion de Jules César jusqu'à l'avènement de Henri VII* (2 vols.; Amsterdam, s.n., 1765).

KANT, E., *Observations sur le sentiment du beau et du sublime*, ed. R. Kempf (Paris, Vrin, 1980).

LA BORDE, J.-B. de *Essai sur la musique ancienne et moderne* (4 vols.; Paris, D. Pierres, 1780), i.

LACÉPÈDE, B.-G.-E. de la Ville, *La Poétique de la musique* (2 vols.; Paris, Imprimerie de Monsieur, 1785).

LA FONTAINE, J. de, *Fables*, ed. J. P. Collinet (2 vols.; Paris, Gallimard, 1974).

LA HARPE, J.-F. de, *Lycée: Cours de littérature ancienne et moderne* (16 vols.; Paris, Firmin-Didot, 1821–2), ii.

——*Lycée: Cours de littérature ancienne et moderne* (3 vols.; Paris, Firmin-Didot, 1847).

*LANGLES, L.-M., *Instituts politiques et militaires de Tamerlan, écrits par lui en mongol et traduits du persan* (Paris, Vve Lottin, Didot fils aîné, 1787).

*LAVATER, J. G., *Essai sur la physiognomie, destinée à faire connoître l'homme et à le faire aimer* (3 vols.; La Haye, s.n., 1783–6).

LEIBNIZ, G. G., *Opera omnia collecta* (6 vols; Geneva, L. Dutens, 1768).
——*New Essays on Human Understanding*, ed. P. Remnant and J. Bennett (Cambridge, CUP., 1981).
*Lessing, G. E., *Du Laocöon*, trans. Ch. Vanderbourg (Paris, A.-A. Renouard, 1802).
LEVÉSQUE DE POUILLY, J.-S., *Théorie de l'imagination* (Paris, Bernard, 1803).
LITTRÉ, E., *Dictionnaire de la langue française* (Paris, Hachette, 1863).
LOCKE, J., *Essai sur l'entendement humain*, trans. P. Coste from the 4th rev. edn., corrected and enlarged by author (Amsterdam, Schelte, 1700).
LUCANUS, Ocellus, *De la nature de l'univers*, trans. l'abbé Batteux (Paris, Saillant, 1768). (This work also contains Timaeus Locrus, *De l'âme du monde*, and a Pseudo-Aristotle, *De mundo*.)
Magasin encyclopédique; ou Journal des sciences, des lettres et des arts, ed. Millin *et al.* (122 vols.; Paris, Imprimerie du 'Magasin encyclopédique', 1795–1819), iii, iv, v, vi; *Table générale des matières* (4 vols.; Paris, 1819).
MAINE DE BIRAN, P., *Journal intime*, ed. La Valette Monbrun (2 vols.; Paris, Plon, 1927, 1931).
MAISTRE, J. de, *Essai sur le principe générateur des constitutions politiques et des autres institutions humaines* (St Petersburg, Pluchart et Cie, 1814), ed. R. Triomphe (Strasburg, Les Belles Lettres, 1959).
——*Considérations sur la France* (Neuchâtel, Louis Fauche-Bovel, 1797), ed. J.-L. Darcel (Geneva, Slatkine, rev. edn., 1980).
*MALEBRANCHE, N., *De la recherche de la vérité, où l'on traite de la nature de l'esprit de l'homme, et de l'usage qu'il en doit faire pour éviter l'erreur dans les sciences* (Paris, André Pralard, 1674).
——*Œuvres complètes*, ed. G. Rodis-Lewis, *et al.* (20 vols.; Paris, Vrin, 1958–68), i–iii. *De la recherche de la vérité*.
MARMONTEL, J.-F., *Eléments de littérature* (3 vols.; Paris, Firmin-Didot, 1846).
——*Éléments de littérature* (3 vols.; Paris, Firmin, 1879).
MERCIER, L. S., *Dictionnaire d'un polygraphe, Textes de L. S. Mercier*, ed. G. Bollème (Collection 10/18; Paris, Union Générale d'Éditions, 1978).
Le Mercure de France (1790–1, 1800–17).
MERSENNE, le père Marin, *Harmonie universelle, contenant la théorie et la pratique de la musique* (Paris, S. Cramoisy, 1636).
MILLEVOYE, C. H., *Œuvres* (Paris, Furne, 1833).
MILRAN, F., *Petite histoire de France ou revue polemique d'un grand historien* (2 vols.; Paris, Garnery, 1792).
*MONTESQUIEU, C.-L. de Secondat, *De l'esprit des lois* (3 vols.; Geneva, Barillet et fils, 1753).
*——*Le Génie de Montesquieu* (Amsterdam, Arkstée and Merkus, 1760).
MOREAU, J. N., *Principes de morale, de politique et de droit public puisés dans l'histoire de notre monarchie* (21 vols.; Paris, Imprimerie royale, 1771–89).

SELECT BIBLIOGRAPHY

MORELLET, A., 'De l'expression en musique et de l'imitation dans les arts', *Mélanges de littérature et de philosophie du XVIIIe siècle* (4 vols.; Paris, Lepetit, 1818), iv.

NICOLE, P., *Essais de morale* (Paris, Vve C. Savreux, 1671).

NOLLET, J. A., *Leçons de physique expérimentale* (6 vols.; Paris, Guérin, 1764).

OCELLUS, see Lucanus, Ocellus.

*OHSSON, C. de, *Tableau général de l'empire othoman, divisé en deux parties, dont l'une comprend la législation mahométane; l'autre l'histoire de l'empire othoman. Dédié au roi de Suède, Par M. de M ... d'Ohsson, chevalier de l'ordre royal de Wasa, secrétaire de S.M. le roi de Suède, ci-devant son interprète, et chargé d'affaires à la cour de Constantinople* (5 vols.; Paris, Imprimerie de Monsieur, 1788).

PANGE, F. de, *Œuvres*, ed. L. Becq de Fouquières (Paris, Charpentier, 1872).

PASCAL, B., *Pensées*, ed. M. le Guern (2 vols.; Paris, Gallimard: Folio, 1977).

PLATO, *Divini Platonis opera omnia Marsilio Ficino interprete. Accesserunt sex Platonis dialogi, nuper a Sebastiano Conrado tralati* (London, 1588).

*——*Extraits* (Paris, Louis Josse, 1698).

——*Collected Dialogues*, ed. E. Hamilton and H. Cairns (Princeton, NJ. 1961).

*PLUCHE, l'abbé, A., *Le Spectacle de la nature* (9 vols.; Paris, Estinnes frères, 1764–70).

*PLUQUET, L'abbé, F.-A.-A., *De la sociabilité* (2 vols.; Paris, Barrois, 1767).

PLUTARCH *Œuvres morales*, trans. J. Amyot (8 vols.; Paris, Vasconsan et Fréderic Morel, 1574).

*——*Œuvres morales*, trans. M. l'abbé Richard (17 vols.; Paris, Desaint, 1787), vii.

QUATREMÈRE DE QUINCY, A.-C., *Considérations morales sur la destination des ouvrages de l'art* (Paris, Crapelet, 1815).

——*Essai sur la nature, le but et les moyens de l'imitation dans les beaux arts* (Paris, J. Didot, 1823).

*RABELAIS, F., *Œuvres de Maître François Rabelais, suivies de remarques publiées en anglois par M. Le Motteux, et traduites en françois par C.D.M.* (rev. edn., 3 vols.; Paris, Ferdinant Bastien, an VI).

——*Œuvres complètes*, ed. P. Jourda (2 vols.; Paris, Garnier, 1962).

REID, T., *Œuvres complètes* (6 vols.; Paris, A. Sautelet, 1828–36), ii. *Recherches sur l'entendement humain d'après les principes du sens commun* (1818), v and vi. *Essais sur les facultés actives de l'homme* (1829).

*RIVAROL, A., *Discours préliminaire du nouveau dictionnaire de la langue française* (Paris, Cocheris, 1797).

——*Esprit de Rivarol*, ed. F. J. M. Fayolle and C. de Chênedollé (Paris, s.n., 1808).

——— *Œuvres complètes*, ed. Ch. Chênedollé and F. J. M. Fayolle (5 vols.; Paris, L. Collin, 1808).

RONSARD, P., *Les Amours*, ed. A.-M. Schmïdt and F. Joukovsky (Paris, Gallimard, 1974).

ROUSSEAU, J.-J., *Œuvres complètes*, ed. B. Gagnebin and M. Raymond (4 vols.; Paris, Gallimard: Pléiade, 1969).

*SAINT-MARTIN, L. C. de, *L'Homme de désir* (Lyons, J. Sulpice Grabit, 1790).

——— *Lettre à un ami, ou considérations politiques, philosophiques ou religieuses sur la Révolution française, suivies du précis d'une conférence publique entre un élève des écoles normales et le professeur Garat* (Paris, J.-B. Louvet, 1795).

——— 'Essai sur les signes et sur les idées', *Mélanges* (Paris, 1799).

——— *De l'esprit des choses* (2 vols.; Paris, Laran, 1800).

——— *Les Cahiers de Saint-Martin*, ii, iv (Collection Bélisaire; Nice, 1978, 1983).

SAINT-PIERRE, Bernardin de, *Harmonies de la nature*, ed. L. Aime-Martin (Paris, Mequignon-Marvis, 1815).

——— *Voyage à l'île de France: Un officier du roi à l'île Maurice, 1768–1770*, ed. Y. Bénot (La Découverte; rev. edn., Paris, Maspéro, 1983).

SAINTE-CROIX, G. DE CLERMONT-LODÈVE, BARON DE, *Mémoires pour servir à l'histoire de la religion secrète des anciens peuples; ou Recherches historiques et critiques sur les mystères du paganisme* (Paris, Nyon, 1784; 2nd edn., ed. S. de Saci (2 vols.; Paris, de Bure, 1817).

*SCALIGER, J. C., *Poetices libri septem* (Geneva, J. Crispinum, 1561).

SCHLEGEL, F., *Dialogue on Poetry and Literary Aphorisms*, trans. and ed., E. Behler and R. Stuc (Pennsylvania State University Press, 1968).

SEBILLET, T., *Art poétique françois* (Paris, G. Corrozet, 1548).

SOBRY, J. F., *Poétique des arts ou cours de peinture et de littérature comparées* (Paris, Delaunay, 1810).

STAËL, A.-L.-G.-N., Mme de, *De la littérature considérée dans ses rapports avec les institutions sociales*, ed. P. van Tieghem (Geneva, Droz, 1959).

——— *Corinne ou l'Italie* (Paris, Didot, 1875).

Tableau général raisonné et méthodique des mémoires de littérature de L'Académie des Inscriptions et Belles Lettres (Paris, P. Didot l'aîné, 1791).

TIEDEMANN, D., *Dialogorum Platonis argumenta exposita et illustrata* (Paris, Biponti, 1786).

TOCQUEVILLE, A., *L'Ancien régime et la révolution*, ed. J.-P. Mayer (Paris, Gallimard, 1967).

TRUBLET, N., *Essais sur divers sujets de littérature et de morale* (4 vols.; (Paris, Briasson, 1768).

TURGOT, A.-R.-J., 'Mémoire sur le voyage du capitaine Cook', *Œuvres complètes* (9 vols.; Paris, Delance, 1810), ix. 416–18.

——— *Œuvres*, ed. G. Schelle (4 vols.; Paris, Alcan, 1919).

*VICO, J. B., *De universi juris uno principio et fine uno liber unus ad amplissimum virum, Franciscum venturam a regis consiliis ad criminum quaestorem alterum* (Naples, Felix Musca, 1720).
*——*Liber alter qui est de constantia jurisprudentis ad amplissimum virum Franciscum Venturam* (Naples, Felix Musca, 1721).
VIGNY, A. de, *Les Destinées*, ed. V. L. Saulnier (Geneva, Droz, 1967).
VILLERS, Ch., *Philosophie de Kant, aperçu rapide des bases et de la direction de cette philosophie. Rédigé à Paris pour Bonaparte et imprimé comme manuscrit* (s.e, s.n, 1801).
VILLOTEAU, G., *Mémoire sur la possibilité et l'utilité d'une théorie exacte des principes naturels de la musique* (Paris, Imprimerie impériale, 1807).
——*Recherches sur l'analogie de la musique avec les arts qui ont pour object l'imitation du langage pour servir d'introduction à l'étude des principes naturels de cet art* (Paris, Imprimerie impériale, 1807; repr. 2 vols.; 1970).
*VINNIUS, A. J. C., *Note in quatuor libros institutionum, sive elementorum juris D. Justiniani, Sacratissimi principis, Nova editione recognita et emendata, Accessit index locu pletissimus, cura et studio, Ludovici Muguet, J. U. Doctoris, Parisiis, Excudebat Franciscus Muguet Regis, Cleri Gallicani, et Illustrissimi D.D. archiepiscopi, Typographus* (2 vols.; 1698).
VOLNEY, C.-F., *Les Ruines, ou Méditations sur les Révolutions des Empires* (Paris, Desenne, 1791).
WINCKELMANN, J. J., *Histoire de l'art chez les anciens* (2 vols.; Amsterdam, E. van Harrevelt, 1766).

SECONDARY SOURCES

(i) Critical books and articles on, or specifically referring to, Joubert

'Actes du Colloque Joseph Joubert', *Association Bourguignonne des Sociétés Savantes* (Villeneuve-sur-Yonne, Société des amis de Joseph Joubert, 1986).
'Actes du Colloque Joseph Joubert', La Vallée-aux-Loups, 28 mai 1988 (Villeneuve-sur-Yonne, Société des amis de Joseph Joubert, 1989).
ALCER, N., *Studien zu Joseph Joubert (1754–1824), mit bisher unveröffentlichten Schriften* (Bonn, Free University, 1980).
AMIEL, H.-F., *Fragments d'un journal intime* (3 vols.; Geneva, Georg et Cie, 1922), i. 29–31, iii. 125.
ARNOLD, M., *The Complete Prose Works*, ed. R. H. Super (11 vols.; Ann Arbor, University of Michigan Press, 1960–77), especially vol. iii.

AUDIGER, G., *Souvenirs et anecdotes sur les comités révolutionnaires, 1793–1795* (Paris, P. D. Persan, 1830), 292–3.

BABBITT, I., *The Masters of Modern French Criticism* (London, Constable and Co.; Boston and New York, Houghton Mifflin, 1913).

BARBEY D'AUREVILLY, J., 'Joubert', in *Les Œuvres et les hommes: Les Critiques ou les juges jugés* (Paris, L. Frinzine, 1885), vi.

BARRIÈRE, P., *La Vie intellectuelle en Périgord, 1550–1800* (Bordeaux, Delmas, 1936), 542–6.

BAUER, G., *Les Moralistes français: La Rochefoucauld, La Bruyère, Vauvenargues, Chamfort, Rivarol, Joubert* (Paris, Albin Michel, 1962).

BEAUNIER, A., *La Jeunesse de Joseph Joubert* (Paris, Perrin, 1918).

—— *Joseph Joubert et la Révolution* (Paris, Perrin, 1918).

—— *Le Roman d'une amitié: Joseph Joubert et Pauline de Beaumont* (Paris, Perrin, 1924).

BELLAUNAY, P., *Joseph Joubert et la littérature* (Groningen, J. B. Walters, 1955).

BIBLIOTHÈQUE NATIONALE, *Joseph Joubert, 1754–1824: Exposition organisée pour le 200ᵉ anniversaire de sa naissance* (Paris, 1954).

BILLY, A., *Joubert énigmatique et délicieux* (Paris, Gallimard, 1969).

BLANCHOT, M., 'Joubert et Mallarmé', *La Nouvelle Revue française*, 7 (1956), 110–21.

——'Joubert et l'espace', in *Le Livre à venir* (Paris, 1959), 63–82.

BONNARDOT, J., 'Au verger de Joubert', *Études Villeneuviennes*, 6 (1983), 29–39.

BUSNELLI, M.-D., 'Une devise de Joubert inspirée par Kotzebue', *Revue d'histoire littéraire de la France*, 38.

CARO, E., 'Joseph Joubert et ses Pensées', *Revue des deux mondes*, 90 (1 Nov. 1870), 27–37.

CESTRE, M., *Joubert* (Auxerre, Gallot, 1912).

CHARPENTIER, J., *Napoléon et les hommes de lettres de son temps* (Paris, Éditions du Mercure de France, 1935).

CHASTENAY, Mme de, *Mémoires de Mme de Chastenay, 1771–1815* (2 vols.; Paris, Plon, 1897).

CHRÉTIEN, J.-L., 'Joseph Joubert: Une philosophie à l'état naissant', *La Revue de métaphysique et de morale*, 4, 34 (1979), 467–92.

CLARENS, J.-P., *Joseph Joubert* (Paris, Savine, 1893).

COCKING, J. C., 'Joseph Joubert and the Critical Tradition', *French Studies*, 37 (1983), 220–1. (This is a review of the book of that title by P. A. Ward.)

CONDAMIN, J. P., *Essai sur les pensées et la correspondance de Joubert* (Paris, Didier, 1877).

DANIEL-ROPS, H., 'Les Carnets de Joseph Joubert', *La Revue hebdomadaire* (June–July 1938), 102–12.

DAUPHIN, J.-L., 'Joubert, Fontanes et le vin de Villeneuve-sur-Yonne', *Bulletin de la Société des Sciences Historiques et Naturelles de l'Yonne*, 113 (1981), 108–19.
——'Les Amis de Joseph Joubert', *Études Villeneuviennes*, 9 (Villeneuve-sur-Yonne, 1986), 65–86.
DURANTON, G., 'Joubert le penseur', *Annuaire de l'Yonne* (Auxerre, 1869), 20–63.
DURIEUX, J., *Joseph Joubert, l'homme et l'œuvre* (Périgeux, Imprimerie de la Dordogne, 1901).
ÉMILE-PAUL, H., 'Les Pensées de Joubert', *Bulletin du bibliophile* (Oct. 1948), 488–90.
ESSARTS, E. des, 'Les Théories de Joseph Joubert', *Revue bleue* (20 July 1907), 75–7.
EVANS, J., *The Unselfish Egoist* (London, Longmans, 1947).
FAIRCLOUGH, G. T., *A Fugitive and Gracious Light. The Relation of Joseph Joubert to Matthew Arnold's Thought* (University of Nebraska Studies New Series, 23; Lincoln, University of Nebraska Press, 1961).
FRESCAROLI, A., 'Estetica e critica in Joseph Joubert', *Aevum*, 35 (July–Aug. 1961), 323–80.
——'La Fortuna di Joseph Joubert', *Aevum*, 36 (Jan.–Apr. 1962), 141–59.
FROMENT, Th., 'Un voisin de Montaigne au XIXe siècle, Joubert', *Revue philomathique de Bordeaux* (1900), 481–99.
GAILLON, MARQUIS de, 'De Joubert et de quelques-uns de ses jugements littéraires', *Bulletin du bibliophile* (1865), 80–4.
GARCIN, P., 'Joubert, ou la rhétorique efficace', *Critique*, 10 (July–Aug. 1954), 592–608.
GAUDEMAR, P. de, 'La Signification du thème de la pudeur dans la pensée morale et sociale de Joubert', *Annales de la Faculté des Lettres de Toulouse, Homo*, 4 (May 1965), 153–75.
GÉRARD, A. S., '"Fancy" in Joubert: Modes of Imagination in Romanticism', *Comparative Literature*, 16 (1964), 158–66.
GÉRUZEZ, E., 'Joubert', in *Nouveaux essais d'histoire littéraire* (Paris, Hachette, 1846), 423–36.
GILMAN, M., 'Joubert on Imagination and Poetry,' *Romanic Review*, 40 (1949), 250–60.
GIRAUD, V., 'Une biographie perdue de Joubert', *Revue de Fribourg* (1908), 347–67.
——'Un moraliste d'autrefois: Joseph Joubert', *Revue des deux mondes*, 58 (15 Aug. 1910), 769–807.
——*Moralistes français* (Paris, Hachette, 1923).
——'Joubert inconnu', *Revue des deux mondes* (15 Mar. 1939), 417–32.

GONCOURT, E. and J. de, *Mémoires de la vie littéraire* (édition définitive publiée sous la direction de l'Académie Goncourt; 9 vols.; Paris, Flammarion, 1935–6), iii.
GOUZE, R., 'Joubert et Alain', unpublished article.
GUITTON, J., 'Tombeau de Joubert', *Journal–Études et rencontres* (Paris, Plon, 1959).
HALDA, B., *Joseph Joubert ou de la perfection* (Paris, Colombe, 1953).
ILLAS JOSA, N., 'La Posteridad de Joseph Joubert', thesis abstract (University of Barcelona, 1981).
——'Joubert et Diderot', *Universitas Tarraconensis, Facultat de Filosofia i Lletres*, viii (Tarragona, University Press, 1985), 85–6.
JOUBERT, A., *Notice historique sur Joseph Joubert* (Paris, Le Normant fils, 1824).
KINLOCH, D. P., 'The Art of the Missing Postscript: Some Unpublished Manuscripts of Joseph Joubert', *Nottingham French Studies*, 24/2 (1985), 12–27.
——'Platonism and the *Carnets* of Joseph Joubert', *French Studies Bulletin*, 32 (1989), 10–14.
KRAUS, F. X., 'Jouberts "Gedanken" und Briefwechsel', *Deutsche Rundschau*, 44 (Berlin, 1886), 348-70.
KRUMMENACHER, M., 'L'Authenticité de l'expérience joubertienne', thesis (Zurich, 1972).
LATAPIE, F. de P., 'L'Industrie et le commerce en Guienne sous le règne de Louis XVI' (Journal de tournée de François-de-Paule Latapie en 1778), *Archives historiques du départment de la Gironde*, 38 (Paris and Bordeaux, Feret, 1893).
LAUDET, F., *Les Semeurs* (Paris, Perrin, 1917), 15–72, 91, 93, 109–111.
LEMAÎTRE, J., 'Un symboliste: Joubert', *Temps* (28 June 1894).
——*Poésies de Jules Lemaître* (Paris, A. Lemerre, 1896), 131–2.
——*Les Contemporains*, 6th ser. (Paris, Lécène Oudin, 1896), 302–7.
LOMBARD, A., *Étude sur Joubert* (Nancy, Imprimerie de Vve. Raybois, 1862).
LOMBARD DE LANGRES, V., *Mémoires anecdotiques pour servir à l'histoire de la Révolution française* (2 vols.; Paris, Ladvocat, 1823), i. 48–51, 76–7, 84–5.
MANGEOT, P., '"20 Janvier 1800. A qui parles-tu?" Joseph Joubert et l'écriture des carnets', *Littérature*, 80 (Dec. 1990), 71–85.
MASSON, P.-M., 'Chateaubriand et Joubert', *Revue d'histoire littéraire de la France*, 16 (1909), 794–7.
MICHEL, A., 'La Parole et la beauté chez Joubert, Jouffroy, et Ballanche', *Revue d'histoire littéraire de la France*, 80 (1980), 195–207.
MONGLOND, A., *Histoire intérieure du préromantisme français de Prévost à Joubert* (2 vols.; Grenoble, Arthaud, 1929).
——'Joubert en Périgord', *Revue des deux mondes* (15 Jan., 15 Feb. 1941), 203–18, 500–8.

SELECT BIBLIOGRAPHY

MONNET, A., *Étude sur Joseph Joubert et son époque (1754–1824)* (Niort, Clauzot, 1887).

NORBERT, Sœur M., 'Joseph Joubert et le culte public', *Revue de l'Université d'Ottawa*, 34 (Jan.–Mar. 1964), 45–62.

PAILHÈS, G., Abbé, *Du Nouveau sur Joubert, Chateaubriand, Fontanes et sa fille* (Paris, Garnier, 1900).

PERCHE, L., *Joubert parmi nous* (Limoges, Rougerie, 1954).

PERROS, G., 'Joubert', *Les Cahiers du chemin*, 13 (15 Oct. 1971), 130–4.

PICHOIS, C., 'Actualité de Joubert', *Revue des cercles d'études d'Angers*, 15–16 (Nov. 1954), 27–8.

PIZZORUSSO, A., 'L'imaginazione e le immagini in Joseph Joubert', *Annali delle Facoltà di lettere e filosofia dell'Università di Cagliari*, xix (1952), 99–115.

——'La poetica di Joubert', *Studi sulla letteratura dell'età préromantica in Francia* (Pisa, Goliardica, 1956), 53–97.

——'Sui "Carnets" di Joubert: Gli spettacoli dell'immaginazione e della memoria', *Paragone*, 35/418 (Dec. 1984), 3–23.

——'Joubert e l'immagine del soggetto', *Belfagor*, 40 (1985), 19–37.

——'Joubert e l'osservazione della scrittura', *Rivista di letterature moderne e comparate*, 39 (Florence, 1986), 25–44.

——'L'Image du sujet dans les *Carnets* de Joubert', *Lettres et réalités. Mélanges de litterature générale et de critique romanesque offerts à Henri Coulet par ses amis* (Aix-en-Provence, Université de Provence, 1988), 295–310.

PRÉVOST, M., 'Les Carnets de Joseph Joubert', in *Marcel Prévost et ses contemporains* (2 vols.; Paris, Éditions de France, 1943), i. 134–9.

RAT, M., 'Joubert: Grammarien et amateur de beau langage', *Vie et langage*, 10 (1961), 17–18.

RAYNAL, P. DE (ed.), *Les Correspondants de Joubert* (Paris, Calmann-Lévy, 1883).

RENDU, E., *M. Ambroise Rendu et l'Université de France* (Paris, Fouraut et Dentu, 1861).

ROUSSEAUX, A., 'Le Penseur Joubert', in *Le Monde classique* (Paris, A. Michel, 1941), 128–35.

SABA, G., 'Profilo di Joubert', in *Memoria e poesia, scrittori francesi dal Préromanticismo al Simbolismo* (Rocca San Casciano, Cappelli, 1961), 5–31.

SAINT-MARTIN, J., 'Les Parentés spirituelles entre la Boétie, Montaigne et les autres penseurs du Périgord et du Bordelais', in G. Palassie (ed.), *Mémorial du 1er Congrès International des Études Montaignistes* (Bordeaux, Tafford, 1964), 173–89.

SAINTE-BEUVE, C. A., *Les Grands Écrivains français*, ed. M. Allem (23 vols.; Paris, Garnier, 1930), xii, pt. i. *Philosophes et essayistes*.

SAINTSBURY, G., *A History of Criticism and Literary Taste in Europe* (3 vols.; Edinburgh and London, Blackwood and Sons, 1900–4), iii.
SAMIE, Mme P. de, 'L'Amitié d'un sage pour un poète. Lettres inédites de Joubert à Chênedollé', *Revue d'histoire littéraire de la France* (Jan.–Mar. 1932), 73–99.
EL SAMMON, J. A., 'The Criticism and Poetics of Joseph Joubert', unpublished thesis (Pittsburgh, 1966).
SCHERER, E., *Études sur la littérature contemporaine* (Paris, Calmann-Lévy, 1891), i. 111–13, 122.
SOREIL, A., 'Sur un mot de Joubert', *Marche Romane*, 5–9 (1955–9), 111–120.
STEELE, A. J., 'La Sagesse de Joubert', in *Studies in Romance Philology and French Literature Presented to John Orr* (Manchester, 1953), 282–5.
STURM, P. J., 'Joseph Joubert', unpublished thesis (Yale University, 1938).
——'Joubert and Voltaire: A Study in Reaction', *Yale Romanic Studies*, 18 (1941), 185–220.
——'Joseph Joubert's Self-Portrait', *Romanic Review*, 32 (1941), 345–58.
TALVART, H., and PLACE, J., *Bibliographie des auteurs modernes de langue française (1801–1949)* (17 vols.; Paris, Chronique des lettres françaises, 1950), x. 160–73. (It should be noted that these pages, useful though they may be, mention a number of works which do *not* refer to Joubert at all or which confuse him with writers of similar-sounding names.)
TESSONNEAU, R., *Joseph Joubert, Éducateur, d'après des documents inédits (1754–1824)* (Paris, Plon, 1944).
——'Chateaubriand Éditeur de Fontanes et de Joubert', *Revue d'histoire littéraire de la France* (May/June 1976), 433–42.
THÉVENAZ-SCHMALENBACH, C., *Joubert: Seine geistige Welt* (Geneva, Kundig, 1956).
TURQUETY, É., 'Réponse à un reproche', *Bulletin du bibliophile* (Nov. 1865), 172–81.
VANDÉREM, F., *Le Miroir des lettres* (8 vols.; Paris, Flammarion, 1929), vii. 166–69.
VERNON, A., 'Amour et amitié dans Joseph Joubert', unpublished thesis (McGill University, 1970).
WARD, P. A., *Joseph Joubert and the Critical Tradition: Platonism and Romanticism* (Geneva, Droz, 1980).
——'Joubert and Vico', *Revue de littérature comparée*, 55 (1981), 226–31.
WILSON, A., *Fontanes 1751–1821: Essai biographique et littéraire* (Paris, De Bocard, 1928).

(ii) Background critical books and articles

ABRAMS, M. H., *The Mirror and the Lamp: Romantic Theory and the Critical Tradition* (Oxford, OUP, 1953).

ACOMB, F., *Mallet du Pan: A Career in Political Journalism* (Durham, NC, Duke University Press, 1973).
ACTON, H. B., *The Philosophy of Language in Revolutionary France* (Dawes Hicks Lecture on Philosophy; London, British Academy, 1959).
ALLEN, M., *The Platonism of Marsilio Ficino: A Study of his Phaedrus Commentary, its Sources and Genesis* (Center for Medieval and Renaissance Studies; Berkeley and London, University of California Press, 1984).
—— *Marsilio Ficino: The Philebus Commentary, a Critical Edition and Translation* (Berkeley and London, University of California Press, 1975).
ALTHUSSER, L., 'Despote et monarque chez Montesquieu', *Esprit*, 26 (1958), 595–614.
ANDERSON, W. C., *Between the Library and the Laboratory: The Language of Chemistry in Eighteenth Century France* (Baltimore, Johns Hopkins, 1984).
ASPELIN, G., 'Ralph Cudworth's Interpretation of Greek Philosophy', *Göteborgs Högskolas Åsrskrift* (1943), 11–43.
BADOLLE, M., *L'Abbé Jean-Jacques Barthélémy (1716–1795) et l'hellénisme en France dans la seconde moitié du XVIIIe siècle* (Paris, Presses Universitaires de France, 1926).
BAHNER, W., 'Le Mot et la notion de "peuple" dans l'œuvre de Rousseau', *Studies on Voltaire*, 55 (1967), 113–27.
BARBER, W. H., *Leibniz in France* (Oxford, OUP, 1955).
BARCLAY, L., 'Louis de Bonald, Prophet of the Past?', *Studies on Voltaire*, 55 (1967), 167–203.
BARDEZ, J.-M., *Les Écrivains et la musique au XVIIe: Philosophes, encyclopédistes, musiciens, théoriciens* (Geneva, Slatkine, 1980).
BARTHOLOMESS, C., *Histoire philosophique de l'académie de Prusse* (2 vols.; Paris, Ducloux, 1851).
BECQ, A., 'Aux sources occultes de l'esthétique romantique: L'Imagination selon Saint-Martin', in P. Viallaneix (ed.), *Le Préromantisme: Hypothèque ou hypothèse* (Paris, Klincksieck, 1975), 414–24.
—— *Genèse de l'esthétique française moderne: De la raison classique à l'imagination créatrice, 1680–1814* (2 vols.; Pisa, Pacini, 1984).
—— 'Esthétique et politique sous le Consulat et l'Empire: La Notion de beau idéal', *Romantisme*, 51 (1986), 23–37.
BÉNICHOU, P., *Le Sacre de l'écrivain* (Paris, José Corti, 1973).
BÉNOT, Y., 'Diderot et le luxe: Jouissances ou égalité?', *Europe*, 661 (May 1984), 58–72.
BERLIN, I., *Four Essays on Liberty* (Oxford, OUP, 1969), especially 'Two Concepts of Liberty', 118–72.
—— *Vico and Herder: Two Studies in the History of Ideas* (London, Chatto and Windus, 1976).
—— 'The Hedgehog and the Fox', in H. Hardy and A. Kelly (eds.), *Russian Thinkers* (Harmondsworth, Pelican, 1979), 22–81.

BLANCHOT, M., *L'Espace littéraire* (Paris, Gallimard, 1955).
—'Sur le journal intime', *La Nouvelle Nouvelle Revue française*, 5 (1955), 683–91.
BOAS, G., *French Philosophies of the Romantic Period* (Baltimore, Johns Hopkins, 1925).
BOYANCÉ, P., 'Le Platonisme à Rome: Platon et Cicéron', *Études sur l'humanisme cicéronien*, 121 (Brussels, Latonus, 1970), 224–47.
BRAHIMI, D., 'Préromantiques en Barbarie', in P. Viallaneix (ed.), *Le Préromantisme: Hypothèque ou hypothèse* (Paris, Klincksieck, 1975), 169–81.
BREMOND, H., *Les Deux Musiques de la prose* (Paris, Le Divan, 1924).
BRODY, J., *Boileau and Longinus*, (Geneva, Droz, 1958).
—'Platonisme et Classicisme', in J. Brody (ed.), *French Classicism: A Critical Miscellany* (Englewood Cliffs, NJ, Prentice-Hall, 1966), 186–207.
—*Du style à la pensée: Trois études sur les caractères de La Bruyère* (French Forum; Lexington, Kentucky, 1980).
BRYANT, D., 'Revolution and Introspection: The Appearance of the Private Diary in France', *European Studies Review*, 8 (University of Wales, 1978), 259–72.
BUSSON, H., *La Religion des classiques (1660–1685)* (Paris, PUF, 1948).
CABEEN, D. C., *A Critical Biography of French Literature* (Syracuse University Press, 1947; supplement, 1968).
CANAT, R., *La Renaissance de la Grèce antique* (Paris, Hachette, 1911).
—*L'Hellénisme des romantiques*, i. *La Grèce retrouvée* (Paris, Didier, 1951).
CASTÉRAS, P. de, *La Société toulousaine à la fin du XVIIIe siècle: L'Ancien Régime et la Révolution* (Toulouse, 1891).
CAVE, T., *Ronsard the Poet* (London, Methuen, 1973).
CELLIER, L., *Fabre d'Olivet: Contribution à l'étude des aspects religieux du Romantisme* (Paris, Nizet, 1953).
CHARDON DE LA ROCHETTE, 'Sur la vie et les principaux ouvrages de Villoison', *Mélanges de critique et de philologie* (3 vols.; Paris, d'Hautel, 1812), iii. 1–61.
CHASTEL, A., *Marsile Ficin et l'art* (Geneva, Droz, 1954).
CHINARD, G., *L'Amérique et le rêve exotique* (Paris, Hachette, 1913).
—*L'Exotisme américain dans l'Œuvre de Chateaubriand* (Paris, Hachette, 1918).
CHOUILLET, J., *L'Esthétique des lumières* (Paris, PUF, 1974).
CIORANESCU, A., *Bibliographie de la littérature française du dix-huitième siècle* (Paris, CNRS, 1969).
CROCKER, L. G., *An Age of Crisis: Man and World in Eighteenth Century French Thought* (Baltimore and London, Johns Hopkins, 1959).
CROUZET, M., 'D'Helvétius à Stendhal: Les Métamorphoses de l'utile', in P. Viallaneix (ed.), *Le Préromantisme: Hypothèque ou hypothèse* (Paris, Klincksieck, 1975), 468–87.

DEGUY, M. *La Poésie n'est pas seule: Court traité de poétique* (Paris, Seuil, 1987).
DELON, M., 'Savoir totalisant et forme éclatée', *Dix-huitième siècle*, 14 (Paris, Garnier, 1982), 13–26.
——*L'Idée d'énergie au tournant des lumières* (Paris, Presses Universitaires de France, 1988).
DERRIDA, J., *L'Archéologie du frivole: Lire Condillac* (Paris, Denoël/Gonthier, 1973).
DIDIER, B., *Le Journal intime* (Paris, PUF, 1976).
DIMOFF, P., *La Vie et l'Œuvre d'André Chénier, jusqu'à la Révolution française, 1762–1790* (2 vols.; Paris, Droz, 1936).
DUCHET, M., 'Le Primitivisme de Diderot', *Europe*, 405–6 (Jan.–Feb. 1963), 126–37.
EGGER, E., *L'Hellénisme en France: Leçons sur l'influence des études grecques dans le développement de la langue et de la littérature française* (Paris, Didier, 1869).
EHRARD, J., *L'Idée de nature en France à l'aube des lumières* (Paris, Flammarion, 1970).
Europe, 661 (May 1984), 'Diderot'.
FARGHER, R., 'The Retreat from Voltairianism, 1800–1815', in W. Moore, R. Sutherland, and E. Starkie (eds.), *The French Mind: Studies in Honour of Gustave Rudler* (Oxford, Clarendon Press, 1952), 220–37.
FAYOLLE, R., *Sainte-Beuve et le dix-huitième siècle, ou comment les révolutions arrivent* (Paris, Armand Colin, 1972).
FESTUGIÈRE, J., *La Philosophie de l'amour de Marsile Ficin* (Paris, 1941).
FOLKIERSKI, W., *Entre le classicisme et le romantisme* (Paris, Champion, 1925).
GILMAN, M., *The Idea of Poetry in France from Houdar de la Motte to Baudelaire* (Cambridge, Mass., 1958).
GIRARD, A., *Le Journal intime et la notion de personne* (Paris, PUF, 1963).
GIRAUDOUX, J., 'Supplément au voyage de Cook, pièce en un acte', in *Théâtre complet* (2 vols.; Paris, Grasset, 1971), ii. 10–43.
GODECHOT, J., *La Contre-Révolution* (Paris, Presses Universitaires de France, 1961).
GOHIN, F., *La Fontaine, études et recherches* (Paris, Garnier, 1937).
GOUHIER, H., *Les Conversions de Maine de Biran* (Paris, Vrin, 1947).
GOYET, T., 'Présence de Platon dans le classicisme français', Congrès de Tours et Poitiers, *Association Guillaume Budé* (Poitiers, 1953).
GROETHUYSEN, B., *Philosophie de la Révolution française* (Paris, Gallimard, 1956).
GUILLOIS, A., *Le Salon de Madame Helvétius* (Paris, Calmann-Lévy, 1894).
GUITTON, E., 'Aspects de la conversion (1790–1800)', *Dix-Huitième Siècle* ('Au tournant des lumières': 1790–1800), 14 (1982), 151–66.

HAIGHT, J., *The Concept of Reason in French Classical Literature, 1635–1690* (University of Toronto Romance Studies Series, 45; Toronto University Press, 1982).
HAMILTON, P., *Coleridge's Poetics* (Oxford, Blackwell, 1983).
HAMPSON, N., *Will and Circumstance: Montesquieu, Rousseau and the French Revolution* (London, Duckworth, 1983).
HARDING, F. J. W., *Matthew Arnold the Critic and France* (Geneva, Droz, 1964).
HAZARD, P., *La Pensée européenne au XVIIIᵉ siècle* (Paris, Boivin, 1946).
HELLAND, G., *Étude biographique et littéraire sur Chênedollé* (Paris, Mortain, 1857).
HOBSON, M., *The Object of Art: The Theory of Illusion in 18th Century France* (Cambridge, CUP, 1982).
HOWELLS, W. S., *Eighteenth-Century British Logic and Rhetoric* (Princeton University Press, 1971).
HUIT, Ch., 'Le Platonisme en France au XVIIᵉ et au XVIIIᵉ siècles', *Annales de la philosophie chrétienne*, iv–vii (Paris, Apr. 1907–Sept. 1908).
IKNAYAN, M., *The Concave Mirror: From Imitation to Expression in French Esthetic Theory, 1800–1830*, Stanford French and Italian Studies, 30; (Saratoga, Anma Libri, 1983).
JANOWITZ, A., 'Coleridge's 1816 Volume: Fragment as Rubric', *Studies in Romanticism*, 24 (spring 1985), 21–39.
JEANNERET, M., 'Les Paroles dégelées, Rabelais, *Quart Livre*, 48–65', *Littérature*, 17 (1975), 14–30.
JORET, Ch., *D'Ansse de Villoison et l'héllénisme en France* (Paris, Champion, 1910).
JUDEN, B., *Traditions orphiques et tendances mystiques dans le Romantisme français (1800–1855)* (Paris, Klincksieck, 1971).
——'L'Esthétique: "L'Harmonie immense qui dit tout"', *Romantisme*, 5 (1973), 4–17.
——'Nerval et le paradoxe du Grand Tout', *Annales de la faculté de lettres et sciences humaines de Nice*, 51 (1985), 251–60.
KLAPP, O., *Bibliographie der französischen Literaturwissenschaft* (Frankfurt, Klostermann, 1956).
KLINCK, D. M., 'An Examination of the *Notes de Lecture* of Louis de Bonald: At the Origins of the Ideology of the Radical Right in France'. Expanded version of a paper given at the 'Sixième Congrès International des lumières'. See *Transactions of the Sixth International Congress on the Enlightenment* (The Voltaire Foundation, Oxford, 1983), 18–20.
KNIGHT, I. F., *The Geometric Spirit: The Abbé de Condillac and the French Enlightenment* (New Haven, Conn., Yale University Press, 1968).

KRISTELLER, P. O., *The Philosophy of Marsilio Ficino*, tr. V. Conant (Columbia Studies in philosophy, 6; New York, Columbia University Press, 1943).
——*Eight Philosophers of the Italian Renaissance* (London, Chatto and Windus, 1965).
LOVEJOY, A. O., 'Kant and the English Platonists', *Essays Philosophical and Psychological in Honour of William James* (Columbia, NY, 1908).
MACAY, J. (ed.), *Essays on the Enlightenment in Honour of Ira O. Wade* (Geneva, Droz, 1977).
MACCUTCHEON, R. P., 'Eighteenth Century Aesthetics: A Search of Surviving Values', *Harvard Library Bulletin*, 10 (1956), 287–305.
MAJEWSKI, H. F., *The Preromantic Imagination of L. S. Mercier* (New York, Humanities Press, 1971).
MANUEL, F. E., and Manuel F. P., *Utopian Thought in the Western World* (Oxford, Blackwell, 1979).
MARTIN, K., *French Liberal Thought in the Eighteenth Century: A Study of Political Ideas from Bayle to Condorcet* (London, Turnstile Press, 1954).
MAUZI, R., *L'Idée du bonheur dans la littérature et la pensée françaises au XVIIIe siècle* (Paris, Armand Colin, 1960).
MCMAHON, J. (ed.), *The Classical Line: Essays in Honor of Henri Peyre* (Yale French Studies, 38; New Haven, Conn. 1967).
MICHAUD, (ed.), *Biographie universelle*, xxxi (Paris, Desplaces, 1843), 495–505 (Gérando on Plato).
MONCEAUX, H., *La Révolution dans l'Yonne, 1788–1800* (Paris, Picard, 1890).
MONTÉGUT, E., 'Souvenirs de Bourgogne: Les Petites Villes: Villeneuve-sur-Yonne', *Revue des deux mondes* (1 July 1872), 164–95.
MOREAU, P., *Le Classicisme des romantiques* (Paris, Plon, 1932).
MORNET, D., 'Les Enseignements des bibliothèques privées (1750–1780)', *Revue d'histoire littéraire de la France*, 17 (1920), 449–96.
——*French Thought in the Eighteenth Century* (Connecticut, Archon Books, 1969).
MORTIER, R., 'La Transition du 18e au 19e siècle', *Dix-huitième siècle*, 14 (1982), 7–12.
——*L'Originalité: Une nouvelle catégorie esthétique au siècle des lumières* (Geneva, Droz, 1983).
MOSSOP, D. J., *Pure Poetry: Studies in French Poetic Theory and Practice, 1746–1945* (Oxford, Clarendon Press, 1971).
MOULINIÉ, H., *De Bonald* (Paris, Alcan, 1916).
NAUDIN, M., *Évolution parallèle de la poésie et de la musique en France: Rôle unificateur de la chanson* (Paris, Nizet, 1968).
NEEFS, J., 'Le Volume des livres (Fragments pour *Bouvard*)', *L'Arc: Flaubert*, 79 (Aix-en-Provence, 1980), 77–80.

PANOFSKY, E., *Idea: A Concept in Art Theory* (New York, Harper and Row, 1968).
PATER, W., 'Diaphanéité', in *Miscellaneous Studies: A Series of Essays* (London, Macmillan, 1895), 251–9.
PATRIDES, C. A., *The Cambridge Platonists* (London, Arnold, 1969).
POMEAU, R., 'Voyage et lumières dans la littérature française du XVIIIe siècle', *Studies on Voltaire*, 57 (1967), 1269–89.
POMMIER, J., 'Les "Salons" de Diderot et leur influence au XIXe siècle', *Revue des cours et conférences* (30 May and 15 June 1936), 289–306, 437–52.
POULET, G., *La Distance intérieure* (Paris, Plon, 1952).
——*Mesure de l'instant* (Paris, Plon, 1968).
QUAINTON, A., *Francis Bacon* (Oxford, OUP, 1980).
REGALDO, M., *Un milieu intellectuel: La Décade philosophique (1794–1807)* (5 vols.; Paris, Champion, 1976).
ROBINET, A., *Malebranche et Leibniz, relations personnelles* (Paris, Vrin, 1955).
ROSSARD, J., *Une clef du romantisme: La Pudeur* (Paris, Nizet, 1975).
SACCARO-BATTISTI, G., 'Changing Metaphors of Political Structures', *Journal of the History of Ideas* (Jan. 1983), 31–54.
SAINTE-BEUVE, C. A., *Les Cahiers*, ed. A. Lemerre (Paris, Lemerre, 1876).
——*Chateaubriand et son groupe littéraire sous l'Empire*, cours professé à Liège en 1848–1849 (new edn., M. Allem, Paris, Garnier, 1948).
SAMIE, Mme P. de, *A l'aube du Romantisme: Chênedollé* (Paris, Plon-Nourrit, 1920).
SCARFE, F., *André Chénier: His Life and Work, 1762–1794* (Oxford, Clarendon Press, 1965).
SELBY-BIGGE, L. A., *British Moralists: Being Selections from Writers Principally of the Eighteenth Century* (2 vols.; Oxford, 1897).
SHACKLETON, R., *Montesquieu: A Critical Biography* (Oxford, OUP, 1961).
SOLMSEN, F., *Aristotle's System of the Physical World* (Ithaca, NY, Cornell University Press, 1960).
SOLTAU, R., *French Political Thought in the Nineteenth Century* (London, Russell, 1959).
SOREIL, A., *Étude littéraire sur le vicomte de Bonald* (Paris, Lebègue, 1942).
STAROBINSKI, J., 'La Nostalgie: Théories médicales et expression littéraire', *Actes du 1er Congrès international des lumières: Studies on Voltaire*, 27 (1963), 1505–18.
——*1789: Les Emblèmes de la raison* (Paris, Flammarion, 1969).
STELLING-MICHAUD, S., 'Lumières et politique', *Studies on Voltaire*, 27 (1963), 1519–43.
SVAGLIC, M. J., 'Classical Rhetoric and Victorian Prose', in G. L. Levine (ed.), *The Art of Victorian Prose* (New York, OUP, 1968), 268–88.

SZENCZI, M. J., 'The Mimetic Principle in Later Eighteenth-Century Criticism', in M. J. Szenczi and L. Ferenczi (eds.), *Studies in Eighteenth Century Literature* (Budapest, Akademiai Kiadö, 1974), 35–54.

TEYSSÈDRE, B., *Roger de Piles et les débats sur le coloris au siècle de Louis XIV* (Paris, La Bibliothèque des Arts, 1957).

TIGERSTEDT, E. N., 'The Decline and Fall of the Neoplatonic Interpretation of Plato: An Outline and Some Observations', *Commentationes Humanarum Litterarum, Societas Scientiarum Fennica*, 52 (Helsinki, Helsingfors, 1974), 42–5.

TRILLING, L., *Matthew Arnold* (New York, W. W. Norton, 1939).

TRIOMPHE, R., *Joseph de Maistre: Étude sur la vie et sur la doctrine d'un matérialiste mystique* (Geneva, Droz, 1968).

VAN DELFT, L., *Le Moraliste classique: Essai de définition et de typologie* (Geneva, Droz, 1982).

VIATTE, A., *Les Sources occultes du romantisme français, illuminisme, théosophie, 1770–1820* (2 vols.; Paris, H. Champion, 1928).

VIELLE, C., L'abbé, 'L'Esquile, origine et fondateurs', *Revue historique de Toulouse* (Jan. 1914).

VIGUERIE, J. de, *Une Œuvre d'éducation sous l'ancien régime: Les Pères de la Doctrine Chrétienne en France et en Italie, 1592–1792* (publications de la Sorbonne, série 'NS Recherches', 13; Université de Paris, IV; Paris, Éditions de la Nouvelle Aurore, 1976).

WALLIS, R. T., *Neoplatonism* (London, Duckworth, 1972).

WELCH, C. B., *Liberty and Utility: The French Ideologues and the Transformation of Liberalism* (New York, Columbia University Press, 1984).

WELLEK, R., *A History of Modern Criticism*, ii. *The Romantic Age* (New Haven, Conn., and London, Yale University Press, 1955).

YATES, F. A., *The French Academies of the Sixteenth Century* (London, The Warburg Institute, 1947).

ZEMEK, Th., 'Mme de Staël et l'esprit national', *Dix-huitième siècle*, 14 (1982), 89–101.

Index

d'Aguesseau, Henri-Cardin-Jean-Baptiste, marquis 74–5
Alcer, Norbert 24, 39, 43
Allen, Michael 133, 140, 141
analogy 125–27, 142, 153–58
L'Ancien régime et la révolution, see Tocqueville
Ancillon, Frederic 151
Ansse de Villoison, J.-B.G.d' 83–5, 117
  De triplici theologia mysteriisque veterum commentatio 84
Aristotle 79, 93, 111, 124, 125, 131, 134
Arnaud, abbé François 73, 77 n. 20
Arnold, Matthew 5, 6, 7, 9, 10, 11, 12, 13, 14
Arthur, Richard 14

Babbitt, Irving 13, 14
Bacon, Francis 145–6, 147, 152, 159, 164, 165
Baif, Jean-Antoine de 73, 91
Ballanche, Pierre Simon 110
Barbey d'Aurevilly, Jules-Amédée 14
Barnes, Thomas 170 n. 15
Barthelemy, Jean-Jacques 73–4
Batteux, Charles 124, 126, 154, 158
Baudelaire, Charles 14
Baurein, Jacques 30
Beattie, James 155
Beaumont, Pauline de 141, 193
Beaunier, André xi, 2, 12, 15, 16–17, 19, 21, 22, 34, 35, 43, 168, 170, 179
Becq, Annie 175
Bénichou, Paul 14 n. 44
Bénot, Yves 39
Berkeley, George 147, 152
Berlin, Isaiah 41, 63
Blanchot, Maurice 14, 17, 18, 19, 20, 196, 197
Blair, Hugh 165
Boileau, Nicolas 175, 177, 183

Bonald, Louis, vicomte de 40, 50, 52, 56, 57, 58, 61–3, 64, 69, 147, 165–7, 171, 172
  Du Divorce 40, 165
  Essai analytique 165
  Législation primitive 165
  Recherches philosophiques 61–3, 165, 166, 167, 171
  Théorie du pouvoir 164
Bonnet, Charles 111, 112–23, 136, 137, 138, 141, 144, 147, 150, 167, 180, 185, 197
  Œuvres d'histoire naturelle et de philosophie 112
Bougainville, Louis-Antoine de 33, 34, 37, 67
Boyé, 94
Brody, Jules 79–80, 175
Buffier, Claude 150
Buffon, George Louis Leclerc, comte de 38, 111, 113, 120
Burke, Edmund 19, 44–5, 51, 53, 54
  Œuvres posthumes 44–5, 51, 53–4
Bus, César de 25

Cabanis, Pierre-Jean-Georges 111, 115–16, 138, 167
  Histoire physiologique des sensations 115
Candide, *see* Voltaire
Cellier, Leon 110
Chabanon, Michel-Paul-Gui de 93–4
  De la musique 93
  Observations sur la musique 93
Chassaignon, Jean-Marie 23
Chastel, André 89
Chastenay, Mme de 4
Chateaubriand, René de 3, 4, 5, 21, 49, 71, 86, 91, 99, 106, 110, 128, 129, 165, 172
  Essai sur les révolutions 110

Chateaubriand, René de—*contd*
  Génie du Christianisme 106, 129
  Mémoires d'outre-tombe 49, 71
Chênedollé, Charles-Auguste Lioult de 113
  Le Génie de l'homme 113
Chénier, André 90, 99, 110, 113, 120 n. 21
Chinard, Gilbert 34
Chrétien, Jean-Louis 18, 159, 161, 163
Cicero, 11, 85, 181
Clausel de Coussergues, Claude-Charles-Jules 23
Cocking, J. M. 170, 175
Coleridge, Samuel Taylor 7, 12, 13, 14, 170
Commentarium in Convivium, see Ficino
Condillac, Etienne Bonnot de 25, 26, 29, 31, 75, 144, 145, 146–58 *passim*, 165, 167
  Essai sur l'origine des connaissances humaines 153
  Traité des sensations 153
  Traité des systèmes 158
Condorcet, Jean-Antoine-Nicolas 142, 159
Considérations sur la France, see Maistre
Constant, Benjamin 41, 56, 57, 58, 59, 63
  L'Esprit de conquête et de l'usurpation 57
  Sur la liberté des anciens 63
Cook, James 34, 36, 38, 39, 66–9, 103, 195, 196, 198
Corinne, see Mme de Staël
Corneille, Thomas 176, 177
Court de Gébelin, Antoine 165
Cousin, Victor 73
Cratylus, see Plato
Critique of Judgement, see Kant
Crito, see Plato
Cudworth, Ralph 139

Dacier, André 72, 74, 76, 77, 78, 81, 82, 85, 87, 88
Daniel-Rops, H. 15, 16
David, Jacques-Louis 182–3
Deguy, Michel 129
De la musique, see Chabanon
De la recherche de la vérité, see Malebranche
De l'expression en musique, see Morellet

Delisle de Sales, Jean-B.-Claude 110
Delon, Michel 131, 188
Democritus 123
Derrida, Jacques 156
Descartes, René 29
De triplici theologia mysteriisque veterum commentatio, see Ansse de Villoison
Dialogues sur l'éloquence, see Fénelon
Dictionnaire de l'Académie (1786) 75
Diderot, Denis 12, 31, 32, 33, 34, 35, 36–8, 39, 40, 67, 94, 170, 193
  Encyclopédie 9, 28, 82
  Lettre sur les aveugles 38
  Supplément au voyage de Bougainville 36–8
Dilthey, Wilhelm 11
Discours préliminaire, see Rivarol
Discours sur l'essence et la forme de la poésie, see Fabre d'Olivet
Discours sur les sciences et les arts, see Rousseau
Discours sur Platon, see Fleury
Dissertations sur l'union de la religion, de la morale et de la politique, see Warburton
Duchesne, J.-B.M. 2, 3
Duchet, Michèle 38
Du Divorce, see Bonald
Du Marsais, César 127
Dupont de Nemours, Pierre-Samuel 32, 110
Dupuis, Charles 19, 82–3, 85
  L'Origine de tous les cultes 82

Egger, Emile 73
Éléments de littérature, see Marmontel
Emeric-David, Toussaint-Bernard 74, 83 n. 45, 85
Encyclopédie, see Diderot
L'Esprit de conquête et de l'usurpation, see Constant
Essai analytique, see Bonald
Essais de morale, see Nicole
Essai sur la musique, see La Borde
Essai sur la physiognomie, see Lavater
Essai sur le principe générateur, see Maistre
Essai sur les révolutions, see Chateaubriand
Essai sur l'origine des connaissances humaines, see Condillac

Index

Fabre d'Olivet, Antoine 93, 96–7, 110, 111, 115, 131
  Discours sur l'essence et la forme de la poésie 93
  La Musique expliquée comme science et comme art 96–7
Fénelon, Francois de Salignac de la Mothe 10, 11, 169
  Dialogues sur l'éloquence 11
  Télémaque 167, 172
Festugière, P. 89
Ficino, Marsilio 72, 75, 76, 81, 88–91, 92, 98–9, 107 n. 121, 118, 132–3, 139, 140, 141, 144, 163, 164, 191, 197
  Commentarium in Convivium 89, 90, 107 n. 21
Flaubert, Gustave 23
Fleury, abbé Claude 81, 85
  Discours sur Platon 81
Fontanes, Louis 47, 65, 89, 101
Forster, Johann Georg Adam 33
Fraguier, le père Claude-François 73
Furetière, Antoine 9

Garcin, Philippe 17, 22
Garnier, J.-J. 82
Gautier, Théophile 15, 118
Le Génie de l'homme, see Chênedollé
Génie du Christianisme, see Chateaubriand
Gérando, Joseph-Marie, baron de 77 n. 20, 139, 140, 151, 165
Gilman, Margaret 12, 14
Gleizes, Jean-Antoine 110
Goncourt, Edmond et Jules de 14
Goyet, Thérèse 87
Groethuysen, Bernard 41, 48
Grou, le père Jean-Nicolas 77, 91–2

Haight, Jeanne 175
Haller, Albrecht von 113, 121
Hamilton, Paul 155
Harmonies de la nature, see Bernardin de Saint-Pierre
Harmonie universelle, see Mersenne
Hemsterhuis, François 150
Hesiod 34
His, Charles 52, 65
Histoire physiologique des sensations, see Cabanis
Hobson, Marian 156, 157
Hogarth, William 185, 189
Homer 105, 142

Howells, W. S. 11
Huit, Charles 72–6
Hume, David 51

Iamblichus, 76, 80, 82, 87
idea 144–63 *passim*
Iknayan, Marguerite 135
illusion 22, 66, 128–37 *passim*, 141–2, 197
image 127–37, 144–63 *passim*, 197
imagination 22, 127–37 *passim*, 158–75
innat ideas 146–52
Ion, see Plato

Jansenism 26–8, 29
Jeanneret, Michel 104–6
Joubert, Arnaud 2
Joubert, Jean 30
Joubert, Joseph:
  La Bienveillance universelle 31, 35, 49, 177
  Éloge de Cook 31, 33–40, 64–70, 101, 102, 106, 141, 175, 193, 195
  Éloge de Pigalle 31, 178–81
Joubert, Madame, *see* Moreau
Joubert, Sophie 2, 191, 192
Juden, Brian 110, 113

Kant, Immanuel 147, 160, 162
  Critique of Judgement 162

La Borde, Jean-Benjamin de 95
  Essai sur la musique 95
La Bruyère, Jean de 4, 10, 14, 145, 183
Lacépède, Bernard-Germain-Étienne de la Ville, cte de 95
  Poétique de la musique 95
Lacroix, Firmin 27
Lacroix, Jean 29
La Fontaine, Jean de 71, 85, 118, 172
La Harpe, Jean François de 96, 127, 128
Lahonton, Louis-Armand de Lom d'Arce, baron de 48
La Mettrie, Julien Offray de 167
La Rochefoucauld, François, duc de 4, 10
Laromiguière, Pierre 25, 29
Latapie, François de Paule 30, 31
Lavater, Johann Caspar 140, 181, 191–2
  Essai sur la physiognomie 191
Législation primitive, see Bonald

Index

Leibniz, Gottfried Wilhelm von 120, 121, 123, 147, 148–9, 151, 152, 168, 172
   Nouveaux essais sur l'entendement humain 148, 151
Lemaître, Jules 12, 14, 23
Lettre sur les aveugles, see Diderot
Littré, Emile 10
Locke, John 9, 29, 145, 146–58 passim, 167
   Nouveaux essais sur l'entendement humain
Longinus 103

Macaulay, Thomas Babington, Baron 11
Maine de Biran, Pierre 29, 116, 150
Maistre, Joseph de 48, 50, 52, 53, 54–5, 56, 57, 60, 69, 70, 80, 138, 195
   Considérations sur la France 50, 52
   Essai sur le principe générateur 52
Malebranche, Nicolas 79, 147, 164, 167–71, 173
   De la Recherche de la vérité 164, 167
Mallarmé, Stéphane 188, 197, 198
Manuel, F.P. and F.E. 33, 67
Marat, Jean Paul 48
Maréchal, Sylvain 110
Marlin, François 42
Marmontel, Jean-François 39, 95–6, 127
   Éléments de littérature 95–6
Mémoires de l'académie des inscriptions et belles lettres 71, 73, 82, 91
Mémoires d'outre-tombe, see Chateaubriand
Menander 178
Mercier, Sebastien 23
Mersenne, Marin 99
   Harmonie universelle 99
Monglond, André 12
Montaigne, Michel de 4, 5
Montesquieu, Charles-Louis de Secondat, baron de 8, 19, 30, 31
Moreau, Jacob Nicolas 42–3
Moreau, Mlle Victorine (future Madame Joubert) 3, 43, 45
Moreau, Pierre 12
Morellet, abbé André 94–5, 96
   De l'expression en musique et de l'imitation dans les arts 94–5
Mornet, Daniel 28
Moulinié, Henri 166
Mozart, Wolfgang Amadeus 64
La Musique expliquée comme science et comme art, see Fabre d'Olivet

Naudin, Marie 91
Navarre, le père Jean 25, 28
Nicole, Pierre 26
   Essais de morale 26
Nodier, Charles 110
Nollet, abbé Jean-François 147, 150, 167, 174
Nouveaux essais sur l'entendement humain, see Locke
Nouvel homme, see Saint-Martin

Observations sur la musique, see Chabanon
Ocellus Lucanus 124–6, 136, 154, 158, 167
Odes, see Ronsard
Œuvres d'histoire naturelle et de philosophie, see Bonnet
Œuvres posthumes, see Burke
L'Origine de tous les cultes, see Dupuis

Parmenides, see Plato
Pascal, Blaise 10, 113, 162
Pères de la doctrine chrétienne 25–30
Perros, George 1
Phaedrus, see Plato
Philebus, see Plato
Pichois, Claude 4, 5
Pigalle, Jean-Baptiste 179–81
Plato 11, 14, 15, 20, 49, 58, 66, 70, 71–109 passim, 111, 113, 116, 121, 123, 125, 126, 129, 133, 134, 138, 142, 146, 149, 152, 165, 168, 169, 171, 193, 197
   Cratylus 58, 77, 121, 165
   Crito 73
   Ion 73, 89, 90, 92, 93, 94, 118
   Parmenides 81
   Phaedo 135
   Phaedrus 89, 135, 140, 141
   Philebus 92, 133, 140
   Republic 73, 92
   Sophist 66, 135
   Symposium 89, 90, 139
   Thaetetus 73, 133, 138
   Timaeus 74, 116, 121, 135, 151, 191
platonism 14, 22, 61, 65, 69, 70, 71–109, 118, 134, 197
Plutarch 81, 87, 88, 193
Poétique de la musique, see Lacépède
Porphyry 76, 80, 82, 87
Poulet, Georges 14, 17, 18, 19
Prévost, Marcel 15
Pythagoras 10, 75, 99, 111, 113, 129

pythagorism 91, 110–11, 142, 188

Quai, Maurice 110
Quart livre, see Rabelais
Quatremère de Quincy, Antoine-Chrysostôme 134, 135, 181–2, 188

Rabelais, François 87, 88, 104–7, 137
  Quart livre 87
Racine, Jean 86, 176
Ramus, Petrus 11
Raphael, D. D. 9
Raynal, Paul de 3, 4, 5, 15, 16, 72
Recherches philosophiques, see Bonald
Recherches sur l'analogie de la musique avec les arts, see Villoteau
Recherches sur les mystères du paganisme, see Sainte-Croix
Reid, Thomas 155
Republic, see Plato
Restif de la Bretonne, Louis 110
Rivarol, Antoine de 172
  Discours préliminaire 172
Rolin, Charles 127
Ronsard, Pierre de 88, 89, 90, 94, 99
  Odes 89
Rousseau, Jean-Jacques 7, 12, 25, 26, 31, 32, 33, 38, 39, 40, 41, 50, 56, 57, 58
  Discours sur les sciences et les arts 57

Saint-Martin, Louis Claude de 60, 70, 85, 86, 110, 189
  Nouvel homme 70
Saint-Pierre, Bernardin de 39
  Harmonies de la nature 110–11
  Voyage à l'île de France 39
Sainte-Beuve, Charles 5–10, 12, 13, 14
Sainte-Croix 19, 84–5
  Recherches sur les mystères du paganisme 84
Saintsbury, George 12, 13, 14
Sallier, abbé Claude 73
Schlegel, A.W. 181
Schlegel, Friedrich 143
Secondat, Jean-Baptiste de 30
Selby-Bigge, L.A. 9, 10
Sénancour, Étienne Pivert de 99, 110
Smith, Adam 32
Socrates 70, 86, 142
Solmsen, Friedrich 126
Sophist, see Plato

Staël, Anne-Louise-Germaine Necker, baronne de 13, 98, 99, 101, 103, 106, 110, 178, 188
  Corinne 98, 101
Starobinski, Jean 64, 65
Steele, Alan 18, 19
Stewart, Dugald 155
Supplément au voyage de Bougainville, see Diderot
Sur la liberté des anciens, see Constant
Symposium, see Plato

Télémaque, see Fénelon
Tessonneau, Rémy 2, 24, 29, 43, 77 n. 20
Thaetetus, see Plato
Théorie du pouvoir, see Bonald
Tiedemann, Dietrich 74, 88, 138, 139
Timaeus, see Plato
Timaeus Locrus 124, 126, 158
Tocqueville, Alexis de 58
  L'Ancien régime et la révolution 58
Torné, Anastase 27
Traité des sensations, see Condillac
Traité des systèmes, see Condillac
Triomphe, Robert 54, 55
Turgot, Anne-Robert-Jacques 32

Van Delft, Louis 8, 11, 20
Vauvenargues, Luc de Clapiers 10
Viatte, Auguste 86, 110
Vigny, Alfred de 118
Viguerie, Jean de 25, 26, 28
Villoteau, Guillaume 92–3, 177, 190
  Recherches sur l'analogie de la musique avec les arts 92, 177
Virgil 34
Volney, Constantin-François de Chassebœuf, cte. de 83, 167
Voltaire, François-Marie Arouet de 7, 179, 186–7, 189
  Candide 167
Voyage à l'île de France, see Bernardin de Saint-Pierre

Warburton, William 85, 159
  Dissertations sur l'union de la religion, de la morale et de la politique 85
Ward, Patricia 4, 7, 12, 13, 14 n. 43, 22, 134, 170
Ward, Mrs Humphry 5
Wellek, René 13, 14